How to

Incorporate
in Any State

Everything you need to form a corporation.

W. Dean Brown

Consumer Publishing Company
Copyright © 2000

How to Incorporate in Any State
W. Dean Brown

This publication is intended to provide accurate information with regard to the subject matter covered. The reader is cautioned that this book is sold with the understanding that the Publisher is not engaged in rendering legal, accounting or other professional service. Since everyone's situation is different, readers are urged to consult their own legal or tax advisor for advice regarding their particular needs.

Since we live in a lawsuit prone society, we feel the following disclaimer is necessary. Although we make every attempt to insure that the information contained in this book is accurate and up-to-date, we make no warranty, either expressed or implied, as to the accuracy of the information contained in this book. Neither do we make any warranty as to this book's fitness for a particular purpose or its merchantability. Consumer Corporation nor the author shall be liable for incidental or consequential damages resulting from the use of this book or the information contained herein.

Distributed in the U.S. and Canada by
Independent Publishers Group
814 North Franklin Street
Chicago, IL 60610
Bookstores and Wholesalers please call 1-800-888-4741

Published by
Consumer Publishing, Inc.
Consumer Corporation
P.O. Box 23830
Knoxville, TN 37933-1830

Internet address
www.consumercorp.com

Telephone numbers
Questions and general information (865) 671-4858
Orders 1-800-677-2462

Consumer Corporation and Consumer Publishing, Inc. are trademarks of Consumer Corporation.

Designed and written by Dean Brown.
Printed in the United States of America.

Library of Congress Cataloging in Publication Data
Brown, W. Dean
         How to Incorporate in Any State / by W. Dean Brown
         1st edition
                  p.   cm. –
                  Includes Index.
                  ISBN 1-879760-85-1 (pbk.)
                           1. Incorporation – Popular works.
                           2. Corporation law – Popular works.
                           3. Private companies – Popular works. – Limited Liability Company

         I. Title.
         II. Series: (Knoxville, Tenn.)

With many thanks to my wife Cherie…

I couldn't have done this without her help.

About the Author

Dean Brown graduated with honors from the University of Tennessee in 1985, with a Bachelor of Science Degree in Accounting. After graduation, he worked for the small business services division of Price Waterhouse, one of the largest public accounting firms in the world. Here, the author worked to help small business owners find better ways to operate their business. Working with these small businesses made him aware that they operate on tight budgets.

Unfortunately, no matter how great the benefits of incorporating are, many small business people can't afford to pay a professional to incorporate their business, and most don't know how to do it themselves. To fill this need, a series of how-to-incorporate books was started. Since 1991, Dean has written over 30 books on the subject of incorporating.

He wrote his first book, an incorporating handbook for Tennessee, on a borrowed computer. He had samples printed up at Kinko's and sent them off to Walden and B. Dalton bookstores. The books were well received and the stores placed orders for almost 300 books. Kinko's printed these first 300 books on a copier, and Dean bound them by hand on his dining room table.

He makes his home in Knoxville, Tennessee where he writes, operates Consumer Publishing, Corporate Publishing, and occasionally speaks at the University of Tennessee School of Business. He loves working out, tinkering around the house, and being in the great outdoors—especially the nearby Great Smoky Mountains National Park. In 1999, he bought a Chrysler convertible and loves driving it through the mountains with the top down. He has a wife Cherie, two daughters Mallory and Amber, and a son William.

Drop Me a Line!

Starting a business is a wonderful, sometimes intimidating event. It's kind of like a roller coaster, a lot of fun, and a little scary. You are off on a fantastic journey. Thank you for taking me along. I've made many friends producing these books for the last nine years. I hope you will be one of them.

If you feel this book has helped you, please drop me a note or a post card of your hometown to let me know. (Tell the manager of your bookstore too!) My four your old son and I thoroughly enjoy these postcards. They're displayed on the wall of my office. Please send them to:

Dean Brown
Consumer Publishing Inc.
P.O. Box 23830
Concord, TN 37933-1830

Table of Contents

Chapter 1
Which Type of Business Organization is Best for You? 7
    Types of Business Organizations 8
    The Sole Proprietorship 8
        Advantages 8
        Disadvantages 8
        Taxes 9
    The Partnership 9
        Advantages & Disadvantages 9
        Taxes 9
    The Corporation 10
        Advantages 10
        Disadvantages 13
        The S Corporation 14
        S Corporation vs. C Corporation 14
    The Limited Liability Company 15
    Of The Four Types, Which is Best? 15
        Sole proprietorship 15
        Partnership 15
        Corporation 15
        Limited Liability Company 16
        The Bottom Line 16

Chapter 2
Forming a Corporation 19
    A Little Background 19
    In Which State Should You Incorporate? 20
        The Bottom Line 20
    The Incorporating Process 21
    Step 1. Choose a Corporate Name 21
        State Requirements 21
        Other considerations for choosing a name 22
    Step 2. Check the Availability of Your Corporate Name 23
        How to do it 23
    Step 3. File Your Paperwork 24
        Completing the Articles 24
        Name 24
        Office 24
        Duration 24
        Stock 25
        Capitalization 26

Purpose 27
Registered agent 27
Incorporator 27
Optional items 27
Step 4. Take Care of Organizational Matters 28
Elect Directors 28
Appoint Officers 30
Shareholders 30
Issuing Stock 32
Authorized vs. Issued Shares 33
Multiple Shareholders 33
Consideration 35
Issuing Stock Certificates 37
Stock Registration 37
Step 5. Prepare Your Corporate Records 41
Buying a Kit 41
Making a Kit 41
Record Keeping 42
Holding Meetings 43

Chapter 3
Incorporating an Existing Business **45**
Dissolve the Existing Business 46
Transfer Assets. 46
Cash 47
Accounts receivable 48
Notes receivable 48
Miscellaneous assets 48
Assets with titles or deeds 48
Liabilities 48
Other contracts 49
Partnership agreements 49

Chapter 4
After Incorporating **51**
Getting an Employer Identification Number (EIN) 52
S Corporation Election 52
IRS Form 2553 52
Completing the form 53
Other Considerations 54
Your Business Name 54
Taxes 54
Permits 54
Insurance 54
Accounting 55
Employees 55
Free help 55

Incorporating Forms and Instructions **57**

Glossary. **189**

Index **195**

Chapter 1
Which Type of Business Organization is Best for You?

If you've never started a business before—relax. Forming a corporation is easier than you might think. As a matter of fact, if you can put your name and address on a form, you can incorporate a business. If you're starting a business for the first time, you're probably a little anxious, maybe afraid you'll do something wrong or leave something out, but don't worry, I've worked hard to make this easy for you. You can't do anything wrong. So please, sit back, relax, and spend a couple of hours with me. We'll have your business incorporated in no time. And by the way, thank you for choosing this book.

If you're unsure whether forming a corporation is the best thing for your business, or if you're not exactly sure what a corporation is, this chapter will give you an overview of the most common types of business organizations—the sole proprietorship; the partnership; the corporation; and the newest type of business organization, the limited liability company, or LLC as it is more commonly known.

If you're sure that incorporating is right for you, skip this chapter and go on to Chapter 2 where you'll learn the incorporating process.

If, *after reading the entire book*, you have a question, we'll be glad to help. Answers to most common questions will be posted on our main website at www.consumercorp.com. You can also call our office and speak to someone on our staff. The telephone number is (865) 671-4858. Our office hours are 9-5 Monday-Friday (e.s.t.). Please note that there are no lawyers on our staff, and we are unable to give legal or tax advice, or do any consulting. We can only clarify subjects or procedures discussed in this book.

Types of Business Organizations

One of the first executive decisions you'll make for your new business is deciding how to organize it. Basically, there are four ways to organize a business.

- The sole proprietorship
- The partnership
- The corporation
- The limited liability company (LLC)

The choice you make here is important because it will determine what your business can and cannot legally do, what will happen if someone sues you, how your business is taxed and things like that.

You see, a business only exists because a group of lawmakers, a legislature, passed a special set of laws that governs its formation and operation, kind of like "the rules of the game." The type of business organization that you choose determines the set of laws that govern it, and therefore how it is formed, how it will operate, and what rights it will have. A corporation only exists because a state legislature passed a special set of laws that governs corporations. These laws spell out what a person must do to form a corporation, what the corporation can and cannot do, and how the corporation will be taxed.

The Sole Proprietorship

A sole proprietorship, as the name suggests, is a business with one owner. Of the four types of business organizations, it is probably the most common. A business organized as a sole proprietorship is not separate from its owner, but merely a different name with which the owner represents him/herself to the public. The owner is the business and the business is the owner. They're inseparable.

Advantages

Since they have few legal requirements, sole proprietorships are easy to form and operate. They can also be more affordable since no legal documents need to be filed in most cases. Basically, all you have to do to organize a sole proprietorship is get a business license and begin operations.

Disadvantages

Although the sole proprietorship does have the advantage of simplicity, the negative aspects steer most entrepreneurs away from this form of business organization. The disadvantages of a sole proprietorship stem from its very nature—the business and the business owner are inseparable. This leads to three potential problems.

1. Unlimited liability – Since the owner and the business are inseparable, whoever sues the business actually sues the owner personally. A single lawsuit can financially ruin a sole proprietorship and its owner

because the owner's personal property can be taken to satisfy judgments against "the business." The owner's personal exposure is unlimited.

2. Responsible for business obligations – The business owner is personally liable for the debts of the company, and unfortunately, personal assets like cars, savings, and homes can be taken to pay company obligations.

3. No tax benefits – Owners can lose some lucrative tax free fringe benefits because they cannot participate in company funded employee benefit plans like medical insurance and retirement plans. Since the owner is the business, he/she cannot be an employee, and therefore can't participate in "employee" benefit plans. (Some owners get around this by hiring their spouse as an employee, and the spouse participates in the employee benefit plans.)

Taxes

Since the owner and the business are the same entity for tax reporting purposes, a sole proprietorship is known as a pass-through entity. This means that all business income and expenses are passed through to, and filed as part of the owner's personal return. If there is a business loss, the owner will enjoy a deduction to offset personal (paycheck) income. However, if the business makes a profit, the owner must pay any taxes due.

The Partnership

A partnership is similar to a sole proprietorship but has two or more owners. Like the sole proprietorship, the partnership is not a separate legal entity from its owners. Also like a sole proprietorship, you don't have to file papers with the state to form a partnership. You should, however, create and adopt a partnership agreement. A partnership agreement outlines the arrangement between the partners for running the business and dividing the profits. You don't have to adopt a partnership agreement, but doing so will help settle arguments before they begin.

Advantages & Disadvantages

In general, the partnership shares the same advantages and disadvantages as the sole proprietorship. However, the partnership has an additional drawback. A partner can be held liable for the acts of the other partners, thus increasing each partner's personal liability. For example, if Brent and Irene are partners and Brent incurs a debt on behalf of the partnership, Irene is also liable for the debt even if she knows nothing about it.

Taxes

Tax treatment of the partnership is also slightly different. Although it is a pass-through entity, the partnership does file an "informational" tax return (Form 1065) with the IRS showing its income and expenses. The pro-rata share of partnership profit or loss is then shown on each partner's personal return. The partners pay any taxes due on their personal tax returns. Conversely, if the company loses money, the partners will share a deduction on their personal returns.

The Corporation

The corporation was conceived to solve the typical problems of the sole proprietorship and partnership forms of business organization. Incorporating allows a group of entrepreneurs to act as one, much the way a partnership does, with one important advantage—since the corporation is a separate legal entity capable of being sued, it can protect its owners by absorbing the liability if something "goes wrong." (This characteristic of the corporation keeps you from losing your home if someone sues your business.) Also, many people incorporate to avoid personal liability for debts and liabilities of the business. In recent years, the corporation has become a tax-reduction and tax-planning tool.

There are all sorts of technical explanations for what a corporation is. Here's a textbook definition: A corporation is an artificial being created by operation of law, with an existence separate from the individuals (shareholders) who are its owners. It is a separate and distinct entity that acts for, or on behalf of a person or group of people.

Corporations are created primarily to operate a business for the benefit of its owners—the shareholders. When you incorporate a business, you actually create an "artificial person" and let this "person" operate your business for you, subject to your control of course. A corporation is essentially a legal "person" created and operated with the permission of the state where it's incorporated. It's a person like you and me, but only "on paper." As a legally recognized person, a corporation enjoys most of the rights and privileges that you and I do. Among other things, a corporation can own property, sue, be sued, and of course, operate a business. Corporations also enjoy many of the privileges enumerated in the Constitution and the Bill of Rights like freedom of speech. The only difference between a real person and a corporation is this—a person has a physical body and a corporation does not.

A corporation is "brought to life" when a person, the incorporator, files a form with their state known as the articles of incorporation. You can think of the articles of incorporation as the corporation's birth certificate. (This document goes by a different name in some states, certificate of incorporation, certificate of organization, and charter are some of the most common.)

Advantages

Some people incorporate for one reason. They like to have "Inc." after their business name, and that's okay. They've always wanted to have a company of their own, and if they're going to have a company, they want it to be a corporation—*it sounds BIG!* In fact, it can sound impressive to customers and suppliers. It may also indicate that your business is larger than it actually is, perhaps making customers and suppliers more willing to do business with you and extend credit.

On a more practical note, the corporation offers benefits to you because of its legal nature. Since a corporation is a separate legal entity, the corporation actually owns and "operates" the business for you. This separation provides a legal distinction between you and your business and thereby provides three important benefits:

1. Incorporating offers you the protection of limited liability for actions of the corporation;

2. You are not responsible for company obligations

3. Incorporating offers some terrific tax breaks.

Limited liability

Since you and your company are now two separate legal entities, lawsuits can be brought against your company instead of you personally. Separating you (the shareholder) from your business offers protection. Since the corporation has the right to sue and be sued, a person bringing a lawsuit will typically sue your corporation instead of you personally. This is usually the case even when the owner is the only shareholder, the only director, and the only officer. If someone sues Ford Motor Company, the person bringing the suit will simply sue Ford Motor Company Inc., not Mr. Ford himself.

Please note that this is what typically happens, or at least what should happen. However, sometimes when a person sues your company, they sue everyone associated with the company, anyone near the building, the janitor, and even the President of the United States if they think it will get them some money. Nevertheless, even if you are personally named in a lawsuit, your corporation can handle the lawsuit and still protect your personal property. The key here is to make sure that your corporation has proper insurance coverage. The corporate entity won't replace insurance and good business practices.

Not responsible for company obligations

When debt is incurred in the company name, you are not personally liable for it and your personal assets cannot be taken to settle the company obligations. Say for example, you lease a computer for your corporation and put it in the company name. Then, at some point down the road the business goes under. The company that leased the computer to your business can't come after you personally for the lease payments. They can only look to the now defunct corporation for the payments. If the corporation has no assets or money in the bank, the creditor will have to be satisfied with the repossessed equipment. The computer company simply extended credit to a corporation that is now out of business. There is no money to collect. The same goes for all your suppliers, the landlord, and so on.

It's important to note here that this limitation only applies for debt incurred in the corporate name that you did not personally guarantee. That is, when you incurred the debt or signed the contract, you didn't personally guarantee payment of the obligation in the event the corporation couldn't make the payments. If you personally guaranteed payment of the obligation, the corporation can't do anything to protect you. You'll have to make the payments. That's why it is important to sign your name on a contract as an officer of the corporation. That is, sign like this, ABC Corporation, by Jane Gray, President.

Tax benefits

Being incorporated allows you, the owner, to hire yourself as an employee (typically as president) and then participate in company funded employee benefit plans. You benefit by receiving these benefits tax-free and the corporation gets a deduction for providing them to you. These tax benefits mainly apply to C corporations because expenses from the S Corporation are reported on your personal return and therefore either reduced or eliminated.

My favorite company provided benefits include retirement plans and medical and dental reimbursement plans. Let me tell you a bit about them. Using a company provided retirement plan or pension plan, your corporation can put away a sizeable amount of money each year for your retirement and deduct the amount from its income as a business expense.

Retirement Plans – Everyone is familiar with retirement plans. They are the company sponsored retirement accounts that most large companies offer to their employees. The best thing about a pension plan is that the contributions made to your account by your corporation are tax deductions for the corporation, but are not taxable to you until you retire. These contributions earn interest and multiply with no tax implications to you, while the corporation's tax bill is lowered by thousands of dollars each year. If you operate as an S Corporation, making these contributions can lower your personal tax bill. It's kind of like an IRA without the small annual limit.

If you operate as a C Corporation, things can be even more lucrative. You can actually borrow money from your retirement account if certain easy to meet requirements are satisfied. Borrowing from your pension fund allows you to use this money now without paying taxes on it.

Medical and Dental Reimbursement Plan – A medical and dental reimbursement plan is an employee benefit plan that allows your corporation to pay your insurance premiums, deductibles, and co-payments. The corporation can also reimburse you for expenses incurred for eyeglasses, braces, and so on. (You're probably beginning to see how beneficial a plan like this can be.) You can spend thousands of dollars annually on these items that even the best insurance doesn't pay for. Fortunately, when your business is incorporated, the corporation can pick up the tab for these expensive items. A benefit plan like this can save you thousands of dollars per year and provide the corporation a tax deduction. A medical and dental reimbursement plan is a standard fill in the blank type form available in our corporate outfits or on the computer disk that comes free with the purchase of this book.

Please note that since the S Corporation passes its deductions to the shareholder's personal tax return, only a percentage of health insurance premiums are deductible. If you want to take full advantage of having your corporation pay your health care costs, you'll need to operate as a C Corporation.

Disadvantages	The typical disadvantages of incorporating are often listed as increased administrative duties, the high cost of incorporating, the inflexibility of having a separate entity, and "double taxation"— none of which are very good arguments against incorporating.
	Administrative – The only real administrative duty is holding an annual shareholder meeting, and all you have to do is use one of our pre-written forms once a year to satisfy the requirement. You may also need to hold a director's meeting to vote on important matters from time to time.
Cost	The cost of incorporating isn't high if you do it yourself. You can put your name and address on a form and send it to the state. Your only cost is the purchase price of this book plus state filing fees.
Inflexibility	The corporate form of operating your business can at times be inflexible, especially if you've previously operated your business as a sole proprietorship. For example, a person operating as a sole proprietorship can co-mingle (mix) his/her personal and business assets. After incorporating, personal and corporate assets must be segregated, and accounted for separately.
"Double taxation"	The "double taxation" aspect of corporations only applies in the case of a large dividend-paying corporation like IBM. Double taxation doesn't usually apply to a small corporation. Let me explain.
	A dividend is *not* a tax deductible expense like salaries, rent, etc. Since it isn't a deductible expense, the corporation has to pay tax on any money paid out as dividends. (There is no offsetting expense for this income.)
	When the dividend is received by the shareholder, it is taxable income to him/her. Therefore, tax on the amount of the dividend is paid once by the corporation and then paid again by the shareholder, resulting in double taxation—but wait—*small corporations never pay dividends*, or at least they *shouldn't* pay dividends. In a small corporation, the owners receive money from the corporation in the form of salaries and bonuses, all of which are tax deductible by the corporation. Since salaries and bonuses are a tax deduction for the corporation, but it pays no tax on these amounts. The money is only taxed when received by the shareholders, resulting in no double taxation.
State taxes	The only real disadvantage of incorporating as I see it is taxation of corporate income by a state government. If a state taxes corporate income, which most do, it can be a problem as your sales increase to the point where you have a profit at the end of the year. When you are starting off, you probably won't have to worry about paying taxes on corporate income, because there won't be any income (profit). Your expenses will usually keep up with sales and leave you with no taxable income at the end of the year. But as your business grows, you will probably begin to have profits at year-end and therefore State and Federal income taxes to pay.

Of course there are ways to lower or even eliminate your tax bill. You can "eat up" a lot of income by giving yourself corporate paid benefits like health insurance and retirement plans. You can also purchase equipment and reduce your income in other ways. Many owners of small companies simply write themselves a bonus check at the end of the year and "zero out" the income of the business by increasing salary expenses. So with a little tax planning, you'll pay little or no state or Federal income tax and get to enjoy the corporation provided fringe benefits too.

The S Corporation

An "S" Corporation is the same as any other business corporation with one important difference, the IRS allows it to be taxed like a partnership, making it a pass-through entity.

When business corporations are created, they are all regular "C corporations." If you want to be an S Corporation, you must file a form with the IRS known as a Form 2553. This form tells the IRS that you want your corporation to be taxed like a partnership, a special filing status. This means that your corporation's profit or loss at year-end will be included as part of your personal tax return. If your corporation makes money at the end of the year, your personal income and income taxes will increase. If your corporation loses money at the end of the year, you will enjoy a deduction on your personal return, up to the amount that you have invested in the company.

Many people begin corporate life as an S Corporation when there are losses to offset their "paycheck" income, and then revert to C Corporation status when the corporation begins to make taxable profits. It is important to remember that being an S Corporation is a tax matter only. It is simply a tax filing status, kind of like "single," "married filing jointly," or "head of household."

S Corporation vs C Corporation

Which is best? Well, everyone's personal tax situation is different, but I prefer operating as a C corporation. Why? Because I don't want my business income and expenses ending up on my personal return like they do with an S Corporation. I want my business income and expenses to stay separate like they do with a C Corporation. You see, if your S Corporation makes a profit at the end of the year, that income ends up on your personal 1040 return increasing your personal income, increasing your personal income taxes. Also, with a C Corporation, you can deduct more medical and dental expenses than you can with an S Corporation, something very important to me. Also, if you have a C Corporation, you can take advantage of "income splitting."

Income splitting is a way to lower your overall tax bill by leaving some of your year-end profits in the corporation, which is then taxed at a lower rate than if you'd paid the tax on your personal 1040 return. Using income splitting helps keep you and the company in a lower tax bracket, lowering your overall tax bill.

The Limited Liability Company

A limited liability company (LLC) is the newest form of business organization. Although it was conceived as a replacement for the "limited partnership" to be used in real estate financing deals, the LLC is becoming an alternative to the corporation. Available in all 50 states, it's a hybrid entity that provides the limited liability of the corporation with the taxation status of a partnership, making it a pass-through entity. You can look at it like this, the LLC is a "corporation" that's taxed like a partnership. It's very similar to an S Corporation, but the S Corporation can't have more than 75 shareholders. I think of the LLC as an "S Corporation without the 75 shareholder limit."

The Limited Liability Company is a popular type of business entity, but it does have a couple of disadvantages. First, its newness means that law regarding the LLC is still evolving and some issues relating to its operation remain unsettled. Also, if the LLC is taxed as a partnership, business owners will lose company funded benefits and the LLC income will end up on the owners' personal tax returns.

Of The Four Types, Which is Best?

Everyone has a different answer to this question. Every book has a chart listing the advantages and disadvantages of the different types of business entities and then tell you to ask your CPA or attorney which is best. I will advise the same, but also realize that not everyone has a CPA or attorney to consult with, so I will try to direct you further. Bear in mind that everyone's business is different and everyone's tax situation is different. You may want to refer to the following chart for guidance.

Sole proprietorship

I only recommend this type of business entity for the person starting a very small, probably part-time business with no employees. This business would have no assets and its product or service would be one of low lawsuit potential. That is, your customers wouldn't be likely to be injured by one of your products. My mother used to make crafts and sell them at local craft fairs. This is the ideal sole proprietorship business. It's usually started just to make a little extra money.

Partnership

The ideal candidate for this type of business entity would fit the same criteria as the sole proprietorship mentioned before except this business would have more than one owner. Like the sole proprietorship, a partnership can be incorporated or converted into an LLC later on if the business grows beyond its initial expectations.

Corporation

This type of organization is best suited for a single entrepreneur who wants a small business that offers tax advantages and tax planning capabilities or a group of entrepreneurs who want to start a business that will grow in size and have employees. Its limited liability aspect makes the corporation ideal for companies with products or services with liability potential.

Limited Liability Company

This type of business organization is ideally suited to those who want the limited liability protection of the corporation but want to be taxed as a partnership, perfect for real estate investment businesses. Partnership taxation means that the business profit or loss ends up on the owner(s) personal return(s), and there are few if any personal fringe benefits.

Many people think that the LLC is best because it's the latest thing. Newer must be better, right? Well, not necessarily. The LLC was designed for real estate investment, and that's what it should be used for. The LLC is really just a new twist on an existing type of business organization, a "close" corporation that elects to be taxed as an S Corporation. The close corporation, if available in your state does away with a lot of the administrative requirements of a regular corporation, and choosing S Corporation tax treatment makes it a pass-through entity.

There are only two cases where I'd favor the LLC over the corporation, (1) if the company invested in real estate or (2) if the company was formed in a state where LLC income is taxed at a lower rate than corporation income.

What I Did

Consumer Publishing started out as an S Corporation. Since I didn't think I'd make a profit with the company for two or three years, I started with the S Corporation because it is taxed like a partnership, a pass-through entity. This allowed me to pass the business losses incurred in the start up period through to my personal return and get a personal tax deduction for losses incurred by the business. The limited deductions offered by the S Corporation didn't matter because there was no profit available to "spend" on deductions.

Later, when the company started to make a profit, I terminated the S Corporation status by sending a letter to the IRS, and reverted to C Corporation status because I needed more tax deductions to offset the income. I also switched back to a C Corporation to take advantage of the medical and dental reimbursement plan and the retirement savings plan. The C Corporation also allows me to benefit from income splitting, that is, leaving some income in the corporation, which enjoys lower marginal income tax rates, resulting in lower overall taxes.

Some people achieve this same effect by starting out as an LLC when there are business losses, and then "kill" the LLC when the business starts to make money. They immediately replace the LLC with a C Corporation to take advantage of the tax breaks. This strategy can be a lot of trouble, especially if the business grows to any size at all. Reorganizing an existing business is a lot of work.

The Bottom Line

Well, after considering the advantages and disadvantages of the different types of business organizations, I lean toward the corporation. The corporation's flexibility in tax planning and tax reduction makes it the winner for most people.

Types of Business Organizations

	Proprietorship	Partnership	Corp. (S or C)	LLC
Suited for	• Single owner business where taxes or product liability are not a concern	• A multiple owner business where taxes or product liability are not a concern	• Single or multiple owner business where owners need company funded fringe benefits and liability protection	• Single or multiple owner business where owners need limited liability but want to be taxed as a partnership • Real estate investment companies and existing partnerships
Type of Entity	• Inseparable from owner	• Inseparable from owner but can have debts or property in its name	• Separate legal entity	• Separate legal entity • Pass-through entity for taxation
Advantages	• Inexpensive to set up • Few administrative duties	• Inexpensive to set up • Few administrative duties	• Limited liability • Company paid fringe benefits • Tax savings through income splitting • Capital is easy to raise through sale of stock.	• Limited liability • Taxed like a partnership • Capital is easy to raise through sale of interest
Disadvantages	• Unlimited liability • No tax benefits • Business dissolves upon death of owner	• Unlimited liability • Also liable for acts of partners • No tax breaks • Legally dissolves upon change or death of partner	• Can be more expensive to organize • Administrative duties (record keeping) • S Corporation limited to 75 shareholders	• Can be costly to form • More administrative duties • Taxed like a partnership
Taxes	• Owner is responsible • File "Schedule C" with Form1040	• Partners are responsible • File Form 1065	• C Corp. pays its own • S Corp. passes through to owners and owners pay • File Form 1120 • S Corp. files 1120 S	• Taxed as a partnership, but can be taxed as a corporation in some states • Usually Form 1065

Chapter 2
Forming a Corporation

Most people think incorporating a business is a difficult and complex thing to do. Actually it's very simple. Basically all you need to do is file "articles of incorporation" with a state agency and pay a fee. The articles of incorporation is a simple document that provides information about the corporation you want to form, and not much more than your name and address.

A Little Background

Until the early 1900's, incorporating wasn't so easy. When the first corporations were formed, a business owner had to petition the state legislature to pass a special law allowing the business to operate as a corporation. Of course, having your own law passed is a complicated and expensive process - an option only available to those with enough money, influence, and legal experts to get the job done.

With the industrial boom of the early 1800's, the corporation became the preferred type of business organization. Operating as a corporation made it easier to obtain the enormous funds needed to build factories and railroads. Instead of going to the bank for a loan, entrepreneurs simply sold shares, or small pieces of their business, to anyone wanting to "share" in the huge potential profits of the venture. Legislatures soon found they were spending too much time granting special corporate charters, and began to pass general corporation laws that made it much easier to incorporate a business.

In 1811, New York passed the first general corporation statute and began to enjoy tremendous revenues from businesses incorporating there. Hungry for a piece of the revenue pie, the neighboring states of New Jersey and Delaware passed more liberal (easier to satisfy) corporate statutes by 1899. The Delaware law basically made incorporating a matter of filing a form with the secretary of state. Of course this lured many corporations away from New York and began the interstate competition for corporations that continues today.

Delaware remained the epicenter for corporations until 1969 when the American Bar Association developed a uniform set of corporation law based on the popular Delaware corporation statute. By simply adopting this "turnkey" set of laws called "The Model Business Corporation Act" any state could have its own set of modern corporation law by simply making the model act a part of its own law. Most states did just this. Today, the model act is the basis for corporate law in most states and single-handedly destroyed the primary advantage of incorporating in Delaware, which brings up an important question...

In Which State Should You Incorporate?

New York was the first to discover that making it easy for businesses to incorporate brings in generous revenues in the way of fees and taxes. New York was the first "best state to incorporate in" followed by New Jersey and then Delaware. Today the king of corporations is the State of Nevada. Why? Well the two most important reasons are that Nevada has no corporate income tax, and secondly, the shareholders of the corporation can remain anonymous.

So, in what state should you incorporate? It's my opinion that you should incorporate in the state where you are doing business. That is, where your office is located. There are only two reasons to incorporate in another state, (1) if you are going to have offices in several states, and (2) for tax planning. If you are going to have offices in more than one state, Nevada makes a good choice because it is "friendly" to corporations. Also, since Nevada has no state corporate income tax, you can lower your taxes by shifting income there from a taxable state. Needless to say, this is a sophisticated tax strategy meant for those with large tax bills and a good CPA.

The Bottom Line

When you first start out, it's best to incorporate in your own state. If you get offices in other states later, you can relocate your corporate headquarters then. Besides, if you incorporate in another state, you'll have to register the corporation as a "foreign" (out-of-state) corporation doing business in your own state.

The Incorporating Process

The incorporating process is very simple and consists of five basic steps, choosing a corporate name, checking to see if another corporation is already using the name, filing your articles of incorporation with the state, attending to some organizational matters like issuing stock, and finally, setting up your corporate records book.

Please read and understand all the steps before filing any paperwork. A mistake could result in having to redo and re-file paperwork, costing you time and money.

The process outlined here is applicable to any state. *The instructions on the back of your state's articles of incorporation (appendix) will cover any specifics for your state.* The steps are:

Step 1. Choose a corporate name

Step 2. Check the availability of your corporate name

Step 3. File your paperwork

Step 4. Take care of organizational matters

Step 5. Prepare your corporate records

Step 1. Choose a Corporate Name

The first step in organizing your corporation is selecting a name. Your corporate name must meet specific requirements outlined by State law.

State Requirements
The name must show that you are a corporation. It must contain either "incorporated" "corporation" "company" or an abbreviation of one of these words like "inc." "corp." or "co."

These words or their abbreviations tell the world that you are operating as a corporation. This way, other businesses, creditors, etc. know that you are not responsible for corporate obligations, and that any lawsuits must be brought against the corporation.

The corporate name must be different from corporate names being used in the state or any other name on file with the secretary of state. This includes LLCs, out of state corporations doing business in the state, and registered trademarks. Also, your corporate name may not be "deceptively similar" to other names in use. This keeps companies from benefiting from the goodwill created by another company.

If another corporation has taken the name you want to use, all you'll need to do is add another word to the corporate name to meet this requirement. For example, if your last name is Brown and you want to use "Brown, Inc." as your corporate name, you'll probably find that another entrepreneur named Brown beat you to it. However, you can still use Brown in your corporate name if you simply add another word or initial. For example, you could name it Brown Ventures, Inc., Brown

Publishing, Inc., or Dean Brown, Inc. Oh, by the way, changing the corporate identifier doesn't change the name. That is, changing from "Inc." to "Corp." doesn't help, "Brown, Inc." and "Brown Corp." is the same corporate name.

Please note that if the corporate name you want to use is available according to the records of the Secretary of State, there may still be an unincorporated business like a sole proprietorship or partnership using the name. According to law, the business that uses the name first in a geographic location has the rights to the name. To check for these types of businesses, you can look in the white pages of your telephone directory. If you plan to do business in other cities, you may want to check those telephone directories too. If you want to do business state wide, regionally, or nationally, you may consider having your name researched by professionals and registered as a trademark with the U.S. Patent and Trademark office. Registering a trademark will give you the right to use the name in all 50 states. For more information on trademarks, see the trademark book listed in the brochure.

The corporate name may not contain a word or phrase indicating that the company is organized to transact business for which it has not been approved. For example, your corporate name can't contain the word "insurance" unless the company has satisfied state requirements for incorporating as an insurance company. The same applies for other types of regulated businesses like banks, securities brokers, hospitals, physicians, etc.

Also, the corporate name may not imply that the corporation is affiliated with, or sponsored by, any fraternal, veteran's, service, religious, charitable, or professional organization unless the authorization is officially granted to the business and the authorization is certified in writing. For example, if you're not associated with the YMCA, you can't make "YMCA" a part of your corporate name. In addition, stay away from names that make your corporation sound like it's a part of the State or Federal government. Although using the word federal in your name is usually okay, be careful not to imply any governmental authority or affiliation.

Other considerations for choosing a name

An assumed name, sometimes called a fictitious name or d.b.a., is a feature of some state laws that allows a business to operate under more than one name. This can be convenient to the small businessperson who operates several businesses but does not want to have several corporations. Using an assumed name, you can name the corporation with a generic name, and then use assumed names that are more descriptive or "catchy." These other names would simply be aliases for a single corporation that has only one set of books and the same shareholders. A notice is filed with a state or local official to let the world know that the corporation and these "other companies" are the same entity.

Step 2. Check the Availability of Your Corporate Name

Since you can't use a corporate name already taken by another corporation, documents submitted with such a name used by another corporation will be rejected. So, before filing your articles of incorporation, you'll want to check to see if another corporation is already using the name. In most states you can find out if "your" corporate name is available by simply calling the secretary of state, or searching the name on their website.

Before you call their office, be sure of the name you want to use, and that it contains one of the required "Inc." words. You should also have one or two alternatives in case your first choice is being used by another company. Checking the availability of your name should only take a couple of minutes. This is a good time to ask any questions you may have and double check the filing fees, etc.

After finding that your name is available, you have the option of reserving it. Reserving a name gives you exclusive rights to the name for a period of 30-120 days, depending on the state. This allows you to "tie up" the name while you're getting ready to incorporate. In Georgia, reserving a name is a free service done over the phone while checking the availability. Of course you'll want to go ahead and reserve the name if you live there.

In all other states, reserving a name requires that you file a form with the state, for which there is a filing fee. In these states, you'll only want to reserve the name if you're *not* ready to file your articles of incorporation. If you *are* ready to file the articles, go ahead and file the articles without reserving the name, but don't delay. Filing the articles will make the name yours permanently.

How to do it

The Secretary of State has computer access to all corporate names being used in the state. The role playing outlined below is designed for a telephone call, but of course face to face conversation will be the same. The conversation will basically go like this:

S/S: Secretary of State's Office, may I help you?

You: Yes. I'd like to check the availability of a corporate name please. (The person will either check the name, or transfer you to the person who will.)

S/S: Okay. What is the name you'd like to check?

You: Brown Publishing, Inc.
(The person will now check their computer for the name.)

S/S: That name appears to be available. (That's great!)

The Secretary of State will usually only say something like the "name appears to be available." That's because someone may walk into their office five minutes later and file paperwork using "your" name. There are no guarantees as to the availability of a name until your articles of incorporation are accepted and filed.

If your first choice for a corporate name is already being used, the conversation will continue like this:

S/S: Brown Advertising does not appear to be available at this time. Are there any other names you'd like to check? (This is when your second and third choices come in handy.)

You: Yes. What about Brown Communications, Inc.?

S/S: (The person will now check for the new name.) That name *does* appear to be available at this time. (Got it!)

If name checks by phone are not offered in your state, you'll have to go ahead and file your articles and hope for the best. If the name you like is already being used, the state will fax, call, or write you.

Step 3. File Your Paperwork

The paperwork required to incorporate a business is a document called the articles of incorporation, also known as the articles of organization, certificate of incorporation, or charter in some states. It is filed with your secretary of state or similar business regulatory agency. Articles of incorporation for each state are in the appendix, listed in alphabetical order. In some states, the articles must be filed with another informational form. Check the instructions on the back of your state's articles for details.

Most states require the articles be typed so that it can be recorded (microfiched) clearly. If you want to type the articles on your computer, the forms in this book are available on disk for Windows or Macintosh computers. Let's discuss the items in a typical articles of incorporation.

Completing the Articles

The articles are easy to complete if you know basic information like your name and address and the corporation's name. (No, there's nothing difficult about it.) The articles usually provide information about the following items.

Name

Make sure the name meets state requirements and includes a corporate identifier like "Inc." or Incorporated.

Office

Some states require that you list an address for the principal office of the corporation. Your home address is okay to use.

Duration

The duration of the corporation is simply how long it will exist. If you are using the corporation to pursue a single project, you may wish to limit its life-span to the length of the project. Most businesses don't have a particular life-span. Most corporations will exist until they go out of business or until the sole owner dies. In this case, the life of the corporation is said to be perpetual, or never ending. Unless you have a particular reason for doing otherwise, the period of duration for your corporation should be perpetual. In some states, it is understood that the duration of your corporation will be perpetual. In other states, the duration must be stated in the articles.

Stock

Stock is issued to a corporation's owners, also known as stockholders or shareholders. A stock certificate is drawn up and given to each shareholder as evidence that he/she is a shareholder. While a corporation is in business, shareholders are entitled to dividends and other perks given to them by the corporation. If the corporation ever goes out of business, they are entitled to their pro-rata share of the corporation's assets after all debts are paid.

In this article, you'll describe the stock that your corporation can issue, listing the total number of shares that the corporation can issue to current or future shareholders; the par value; and any particular rights and privileges that the stock allows a shareholder, like voting rights. Providing this information in the articles of incorporation makes it public information, available to all shareholders and potential shareholders. In some states, the information is used to calculate your filing fee.

Authorized Shares – The first piece of information we'll provide about the stock is the number of authorized shares. *This is the total number of shares your corporation will ever have.* You can only change this number with the approval of a majority of shareholders and by amending the articles of incorporation. Needless to say, authorizing too many shares is better than not authorizing enough. I usually authorize one hundred thousand or a million shares of stock unless I'm forming a corporation in a state where the filing fee for the articles of incorporation is based on the number of authorized shares. In which case, I'll authorize the maximum number of shares allowed without increasing the minimum filing fee. Nevada, for example, will let you authorize 25,000 shares of no-par value stock without increasing the $125 minimum fee. Issuing more than 25,000 shares will increase the fee.

Common vs. Preferred shares – There are basically two different types of stock your corporation can issue, common and preferred. Common stock is what corporations usually issue to shareholders. It's what they trade on the New York Stock Exchange. The holders of common stock choose the directors of the corporation by voting their shares at an annual shareholders meeting. They also get to vote on other important matters that affect the corporation. Common stock holders of larger corporations get paid a quarterly dividend based on corporate profits. If there are no profits, a dividend is not usually paid.

Preferred stock, on the other hand is more like a bond or promissory note. It carries a fixed dividend percentage rate that is stated on the face of the certificate like this "8% Preferred."

Holders of preferred stock get paid dividends first. If there are profits left after paying the preferred dividends, then dividends are paid to the common shareholders. That's why it's called preferred stock, dividends on it are paid first. There is a drawback however. As a trade-off for getting dividends first, preferred shareholders don't get to vote on matters affecting the corporation. *Preferred stock is nonvoting.* I occasionally talk to a reader who wants to issue preferred stock. My advice is not to. Issue common stock only. If you want nonvoting stock, divide the common shares into two series, voting and nonvoting.

Voting and Nonvoting Stock – There are two types of common stock, voting and nonvoting. Owners of voting stock get to vote on matters that affect the corporation, like the election of directors. Owners of nonvoting shares do not. Nonvoting stock comes in handy when you want to give someone ownership in the company but you don't want them to have the power to elect directors. Nonvoting stock is good for issuing to your kids, in-laws, investors, or anyone who wants ownership without voting power. To show the difference between voting and nonvoting, you will divide the stock into classes and note the class on the face of the certificate.

To have voting and nonvoting stock in your corporation, you should describe it in your articles of incorporation like this:

> "The corporation is authorized to issue 100,000 shares of stock described as follows:
>
> > 50,000 shares of voting common stock without par value designated as Class A.
> >
> > 50,000 shares of nonvoting common stock without par value designated as Class B."

Par Value – Par value of stock is a bookkeeping term that basically equates to price. That is, the par value of a share of stock is usually the price per share that a shareholder must pay the corporation when buying the stock. It's really an outdated term because most stock issued these days is "no par" stock. That is, it has no fixed price per share. It is sold to different shareholders at different prices depending on the needs of the corporation.

Capitalization

A corporation's capitalization is defined as the number of shares of stock that the corporation is authorized to issue, multiplied by the stock's par value (# shares x par value).

If all the corporation's stock is issued (sold) to the shareholders at par value, then the company will have a known amount of cash in the bank after the stock is issued. This amount of money is known as the corporation's capitalization, or the amount of money (capital) that the corporation started business with.

I only explain this because in some states the fee for filing the articles of incorporation is based on the dollar amount of capitalization, usually stated something like this, "For capitalization up to $25,000, the filing fee is $100." If you've already done the math, no-par stock (with a par value of $0), doesn't work very well in this calculation. So, when corporations have no-par stock, a state usually assigns a par value for purposes of the calculation. This amount is typically one dollar.

Purpose	Some states require a purpose clause. A purpose clause simply states what the corporation's principal business is going to be. Once upon a time, you had to specifically state what type of business you were going to operate, but most states now accept the "general purpose clause." Using this clause, you can operate any type of business that you choose. This clause will also allow you to change the type of business your corporation transacts as you need.
Registered agent	A corporation's registered agent, sometimes called the resident agent, is the person appointed to accept legal documents on behalf of the corporation. If someone sues your corporation, the papers will be served on the registered agent at the "registered office." Therefore, a registered agent must have a street address. You can be your own registered agent and use your home address.
	If you choose to incorporate in a state where you do not have an office, you'll need the services of a registered agent service company. A list of agent services is typically available from the secretary of state for the state in which you want to incorporate, usually on their website. Consumer Publishing can serve as your registered agent in Tennessee or Nevada.
Incorporator	The incorporator is simply the person who files the articles of incorporation with the state. The incorporator really has no rights except appointing the initial corporate directors. You only need one person to be the incorporator. After the directors are appointed, the incorporator resigns.
Optional items	There are many different things that are not required to be in your articles of incorporation that you can include, providing they are not prohibited by state law. Something I usually include is a statement limiting the liability of the directors. As you can tell from reading it, it keeps lawsuit happy shareholders from suing you (the director) for money.
	Delayed effective date – If you are incorporating toward the end of the year, you may want to include a delayed effective date of incorporation. For example, if you're incorporating in the month of December, and you aren't going to start your business until the first of the year, you can include a statement in your articles that says the filing won't be effective until January first. This way, you won't have to file any tax returns for this "short" tax year beginning in December. State and Federal agencies won't be expecting you to be open for business until after the first of January. To make sure the secretary of state sees this, put a yellow Post-it® Note on the articles that says: "Delayed Effective Date."
Signing the articles	All those involved in the corporation do not need to sign the articles because they will be formally adopted by all shareholders and directors after they are filed with the secretary of state. So, only the person completing the articles (the incorporator) needs to sign.
	Now you are ready to file your articles. You can either mail, send them by overnight courier, or take them to the secretary of state's office yourself. Some states offer expedited service for an additional charge.

Step 4. Take Care of Organizational Matters

After your articles of incorporation are filed, state law requires that you take care of a few other important details before the organization of your corporation is complete. You must officially adopt the articles of incorporation filed with the state, adopt the bylaws, elect officers, approve the corporate seal, and issue stock. These actions are usually taken at a meeting known as the organizational meeting.

At the organizational meeting, all proposed directors, officers, and shareholders meet to discuss these organizational matters, take action on them and record the results as "minutes" of the meeting.

To make this easier than it sounds, a pre-written form is included in the appendix for your use. It is called the "Minutes of the Organizational Meeting of the Board of Directors." To use this form, all you'll need to do is read it carefully and insert the information pertaining to your corporation in the appropriate spaces. The next few pages will discuss topics and terminology related to completing the form.

Elect Directors

Although it is a legal "person" with rights of its own, a corporation can't walk, talk, think, or act for itself. It can't hold a pen to sign contracts. It can't go to the bank to make a deposit. It can't market its products or perform any of the physical tasks required to operate a business. Since it has no mental or physical capabilities, the business affairs of the corporation are managed and "directed" by directors. The group that oversees a corporation's activities is known as "the board of directors." Directors are like the guardians of an incompetent adult, who has rights, but can't think or act for him/herself. Directors meet from time to time to plan and approve actions the corporation will take to conduct its business.

Following correct procedure, directors are like trustees, charged by law to oversee the business affairs of the corporation. More like special consultants who come in periodically to plan and approve corporate actions, directors are usually not employees of the corporation. In return for their efforts, directors usually receive a token compensation, and other perks.

Deviating from the procedure envisioned by state law, the directors of large corporations don't actually oversee the business affairs of the corporation. In these corporations, directors are usually well known business people, celebrities, or former politicians who lend credibility to the corporation. In this case, being a director is more a position of status and the directors merely meet from time to time to "rubber stamp" what the officers they appointed have already decided is best for the corporation. This rubber stamp approval of corporate action is not the ideal procedure, but is reality in many cases.

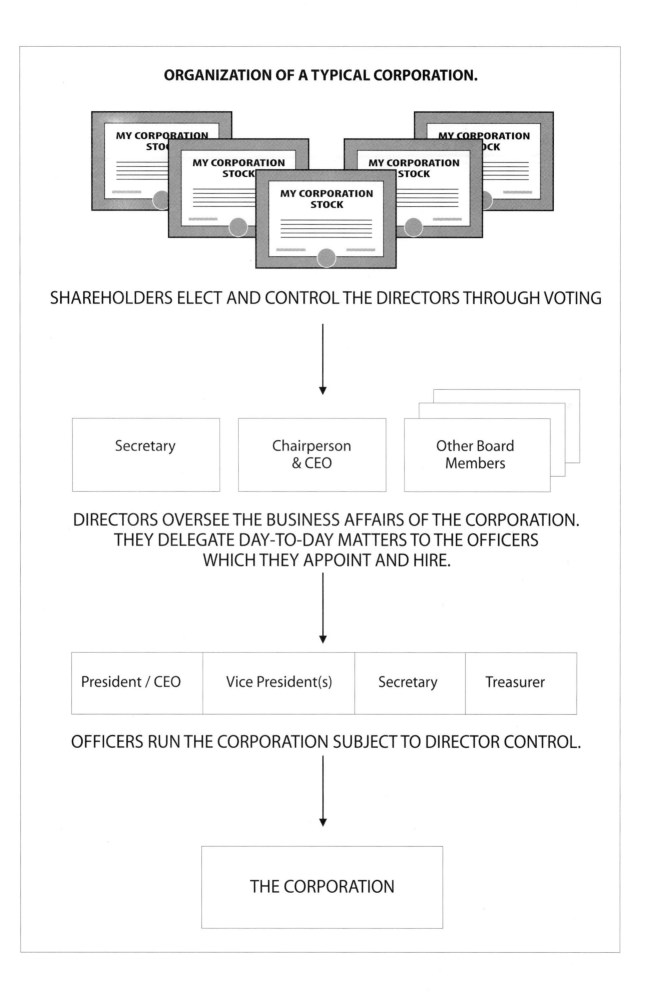

Appoint Officers

Although directors are responsible for managing and directing the business affairs of the corporation, they mostly oversee the "big picture." To manage the day to day activities of the corporation, the directors appoint and hire officers. Officers handle all of the daily decisions required to run a business, and the scope of their duties usually depends on the size of the corporation.

That is, the president of a corporation like Sears probably delegates the important duty of selecting new store sites to a subordinate, checking in periodically to make sure things are running smoothly. In contrast, the presidential duties of a small business corporation would probably include everything from selecting the store location, to selling the merchandise. A corporation usually has the following officers. You can change the titles and responsibilities to meet your needs. You can also add officers and titles if you wish, having more than one vice-president for example.

- President   Carries out the most important functions.

- Vice-President Acts for the President when needed.

- Secretary   Responsible for corporate records and meetings.

- Treasurer   Manages the financial affairs of the corporation.

When managing the daily activities of the corporation, the president is generally responsible for the more important or "glamorous" responsibilities like signing contracts or developing strategies for the corporation. The vice-president fills in for the president when necessary, or assists the president. The secretary maintains corporate records and correlates the organizational affairs of the corporation. The treasurer is responsible for the financial welfare of the corporation, from obtaining loans, to overseeing the accounting department.

Although large corporations can delegate duties the way state laws intended, the officer positions of a small corporation are usually filled by a single person who will carry out most, or all of these responsibilities.

Many times, in a small corporation, the directors and the officers are actually the same people who simply "wear different hats." That is, when you're carrying out director responsibilities, you're a director, and when taking care of officer duties, you're an officer. Officers are most always employees of the corporation. Being an employee of your own corporation is important because it makes you eligible for lucrative employee benefits, like retirement plans and hospitalization insurance. The corporation, of course, pays for these benefits.

Shareholders

Now you know what roles the directors and officers play, but the most important players in the average corporation aren't the directors or the officers. The most important people are those for whom the corporation was formed—the stockholders. The stockholders are the people who started, and own the corporation for their mutual benefit. The stockholders invest money, property, or something else of value into the corporation. In return, the stockholders will own a part of the corporation relative to the amount they invested. These people provide the means by which the corporation is able to begin operating.

To provide evidence of their ownership and investment, the corporation will issue these individuals a stock certificate. That's why these people are called "stockholders." These stocks represent ownership in a particular corporation, and are similar to those bought and sold on the stock exchanges in New York. In fact, stocks of small corporations sometimes trade just as fervently as those on Wall Street. Of course, only the stocks of larger corporations are traded on an exchange.

Since we couldn't have a corporation without them, the stockholders are at the top of the power structure. They control the corporation for their common good by appointing the directors who will oversee the activities of the corporation. Ideally, in large corporations where shareholders are spread over a large geographic area, the directors are like independent observers appointed by the shareholders to help insure their interests are protected.

Of course, what's been described here is the textbook example of how a large corporation works, and is very different from how a small one works. However, all of this needed to be explained so that you might gain a complete understanding of all the participants in the corporate world. You may understand the process better by reviewing the diagram on the previous page. Your corporation will look and function exactly like this diagram. Shareholders will start the corporation by giving money or property in exchange for its stock. The shareholders will then appoint directors to monitor their investment. Finally, since being a director isn't a full time calling, the directors appoint and hire officers to actually run the corporation on a daily basis.

Your corporation, however, will have one very important difference, only one or two people will hold most or all of these positions. Most small corporations will only have one or two people acting as all the directors, officers and stockholders. That's fine. I would suggest, however, that you fill at least two of the officer positions, those of president and secretary. A president is needed to run the day-to-day operations of the corporation like hiring, firing, dealing with the accountant, signing contracts, etc. The secretary is needed to keep up with the internal corporate paperwork—meeting minutes, issuing stock certificates, and drafting corporate resolutions.

When completing the minutes of organizational meeting form (appendix), put a nominal figure in the salary column if you haven't decided what the officer salaries will be. One hundred dollars per year will be okay. When you decide what the salaries will be, hold a director's meeting on the subject and make the change. The directors will officially approve of the salary, and this approval will be noted in the minutes of the meeting.

In reality, most people simply pay themselves whatever they can. Then, at the end of the year (at tax time), part of the total amount paid is allocated to officer salary and the rest to "regular" salary. The allocation is usually based on the amount of time spent performing officer duties relative to the time spent at other tasks. For example, if you paid yourself $50,000 and spent 10% of your time performing officer duties, then it would be reasonable to pay yourself a $5,000 officer salary and a $45,000 salary for your other efforts. (.10 X $50,000 = $5,000 and $50,000 - $5,000 = $45,000) You may want to speak with your accountant about this. I think most people just leave this blank until they know how much they can pay themselves.

Issuing Stock

A business corporation cannot exist without stockholders. Stockholders, or shareholders as they are often called, invest money in a corporation in exchange for a part or "share" of the corporation. In return for their investment, shareholders receive dividends based on the future earnings of the corporation or some other monetary reward. In many cases, shareholders invest in a corporation hoping that its value will increase and enable them to later sell their stock at a profit. Shareholders who buy stock in a corporation for its profit potential are known as investors. Shareholders like you who are not investors usually work for the corporation and receive a salary in addition to or instead of dividends.

There are basically two ways to buy stock in a corporation—either directly from the corporation, or in the open market. Initially, all stocks are purchased directly from the corporation that issued them. However, many shares are bought by investors who will sell them at some point in the future. This is how shares become available in the open market, investors selling them to other investors. There is such a demand for these shares as investments, huge companies that facilitate stock trading, like the New York Stock Exchange, were created to facilitate the purchase and sell of these secondhand securities.

Unlike the investor who buys for speculation, you are buying stock in your corporation to start a company. Like most small business owners, you'll probably hold on to your stock and someday leave it to your kids. But, like the investor, you will still have to "purchase" the stock from your corporation and give something of value for it. You must bargain with the board of directors to determine a price acceptable to both you and the board. Your situation is a little different because you will play both the role of the prospective shareholder wanting to buy stock and the director wanting to receive something of acceptable value for it. In reality, however, prospective shareholders like yourself will give what they can afford for the stock and of course "the board" will accept your offer.

In this case, issuing stock boils down to three things:

1. Who will the shareholders be?

2. What percentage or part of the corporation will each person own?

3. How much will the shareholders pay for each share of stock?

Once you know the answers to these questions, issuing the stock is simply a matter of completing the last section of the form entitled "Minutes of the Organizational Meeting of the Board of Directors" and issuing stock certificates (appendix) to each new shareholder. Be sure to read the remainder of this section before issuing the stock. Also, remember the price per share of all initially issued shares must be the same.

Authorized vs issued shares

Before you issue stock, let's discuss the difference between authorized shares of stock and issued shares of stock. "Authorized shares" is the number of shares set by the articles of incorporation that the board of directors is "authorized" to issue. The board of directors is the body that controls the issuance of stock. In large corporations, this authorized limit on the total number of shares prevents the board from issuing too many shares. Too many new shares lower the value of your stock.

The board may issue all the shares now, or issue some now, and some later. Your articles of incorporation state the number of shares that the corporation is authorized to issue and make this number a matter of public record for all to see. The number of authorized shares equals the total number of shares that may be issued now, or at some point in the future. Issued shares is the number of shares "issued" or distributed to shareholders. Only issued shares count for ownership purposes. Shares that are not issued are called authorized but unissued shares. They are technically worthless until they are issued to a shareholder. Usually when a corporation issues shares of stock to its initial shareholders, a few shares are left unissued so that they may be issued later to new investors, family members etc.

It is a good idea not to issue (distribute) all of the authorized shares now, because you may need a few shares to issue later. You may want to issue some stock to a son or daughter entering the business, or to a new business partner. The main point to remember is that only issued shares count for ownership.

Take the following example for a corporation that has 1,000 authorized (another word for total available) shares of stock, and two owners:

Owner A is issued 100 shares 100/200=50% ownership
(Number owned divided by total issued.)

Owner B is issued 100 shares 100/200=50% ownership
(Number owned divided by total issued.)

The two shareholders in this example own 50% of the corporation because the 800 unissued shares are not considered in the calculation. One thousand authorized shares less 200 issued shares leaves 800 available for future use. Since only the 200 issued shares count for ownership, owners with 100 shares each own one half of the corporation. (One hundred is half of two hundred.) Only issued shares count for ownership percentages.

Multiple shareholders

Issuing stock in a corporation with more than one owner can sometimes be tricky, especially if the percentage of ownership or consideration is unequal. Let's take a minute here to talk about the different combinations and possible solutions. (Consideration is the money or property given for stock.)

For the purposes of these examples, let's say that there are three owners (shareholders) in the corporation and 100,000 authorized shares of stock. Remember from the previous section, it's a good idea not to issue all of your authorized shares so we won't in these examples. Many readers that I talk with get caught up in the stock's price per share upon issue. Don't worry about the price per share. It doesn't matter. Instead, concentrate on how much of the corporation each shareholder will own. The price per share will simply be a function of how much of the corporation the shareholder owns and the amount given for the stock. Price per share will be equal to the amount the shareholder gives for the stock divided by the number of shares they get.

Equal ownership / Equal consideration – This is an easy one. All three shareholders put in an equal amount of cash (the amount doesn't matter) and will divide ownership evenly, one third each. To make the math easy, let's issue each owner 10,000 shares of stock, leaving 70,000 shares unissued. A total of 30,000 shares (10,000 + 10,000 + 10,000) of stock will be issued. Let's check our math, 30,000 total issued shares, divided by 10,000 shares issued to each owner equals .333 or 1/3 ownership each. Each shareholder will invest an equal amount of money, depending on how much money the corporation needs to start operations. To show their ownership, we'll issue one stock certificate to each shareholder for 10,000 shares.

Equal ownership/ Unequal consideration – This is a typical example. People of different financial means often start businesses together. Some owners put in money, and some put in effort. This situation occurs when a certain amount of money is needed to start the business, and only one person can contribute it.

For this example, let's say that $10,000 is needed to start the business. The best way to handle this is to have all three shareholders contribute the same amount of money for their stock, and the additional amount is given as a loan. Two of the shareholders will put in what they can, say $500 each. The third shareholder puts in $500 too. Now the business has $1,500 of the $10,000 it needs. The additional $8,500 needed will be *loaned* to the corporation by the third shareholder. The officers of the corporation will sign a promissory note guaranteeing payment of the $8,500 to the third shareholder.

Again, let's issue each owner 10,000 shares of stock, leaving 70,000 shares unissued. A total of 30,000 shares (10,000 + 10,000 + 10,000) of stock will be issued. Let's check our math, 30,000 total issued divided by 10,000 shares to each owner equals .333 or 1/3 ownership each. To show their ownership, we'll issue one stock certificate to each shareholder for 10,000 shares.

Unequal ownership/ Unequal consideration – In this example there are three shareholders. Shareholder 1 will own 10 percent of the corporation, shareholder 2 will own 20 percent and shareholder 3 will own the remaining 70 percent. All we do here is simply issue the needed number of shares to each person, and adjust the consideration to match.

For example, lets issue 10,000 of our 100,000 shares to make the numbers easy to work with. We will give the first shareholder 1,000 shares, the second shareholder 2,000 shares, and the third shareholder 7,000 shares for a total of 10,000 shares issued. (1,000 is 10% of 10,000 and 2,000 is 20% of 10,000 and 7,000 is 70% of 10,000)

For consideration, the shareholders contribute $1,000, $2,000 and $7,000 respectively. If the shareholders don't have that much money, they could contribute $100, $200, and $700 respectively. Still too much? Then let them contribute $10, $20, and $70 respectively. The amount of the consideration doesn't matter as long as it makes the ownership percentages what we need them to be.

Consideration

Stock in a corporation represents various rights and privileges to the shareholder. So, in exchange for the stock of a corporation something of value must be given. The payment given to a corporation for its stock is known as consideration. State law governs the type of consideration you give for your stock. You can pay money, give property, or have already provided labor or services to the corporation for which you were not paid.

Some states have a minimum capital requirement, that is, a minimum amount of money is required to be in the company's bank account before operations can begin. If there is no minimum capital requirement in your state, any amount of consideration approved by the Board of Directors is acceptable. This amount can be all cash, all property, all services, or various combinations of the three. (Since giving property that has appreciated in value since you acquired it can cause tax problems, you should see your CPA before doing so.)

Please note that money given to the corporation doesn't "disappear." In reality, the corporation will spend this much money just opening its doors and you would have put money into the corporation anyway. The corporation will spend this amount reimbursing you for filing fees, taxes, buying office supplies, printing stationery, paying rent and so forth. If your initial cash contribution isn't enough to get the corporation up and running, you'll have to put more money into the corporation from time to time.

If you have to put money into the corporation, you can account for the contribution in three ways:

1. You can put money into the corporation in return for additional stock. This is usually done when other partners are involved.

2. You can put money into the corporation, issue no more stock and simply call this an owner's contribution. This is usually done when there is only one shareholder. This money is not taxed when taken back out of the corporation. It's a return of capital.

3. You can put money into the corporation, call it a loan, and receive the money back with interest. Discuss this with your CPA first. This is the preferred method. The best way to do it is to set up an account on

your books called something like "Payable to Shareholder" and whenever you lend money to the company, account for it with this account.

Giving property for your stock – If you give real estate, vehicles, equipment or other big dollar items to the corporation in exchange for your stock, you'll need to make up a list of the assets and also transfer title of the property to the corporation. Transfer land to the corporation with a deed, perhaps with the help of a title company. Transfer vehicles to the corporation by signing the title over to the corporation, then have the corporation register the vehicle at the county courthouse. Transfer equipment by giving a bill of sale to the corporation.

If you owe money on the asset, you can't transfer title since the lender has rights to it. If you want your corporation to use and make payments on a car for example, keep everything the way it is and simply lease the car to the corporation. Have the corporation pay you enough each month to make the payment. Also, make the corporation pay for gas and repairs. You'll need to draw up a lease that outlines the details. Be sure to have the vehicle insured in the corporate name in case you're in an accident. You should chat with your accountant and insurance agent about this.

Many people retain ownership to their property and simply rent or lease it to the corporation. This way, they can receive lease payments from the corporation for its use, making it lease or rental income. This is a good way to get money out of the company without paying Social Security taxes. (Rental income is only subject to regular income taxes.) One word of caution here, be careful when leasing vehicles or dangerous equipment to the company. If someone gets injured by the vehicle or equipment, the injured party may try to recover from you as the lessor of the equipment.

Tax considerations – Sometimes, giving property or services for your corporation's stock leads to tax problems, and you should see your CPA accordingly. If you simply give property to your new corporation in exchange for at least 80% of the stock, you usually don't have to worry about taxes. Internal Revenue Code Section 351 calls this a tax-free exchange and allows it. However, exchanging property in the following cases will lead to problems. If you want to exchange property for stock in a manner similar to any of these examples, or are transferring property to the corporation to avoid taxes, see your CPA or tax advisor first. A list of property transfers to avoid:

1. An exchange of property to a corporation when you will own less than eighty percent of the stock.

2. An exchange where you receive cash, or property, or benefits other than stock for your property.

3. An exchange where your liabilities against the property exceed your adjusted basis in that property.

4. An exchange of property that has increased in value since you bought it.

Issuing Stock Certificates

Although stock certificates are not money and this is only an analogy, you may compare stock certificates to checks in a checkbook and authorized shares to the amount of money in your checking account. Stock certificates and checks are similar, but of course are not the same. Instead of representing money like checks do, stock certificates represent shares of ownership in a corporation. When you write a check, you give someone money. When you issue certificates, you give someone ownership in your corporation. With a checkbook, you can write checks in any dollar amount to as many people as you want until you either run out of money or out of checks. With stock, you can issue certificates for any number of shares to as many people as you want until you either run out of authorized shares or certificates.

To issue stock certificates to each shareholder, you must complete the face of the certificate by typing the name of the corporation, the name of the shareholder, the date, the state of incorporation, the number of authorized shares, the par value, and the number of shares being issued to the shareholder all in their appropriate spaces. Next, number the certificates sequentially, (01, 02, 03, 04, 05…) and have the President and Secretary of the corporation sign the certificates at the bottom left and right. The circle near the bottom is where you will press the corporation's seal. Check the example stock certificate on the next page to see how to complete yours.

On the back, do not complete the section that begins with "For value received." This section is completed when, and if you ever sell your stock. Completing this section is like endorsing a check, and makes the certificate transferable.

Stock Registration

The registration of securities, stocks, bonds, partnership interests, etc., is a process designed to protect investors from fraudulent securities offerings. Stock in your corporation is considered a security. Registration usually involves the filing of information related to the offering with a state agency. Securities offered to people in your state fall under state regulation, and securities offered to people outside your state fall under Federal regulation.

If you are simply incorporating your existing business or issuing stock to family members or other organizers and officers of the corporation that live in your state, the issuance is usually exempt from state and Federal registration. Generally, the issuance of stock is exempt from registration if:

1. The stock is only issued to corporate officers and organizers, people who actively participate in the operation and management of the corporation.

2. The stock is issued by the corporation and not a securities dealer.

3. The issue is not advertised or offered to the general public (outsiders).

4. The stock is issued to a limited number of people. (See the notes on the back of your state's articles for this number.)

5. A commission for selling the security is not paid.

If you are starting a business and wish to attract investors (either in-state or out-of-state), are trying to make money from the sale of the stock, or will be paying commissions to a broker for selling the stock, you will need to register your stock, for which you will need professional help.

If you are simply incorporating your business and issuing stock to family members or others that are involved in running the corporation, you will not need to register your stock.

The main point to remember is this. Registration is designed to protect consumers from fraudulent stock offerings. So, do *not* offer stock to someone unless they are intimately familiar with you and the financial condition of the corporation, and they will be helping you operate the business.

Corporation Bylaws

The bylaws of the corporation are the internal rules by which it operates. Just as a city has laws for its citizens, a corporation has laws for its shareholders, directors, and officers. A standard set of corporate bylaws for your use is in the appendix. The only thing you'll need to do with the bylaws is read and become familiar with them. Become especially familiar with the procedure a shareholder must follow before selling any stock as outlined in article four of the bylaws. Also, note in article five you must complete the time and date of the annual meeting of the corporation. This can be any date and time that is convenient for you that allows enough time to prepare financial reports for the year just ended.

It is important that you hold an annual meeting or at least sign the pre-written minutes because the directors and officers are only appointed for one year terms and are reappointed every year at this time. Remember, the minutes of the annual shareholders meeting have already been prepared, so all you really need to do is sign and date them. Most people never really have an annual shareholder's meeting, they just sign the minutes and file them away. Since these bylaws are standard and written for most corporations, you may feel the need to customize or add to the bylaws. You may want to customize your bylaws in these areas:

- Dividends – if, when, and how much will be paid.
- Officer salaries.
- Directors compensation – if, when, and how much will be paid.
- Further conditions for the transfer of stock, like what to do in the event of the death of a shareholder. Will the stock be left to the spouse, or must it be sold back to the corporation?
- What happens if the corporation dissolves? How will the assets be distributed?

At some point in the future a shareholder may want to leave the corporation and sell his stock. How do you determine what the stock is worth? It's better to determine this in advance to prevent arguments. Many corporations value stock by taking the stockholder's equity (Assets - Liabilities) and dividing it by the number of shares. Other corporations have director meetings about once every six months to set a value for the shares. The method is up to you.

1,000

Number of Shares

01

Certificate Number

Certificate of Stock

MY COMPANY NAME

This Certifies that Dean Brown

One Thousand (1,000)

is the registered holder of

shares of the above named corporation.

This certificate is transferable on the books of the corporation only by the shareholder named herein or by the shareholder's duly appointed representative upon surrender of the certificate properly endorsed. This series is designated as Class **A** *and its total authorized issue is* **100,000,000** *shares with* **No** *par value. This stock has not been registered with any State or Federal agency and its transfer is subject to restriction. The corporation is organized in the State of* **Tennessee**

In Witness Whereof, said corporation has caused this certificate to be signed by its duly authorized officers and its seal to be hereunto affixed this **3rd** *day of* **February** *20* **00**

Dean Brown

President

Cherie Brown

Secretary

For value received, I *hereby sell, assign, and transfer unto* **William Brown**

1,000 *shares of stock represented by this certificate, and do hereby irrevocably*

constitute and appoint **Cherie Brown** *Corporate Secretary as Agent to transfer said*

shares on the books of the within named Corporation with full power of substitution in the premises.

Dated: **October 6, 2015**

Signature of Shareholder: *Dean Brown*

Signature of Witness: *Sandy Thomas*

The following abbreviations, when used in the inscription on the face of the certificate, shall be construed as though they were written out in full according to applicable laws or regulations:

TEN COM   as tenants in common
TEN ENT   as tenants by the entirety
JT TEN   as joint tenants with right of survivorship and not as tenants in common
UNIF GIFT MIN ACT (insert name of custodian) as custodian for (insert name of minor child)
under the (insert name of state) Uniform Gifts to Minors Act

Step 5. Prepare Your Corporate Records

Since you are required by law to keep meticulous records of the activities of your corporation, you will need to set up and maintain a corporate record book. Properly organized records are one of the first things the IRS will ask to see if you ever get audited. Plus, if you intend to seek financing for your new venture, your banker will want to see your corporate records as well. The corporate record book is the only proof that your corporation is properly organized and maintained, so don't skip this step.

Although you can organize them in any convenient manner, most people use a corporate records book, or corporate "kit" as they are sometimes called, for storing their records. A record book is simply a nice binder with divided sections for storing your company documents, minutes, and certificates and includes the corporate seal. When preparing a corporate record book, you have two choices, either prepare your own, or purchase one.

Buying a Kit

If you choose to purchase one and are unable to find corporate supplies in your area, corporate kits and corporate seals are available from Consumer Publishing. Please see the order form in the back of the book for more information. Corporate kits are shipped within 24 hours. Next day service is also available. Corporate kits are available for C and S Corporations as well as nonprofit corporations, professional corporations, and close corporations. Each outfit includes:

- A deluxe binder with the corporate name embossed in gold letters on the spine,
- A matching slip case to protect your records from dust,
- A corporate seal,
- 20 Stock certificates typeset with the corporate name, the number of authorized shares of stock and par value, shareholder names can even be typeset if you like.
- A stock transfer ledger,
- Preprinted minutes and bylaws,
- A special forms section and a review of IRS requirements for S Corporations,
- Medical and dental reimbursement plan
- Annual meeting forms.

Making a Kit

If you prefer to prepare your own corporate kit, you'll need to visit a legal stationary or lawyer supply store and purchase the following:

- A three ring binder,
- At least 8 tabbed index dividers to divide the book into sections,
- Pre-punched three ring binder paper to keep minutes on,
- A corporate seal.

A corporate seal should be included with the corporate record book because the seal is how the corporation "signs" contracts, minutes, and other official documents like stock certificates. The seal is maintained by the corporate secretary and is used to show that the corporation approves of documents that the seal is applied to. After you have all of your supplies together, you should assemble them as follows.

1. Prepare these headings for the tabbed index dividers; APPLICATIONS & PERMITS; STATE FILINGS; BYLAWS; MINUTES; STOCK CERTIFICATES; S-ELECTION; FORMS; and JOURNAL LEDGER.

2. Three hole punch the documents already filed with the state and/or the IRS, as well as the directors meeting minutes completed in the previous step and insert them into the appropriate sections of the corporate record book.

3. Copy or remove the bylaws from this chapter and insert them into the BYLAWS section.

4. Copy or remove the pre-written minute forms from this chapter and insert them into the MINUTES section. Remember to make copies of the blank originals for your future minute keeping needs. The minutes from all your meetings will be kept in this section.

5. Prepare a separate list of stockholders, directors, and officers of the corporation and include these lists in the JOURNAL LEDGER section. These lists may seem insignificant but are required by law. Be sure to update these lists if anything changes.

Record Keeping

Every list of pros and cons of incorporating I've ever seen usually lists increased record keeping at the top of the cons list. Although there is more record keeping involved with a corporation, listing increased record keeping as the top reason not to incorporate is shortsighted. Corporate record keeping is not a big deal.

To understand the reason a corporation requires more records than an unincorporated business, lets review for a minute. Remember that a corporation is a separate and distinct entity with legal rights of its own that acts for or on the behalf of its shareholders. Owners incorporate their business to allow them to act through the corporation. Although the corporation is a legal "person" it cannot act for itself. So, to allow the corporation to carry out its business, the shareholders appoint directors to manage and direct the business affairs of the corporation. The directors act like the trustees of an incompetent adult, planning and directing the activities of the corporation. Since the directors are acting in a trustee type arrangement, states require that everything done by the directors on behalf on the corporation be documented. That's why every time a meeting is held to take action on behalf of the corporation, it must be documented, and minutes of the meeting must be recorded.

Another reason extensive records of corporate activities are kept is the shareholder. Remember that when corporate laws were originally drafted, the idea of a one or two person corporation had not been considered. Laws were originally drafted to match the textbook example of a corporation with many investor shareholders. In such a case, the shareholders, officers, and directors were all different people. Laws were written to protect the shareholder from unscrupulous directors and officers who would run a corporation broke to make themselves rich. This is another reason things must be documented and annual shareholders meetings held, to keep officers and directors honest by documenting their every move.

Of course, your corporation will probably be formed with less that four shareholders. These shareholders will probably be the officers, and directors as well. In this case, the shareholders will know the events within their corporation. Considering this, record keeping may seem like a waste but you must remember one thing. Operating as a corporation can give you great benefits, legally, and in the area of taxes too. To make sure that these abilities are not abused, states and the IRS require that you keep records of all corporate activities. Basically records must be kept of all important events within the corporation.

Here is a list of the records you must keep for your corporation. These records must be available for shareholder inspection and accordingly should be kept at the offices of the corporation in an orderly manner.

- Minutes of all shareholder and director meetings, generally for the last 3 years.

- Appropriate accounting records and financial reports.

- An alphabetical list of all shareholders with their addresses.

- An alphabetical list of all directors with their business addresses.

- An alphabetical list of all officers with their business addresses.

- Copies of all formal documents used to incorporate the business.

- All written communications to shareholders for the past 3 years.

- Financial statements for the past 3 years.

- A copy of the most recent annual report.

- All contracts entered into by the corporation.

- Amendments to, or changes in the corporate bylaws.

- Records of stock issues and transfers.

- Promissory notes.

- Life insurance policies held on corporate officers and directors.

Holding Meetings

The recording of meetings and even the meeting itself need not be made overly formalized. For example, many people formally call the meeting to order; formally ask for turns to speak; formally make, and second motions; and formally adjourn the meeting. This formality comes from directors meetings of large corporations, and is not necessary for small corporate meetings.

When holding a meeting, all you need to do is sit down, discuss what needs to be done, vote on the matter, summarize it on paper, and have everyone sign it. The best way to do this is to write down everything that happens on a plain piece of paper, summarize and organize the information, then transfer it to a formal minutes type form.

If you have no other meetings, you must have an annual shareholders meeting to "discuss" the results of operations for the year with the shareholders. Many people don't actually hold a meeting, they just sign the minutes of the meeting and file it in your corporate records binder. Before using them, make extra copies of the forms in this chapter for your future use.

This concludes the incorporating process. If you're incorporating an existing business, read on. If not, proceed to Chapter 4 and read about some things you'll need to after incorporating.

Chapter 3
Incorporating an Existing Business

Since an existing business has employees, leases, existing liabilities, bank accounts and other contractual arrangements, incorporating a pre-existing business is not quite as simple as incorporating a new one. It's more complicated and will take more time. It's more than simply changing stationery.

Because a corporation is a separate and distinct entity and not simply an extension of the owner, incorporating an existing business is not as simple as just changing the name and doing business as usual. After incorporating, the corporation will actually be doing business with your customers, selling your products, making your loan payments and so on.

If you wish to conduct business as a corporation, the corporation will, in effect, need to "take your place" and formally adopt all contracts you've undertaken to conduct business. In some cases, the corporation may simply ratify the contracts that you have entered. In other cases, the old contracts will need to be voided and new ones entered into. In any case, the business that you have known and operated in the past will legally cease to exist and the corporation will take its place as a totally new entity. You're basically selling your business and its assets to the corporation. For this, the corporation will pay you with its stock. When this happens, the corporation essentially owns your business, and you in turn own the corporation. This is how you become separated from your business, thus gaining personal liability protection, and generous tax benefits.

Now that you understand the basics of incorporating a preexisting business, we need to discuss some of the details you'll need to consider when incorporating. However, at this point a word of caution is in order. Incorporating a preexisting business is a fairly straightforward event, but if you don't have a working knowledge of contracts and business law, you may be asking for trouble by going it alone.

Before beginning this process, you may want to do some research on contract law. Many books on the subject are available at your local bookstore or library. Also, your CPA is a good source of information. CPA's have formal training in business law and contracts, and your's may be able to help. As a last resort, you may want to consider hiring an experienced lawyer.

Please understand that this book was written to help you incorporate a business. Since incorporating an existing business includes areas of law beyond the scope of this book, some of which could take volumes to explain, an attempt to fully cover these areas cannot be made. This is merely a basic outline of things you'll need to consider when incorporating an existing business, and is in no way to be considered a complete discourse on the subject, or a how to manual. Also, please remember that transferring property to a corporation may have tax implications, and you should see your CPA before doing anything.

Dissolve the Existing Business

When incorporating an existing business, you must first formally dissolve the old business. Any property held by the existing business will again be held by you personally. After you regain title to the property, there are basically two ways of proceeding:

1. You can keep some of the property in your name personally or

2. You can simply transfer everything to the corporation.

If you choose to keep some of the business assets in your name, you may do so for the following reasons:

1. To help maintain control when you are not the only shareholder and

2. To receive personal income at a lower tax rate.

Transfer Assets

In a corporation where you are not the only shareholder, it is important to retain as much control over the corporation as possible. One way of exercising control is through your voting stock. Another way is to control the assets that the corporation needs to operate. Simply stated, when the equipment needed to operate is under your control, you will usually be treated more fairly by other shareholders because you have the ability to "take your equipment and go home" when things don't go your way.

Secondly, keeping property out of the corporation can be very tax advantageous, especially if your salary income is high. When you retain title to property the corporation needs to operate, you can lease the property back to the corporation, and in return, receive lease payments.

You can then lower the taxable effect of these lease payments with depreciation and other expenses related to the property's operation.

Usually, when a preexisting business is incorporated, everything, or most everything, is transferred to the corporation. This might include all the company assets, liabilities, and other contracts. Assets are usually transferred by conveying your title in them to the corporation. Liabilities, and other contracts are transferred to the corporation when the corporation formally adopts them.

Basically, you will "transfer and assign all your rights" in an item to the corporation with a written agreement stating that you do so. If the item has a title or deed, new documents must be prepared to show that the corporation now legally owns it.

The corporation must then formally adopt and approve everything that is done. To do this you will need to prepare director's consents to corporate action stating that the directors "approve and adopt" everything that is done. Also, if deeds or titles are involved, the corporation president will sign the documents needed to transfer the assets to the corporation. If you "transfer" all your business assets to your corporation, you should do so in return for the stock that the corporation will issue to you. This way, you will reduce or eliminate any chance that the transfers will cause tax problems. Assets to be transferred will include things like:

- Cash in the bank
- Accounts receivable (Money your customers owe)
- Notes receivable (Other monies owed)
- Inventory
- Prepaid Expenses (Insurance)
- Deposits
- Cars and other vehicles
- Plant equipment & machinery
- Office equipment & computers
- Buildings
- Land

Cash

Transferring assets like cash is an easy thing to do. It's done by opening a new bank account in the name of the corporation, and putting the cash from your old account into the corporation's. You will actually close your old account and transfer all the funds with a check made payable to the corporation. You will then be authorized by corporate resolution to write checks on this new account. You will no longer "own" this money the corporation will.

However, by owning the stock of the corporation, you still indirectly "own" the money. But, you will no longer be able to dip into this cash whenever you please, because it now is the property of the corporation.

But don't worry, the tax advantages gained by incorporating will make it worth the inconvenience.

Accounts receivable	Accounts receivable is a formal contractual agreement between you and your customers in which they promise to pay you for goods and services provided to them. Since your business has actually ceased to exist, you'll need to assign your "rights" to collect this money to the corporation. All monies received in the future should be deposited into the corporate account, and you should notify your customers to make their checks payable to the corporation. This is a good chance to let your customers know that you have incorporated your business.
Notes receivable	Notes receivable are like accounts receivable, except that notes receivable usually have promissory notes to back them up. For example, if you own a car lot where you sometimes finance your customer's purchases, your customers will sign a note promising to pay a fixed amount of money at certain intervals. When these promissory notes were made, they were made on behalf of your old business, which no longer exists. Therefore, you'll need to "assign the rights to collect payments" to the corporation, and similarly, tell the borrowers to make their payments to the corporation.
Miscellaneous assets	Miscellaneous assets like inventory, prepaid expenses, office furniture, computers, and deposits are usually transferred to the corporation when the stock is issued. Documentation will include a listing in the corporate records that the property is being transferred to the corporation in exchange for corporate stock. For things like computers, and other small, yet expensive items, you will also need to give the corporation a "Bill of Sale" so that the corporation may prove it has legal title to the property. This is necessary to enable the corporation to sell the item in the future.
Assets with titles or deeds	Some assets, like cars, machinery, buildings, and other larger items, have a title or a deed that shows who legally owns them. The titles or deeds to these items will need to be re-drawn and re-filed in the name of the corporation. This may involve lawyers, title companies, and local governments, all of which will cost you time and money. However, for reasons listed above, these are sometimes not transferred to the corporation.
Liabilities	For a minute, lets discuss the other side of the balance sheet, the liabilities side. Before incorporating, you are personally responsible for all your business's liabilities and loans. Since you now want your corporation to make these payments, the corporation will need to formally adopt the debts as its own. To do this, you will need to meet with your banker and other creditors to arrange for the notes and other liabilities to become the corporation's.
	At best, the creditors will totally release you from the debts in exchange for new promissory notes signed by the corporation. This is ideal for you, because you will no longer be responsible for the payments, and your personal assets will probably not be taken to collect the debts.

In reality however, the creditors will not only want you to stay on the notes, but they will also insist that the corporation be made responsible as well. Of course, the corporation must become liable for the loans. Otherwise, the corporation will be making payments on your personal debt. Obviously, the corporation can't do this, because the IRS would consider these payments as taxable income to you.

Other contracts

Since there are many contracts involved in operating a business, it will be easy to overlook some. Contracts entered into by you will not be enforceable by the corporation, and this could cause problems. Some contracts, like insurance policies, may be changed by transferring the policy to the corporation and having the corporation formally adopt it. Other contracts, like leases or employment agreements should be formally rewritten and entered into by the corporation. This will make enforcing these contracts easier for the corporation, while reducing some of your personal liability exposure. While the incorporation of an existing business includes many variables, I hope that this short discussion on the subject has been helpful to you.

Partnership agreements

A partnership agreement is a special contract entered into by the partners of a business that is organized as a partnership. A partnership agreement is used to outline the basic "rules" by which the partnership will operate. All partners are bound by this agreement. The following list outlines some, but not all of the items covered in a typical partnership agreement:

- Who "owns" the business and how much of the business each partner owns

- How income and expenses will be split between the partners

- What happens to business assets if the partnership splits up

- Who will manage the business

- Who takes care of the money

- Whether one partner can sign contracts without the other's approval

- Salaries and other compensation

- The length of time for which the partnership will exist

- The purpose of the partnership

If you are currently operating your business as a partnership and want to incorporate, you'll need to do things a little differently. You see, corporations do not have "partnership" agreements. Instead, corporations have bylaws. Corporation bylaws should address most of the items listed above. After incorporating, your bylaws will determine how the business is operated. Accordingly, you should no longer use a partnership agreement if you incorporate. All of the items addressed in your current partnership agreement should be addressed by your corporation bylaws instead.

Chapter 4
After Incorporating

Incorporating your business is really only the first step of starting a business. After a business is legally organized, there's a list of things you'll need to do before opening for business.

I like to look at it like this, incorporating is like having a baby. Your articles of incorporation is like a birth certificate for your business. And, just as if you had a baby, there are a few things you'll need to do. First, you'll get him/her a Social Security number. (A corporation gets an Employer Identification Number, or EIN.) Next, you'll open a bank account and deposit all that money the grandparents gave the little bundle of joy. (You'll actually be depositing the money you gave to the corporation for your stock.)

In this chapter, we'll discuss some of the more important things you'll need to do after incorporating.

By the way, if you've never started a business before, you may want to take a look at the "Smart Start" Series of books. There's one for each state, and they cover everything you need to know about starting a new business in a particular state—things like permits, licenses, business taxes, insurance, employees, payroll and unemployment taxes, workers comp. etc. It's listed in the brochure at the back of the book if you're interested.

Getting an Employer Identification Number

Basically, an Employer ID number is a Social Security number for your business. The IRS uses this number to keep up with your business, and maintain a record of the various tax reports and returns that you are required to file, as well as your tax payments. Your bank will require one to open a checking account.

To get an EIN, you'll need to complete the IRS Form SS-4 included in the appendix and send or fax it to the IRS office listed on pages two and three of the instructions to the form. Your assigned number will arrive by mail or fax depending on how you sent it to them.

Completing the Form The date of your incorporation is found on the information you receive from the state after incorporating. The other requested dates will be your best estimates. The name of applicant (Line 1.) is the legal name of the corporation, not your name. (Put your name in item number 3.)

S Corporation Election

This section will cover the subject of S corporations, what they are, and how to form one. Before we proceed, let me make one thing perfectly clear. An S Corporation is not a special kind of corporation. It is simply a corporation that elects special tax treatment allowed under Subchapter S of the Internal Revenue Tax Code. Being an S Corporation is a tax matter only.

When you complete the formation of your corporation by following the steps outlined in this book, a new taxpaying entity will exist. The Internal Revenue Service and your state department of revenue will expect to receive taxes on the income of your new corporation and the income of its employees. It's almost as if you had a newborn baby and the baby was expected to start paying taxes immediately.

Just as individuals may choose to file as either "Single," "Married" "Head of household" etc., corporations have similar filing options. A corporation may choose to file as either a "C" corporation, or an "S" corporation. If a corporation chooses to be a C Corporation, it will be taxed according to Subchapter C of the IRS tax code. If a corporation chooses to be an S Corporation, it will be taxed according to Subchapter S of the IRS tax code.

IRS Form 2553 All new corporations are classified by the IRS as C corporations. You don't have to do anything to be a C Corporation. But, if you want to be an S Corporation, you must elect to be treated as an S Corporation and then notify the IRS of your choice. Notifying the IRS is a simple procedure that is accomplished by filing a single form with them, Form 2553.

To be treated as an S Corporation, you may also have to file a form with your state. To see if you do, contact your state department of revenue.

Please remember that time limits exist regarding the filing of S Corporation forms. Filing a form late may exclude you from obtaining S Corporation status.

Prior to filing the Form 2553 with the IRS and perhaps a similar form with your state department of revenue, you'll need to get director and shareholder approval to make the S Corporation election. Director approval can be granted in a meeting of the directors. Their approval will be noted in the minutes of the meeting. Simply complete and sign the "Minutes of Director Meeting to Elect S Corporation Status" form in the appendix. Do not send this form to the IRS. This form is for your records only. Keep it in your corporate records book.

Shareholder approval is also recorded on Form 2553. All you need to do is simply record the information for each shareholder and have them sign and date the form. Be sure to keep a copy of this form in your corporate record book. Send the original with original signatures to the IRS via certified mail. Technically, election of S Corporation status is subject to IRS approval. Accordingly, you will receive their approval or disapproval by mail.

If you live in a community property state or own the shares of stock jointly with another person, then both people will be listed as shareholders and both will sign the form. Each person will show that they own half the number of shares jointly owned. For example, if a husband owns stock in a corporation and lives in a community property state, his wife legally owns half of the stock. So, both names, SSN's, and signatures will appear on the form. The number of shares that he owns will be divided in half for the purpose of completing the form. Half the number of shares will appear next to his name and half will appear next to hers.

Which is best, an S Corporation or a C Corporation? It depends on your personal tax situation, but here's my opinion. Newer corporations that have net losses should be S Corporations and more mature corporations that are making profits should be C corporations. Many people start out as an S Corporation and then change filing status when the company starts to make a profit.

Completing the form

Completing the IRS Form 2553 is not difficult. The only hard part is remembering to file it before you run out of time. The form must be filed before the 16th day of the third month of the tax year to be effective for your first year in business. If you miss this deadline, your S Corporation election won't be effective until next year. Does that mean that a corporation formed June 1st is out of luck? Well, the instructions would make you to think so, but that's not the case. You see, the tax year of a corporation formed June 1st doesn't begin until June 1. This makes August 15th the deadline for filing. My advice-file the form when you get incorporated and send it via Certified Mail. Most importantly, don't complete the back of the form. The back is for special situations and trust entities.

When you're finished, send the form to the address listed in the instructions to the form. If you have any questions, call the IRS at 1-800-829-1040. The form is available on our forms disk and in the Appendix.

Other Considerations

Your Business Name

If you plan on operating your business under a name that is different from the legal name of the business, you'll need to register the name with the secretary of state or county clerk in which the business operates. See the instructions for your state's articles in the appendix, for details.

Operating your business under a different name is known as operating under a fictitious or assumed name. It is also known as a DBA or "doing business as."

Taxes

You can guess that there are plenty of local, State and Federal agencies that want taxes from your business. You'll need to get in touch with these folks to let them know you're a new taxpaying entity.

You'll need to get in touch with your state department of revenue or taxation to let them know your business is a new taxpayer. Have them send you any information they have outlining their requirements for new businesses.

Filing your SS-4 will notify the Federal government that you are in business. You should also call them to get the free information that they offer. Call them at (800) 829-3676 and request a booklet or find it on their website at: www.irs.treas.gov/prod/forms_pubs/pubs.html

Getting a business permit in the city or the county will put you on their tax rolls. You won't have to notify them. Most telephone books have a government section that lists local, State, and Federal telephone numbers. In most telephone directories, it is the blue pages in the middle of the book.

Permits

There can be many licenses or permits you'll need depending on the type of business you're in. You'll at least need a county business permit, and a city permit if you're in the city. Some states have state business permits, but they're usually for out of state businesses. There are also Federal permits if you engage in any sort of Federally regulated business like alcohol, tobacco, firearms, drug, or food manufacturing.

Insurance

Incorporating your business offers good protection against lawsuits, but it is no replacement for insurance. There are all types of insurance for businesses, but they usually come in a package called "General Business Insurance" or a "Business Policy." It can cover everything from product liability to company vehicles. If you have several employees, you'll need to get workers compensation insurance to cover potential on the job injuries. Your insurance agent can help you get the right coverage for your business.

Accounting

Keeping the books is a new and sometimes difficult chore for many small business owners. If you turn the job over to a bookkeeper or CPA, expect to pay a monthly fee based on the number of checks that you write. For this fee you can expect to have your books posted and your checkbook balanced. You can also get your quarterly and annual tax returns prepared for an extra fee based on the amount of time it takes to prepare the returns.

If you plan to do your own accounting, you'll save money but doing it yourself will take time away from making money. Accounting isn't hard. It just takes a little getting used to. If you're new at accounting, you may want to take a look at the book "Business Owners Guide to Accounting and Bookkeeping" listed in the brochure in the back of the book.

Keeping your books on the computer will make your life a lot easier because the computer will even prepare some or all you your tax returns. There are many software packages available, and I've tried them all. I like Quick Books the best.

Employees

If you have employees other than yourself, you'll need to consider all the State and Federal regulations regarding employees. The book entitled "Legal Guide for Starting and Running a Small Business" and the "Smart Start" series of books are excellent sources of information in this area.

Free help

Volumes can, and have been written about the subjects in this chapter. If you desire additional information on any of these subjects, or how to start a business in general, there are several excellent places to get free or low cost information about starting a business. Here's a list of the best:

- The U.S. Small Business Administration sponsors small business development centers (SBDCs) at community colleges in your area. These SBDCs offer free consulting to small business owners. These offices are staffed by experienced business people and can provide invaluable help to you. To find one in your area, call the community colleges in your area and ask them if they have a small business development center on campus. If you have no luck, call your local chamber of commerce and ask them. Take advantage of this program funded by your tax dollars.

- The U.S. Small Business Administration also sponsors SCORE offices in your area. Separate from the SBDCs, these centers are staffed by retired executives in your area, and also provide free consulting. To find SCORE offices in your area, look in your telephone directory under the Federal Government listings under Small Business Administration SCORE office.

- The SBA publishes books, videos, and pamphlets at little or no cost to you. For a list of these publications, write SBA Publications, P.O. Box 30, Denver CO 80201-0030, and request a catalog.

- Your chamber of commerce is there to help local businesses. They are familiar with the requirements of local and state governments and can provide you with invaluable information that will save you a lot of time and mistakes. Call them and ask if they have any information about starting a new business.

- The IRS, believe it or not, has a lot of free booklets that deal with starting a business, especially the income tax area. Call them at (800) 829-3676 and request a booklet or find it on their website at: www.irs.treas.gov/prod/forms_pubs/pubs.html

Appendix
Incorporating Forms and Instructions

Contents

Articles of incorporation and instructions for each state

Minutes of Organizational Meeting

Bylaws

Stock certificates

IRS Form SS-4 Application for Employer Identification Number

IRS Form 2553 for S Corporation Election

Minutes of Director Meeting to Elect S Corporation Status

State of Alabama
ARTICLES OF INCORPORATION

Pursuant to the provisions of the Alabama Corporation Act, the undersigned hereby adopts the following Articles of Incorporation.

1.   The name of the corporation is:

2.   The names and addresses of the directors are:

3.   The name and address of the sole incorporator is:

4.   The corporation is authorized to issue   shares of no par value, common stock, with identical rights and privileges, the transfer of which is restricted according to the Bylaws of the corporation.

5.   The corporation is organized for profit and may engage in the transaction of any or all lawful business for which corporations may be formed in Alabama.

6.   A director of the corporation shall not be held liable to the corporation or its shareholders for monetary damages due to a breach of fiduciary duty, unless the breach is a result of self-dealing, intentional misconduct, or illegal actions.

7.   The period of the corporation's duration is perpetual.

In witness thereof, the undersigned incorporator executed these Articles of Incorporation on the date below. The incorporator prepared this document.

Date:

Incorporator:

Signature of Incorporator: _____

State Information	Alabama Secretary of State	**Telephone:**	(334) 242-5324
	Corporation Division	**Web address:**	www.sos.state.al.us/index.cfm
	State Office Building, Room 536		
	P.O. Box 5616	**Filing fees:**	$35 to the Judge of Probate and
	Montgomery, AL 36103-5616		$50 to the Secretary of State
		Office hours:	8 - 5 Monday - Friday

Filing Procedure   For clarification on any step, refer to Chapter 2.

Choose a name   The name must include incorporated, corporation, or an abbreviation of one of these words.

Check name availability   Call the Secretary of State at the telephone number above to check the availability of your corporate name. Reserve the name that you find to be available. You will recieve a certificate showing that you have reserved the name. (You can also search a name on their website.)

File your paperwork   Complete the articles of incorporation form. File it and two copies with the Judge of Probate in your county. You will file the name reservation certificate as well. Take a check for the filing fees.

Organizational matters   Choose officers (at least one) and directors (at least one). After filing your articles, complete the Minutes of Organizational Meeting form (appendix) and issue stock certificates to each shareholder.

Prepare corporate records   Prepare or purchase a corporate record book and corporate seal. Place all of your documents in the record book. Use the corporate seal to emboss the stock certificates and Minutes of Organizational Meeting. Review Chapter 4 for a checklist of things to do after incorporating.

Form Instructions

1. Enter your corporate name.
2. Enter the names and addresses of the Directors. You are required to have at least one.
3. Enter your name and address.
4. Enter the total number of shares of stock that your corporation is authorized to issue. You do not have to issue all the shares now. Authorize enough for present and future use.
5. This statement is required.
6. This statement is for your protection.
7. This statement is required.

Sign and date the Articles with black ink. The Articles should be typewritten.

Notes:

In Alabama, unlike any other state, articles of incorporation are filed with the Judge of Probate in the county where the corporation is located. The county then forwards a copy to the Secretary of State. Of the total filing fee of $85 collected by the county, $50 is forwarded to the Secretary of State. The Secretary of State is responsible for name availability checks and reservations, and is the ultimate depository for all corporation filings, however, the actual filing of documents is done at the county.

Usually, purchase of stock by 10 or fewer shareholders within a 12 month period is exempt from registration. Regulated by the Alabama Securities Commission. (334) 242-2984.

For your corporation to use a fictitious name or "d.b.a.", you'll need to register the name with the Secretary of State.

State of Alaska
ARTICLES OF INCORPORATION

Pursuant to the provisions of the Alaska Corporations Code (AS 10.06), the undersigned natural person of the age of 18 years or more, acting as incorporator of this corporation hereby adopts the following Articles of Incorporation for the purpose of forming a for-profit corporation.

1. The name of the corporation is:

2. The corporation is organized for the purpose of:

3. The corporation is authorized to issue   shares of no par value, common stock, with identical rights and privileges, the transfer of which is restricted according to the bylaws of the corporation.

4. The name of the corporation's registered agent is:

5. The street address of the registered agent's office is:

6. The mailing address of the registered agent's office is:

7. The name and address of each alien affiliate is:

8. A director of the corporation shall not be held liable to the corporation or its shareholders for monetary damages due to a breach of fiduciary duty, unless the breach is a result of self-dealing, intentional misconduct, or illegal actions.

9. The name and address of the sole incorporator is:

STATEMENT OF STANDARD INDUSTRIAL CODE (SIC)

The SIC which most clearly describes the initial activities of the corporation is:

In witness thereof, the undersigned incorporator has executed these Articles of Incorporation on the date below. The incorporator prepared this document.

Date:

Incorporator:

Signature of Incorporator: _____

State Information	Department of Community	**Telephone:**	907-465-2521
	and Economic Development		907-269-8140
	Corporations Division	**Web address:**	www.dced.state.ak.us/bsc/
	P.O. Box 110808		corps.htm
	Juneau, AK 99801-0808		
		Filing fee:	$250
	Hand delivered:		
	150 Third Street, Suite 119	**Office hours:**	8-5 Monday-Friday
	Juneau, AK 99801		

Filing Procedure

For clarification on any step, refer to Chapter 2.

Choose a name
The name must include incorporated, corporation, company, limited or an abbreviation of one of these words.

Check name availability
Call the telephone number above, or check the name on their web site.

File your paperwork
File the Articles of Incorporation and one copy with the Corporations Division at the address above. Be sure to include a check for the filing fee.

Organizational matters
Choose officers (see notes) and directors (at least one). When the Articles return from the State, complete the Minutes of Organizational Meeting form (appendix). Issue stock certificates to each shareholder.

Prepare corporate records
Prepare or purchase a corporate record book and corporate seal. Place all of your documents in the record book. Use the corporate seal to emboss the stock certificates and Minutes of Organizational Meeting. Review Chapter 4 for a checklist of things to do after incorporating.

Form Instructions

1. Enter your corporate name.
2. Enter the corporation's primary business activity.
3. Enter the number of shares of stock your corporation is authorized to issue. All of the shares do not need to be issued to shareholders at this time. You must have at least one share of stock
4. Enter your name here.
5. Enter the street address of the registered agent's office.
6. Enter your P.O. Box if you have one. If not, put SAME AS ABOVE.
7. Enter the name and address of each alien affiliate (a non-resident or non-citizen). Put N/A if there are none.
8. This statement is for your protection.
9. Enter your name and address here.

   At the bottom, enter the SIC code that applies to your business. (see notes)

   Sign and date the Articles with black ink. The Articles should be typewritten.

Notes:

The articles must include a statement of codes from the Alaska Standard Industrial Classification Code List describing your business type. To review this list, refer to the website or call (907) 465-2530 and ask them to send you a copy. You can choose from one of the following general codes: 3900 Misc. Manufacturing Industries, 5900 Misc. Retail, 7200 Personal Services, 7300 Business Services, 8999 Misc. Services not elsewhere classified (Artists, Writers).

If one person owns all issued stock, then that person may hold all offices.

The Secretary of State maintains a satellite office in Anchorage at 3601 C Street, Suite 724, Anchorage, AK 99501.

Usually, stock is exempt from registration with the state if the stock is sold to 10 or fewer Alaska residents within a 12 month period of time. Regulated by the Department Of Community and Economic Development, Securities Division.

State of Arizona
ARTICLES OF INCORPORATION

For the purpose of forming a corporation under The Arizona Business Corporation Act, the undersigned natural person, being at least eighteen years of age, adopts the following Articles of Incorporation.

Article 1. The name of the Corporation is:

Article 2. The purpose of this corporation is the transaction of any and all lawful business for which corporations may be incorporated under the laws of Arizona as amended.

Article 3. The initial business of the corporation is

Article 4. The corporation is authorized to issue   shares of no par value, common stock, with identical rights and privileges, the transfer of which is restricted according to the bylaws of the corporation.

Article 5. The street address of the known place of business of the Corporation is:

Article 6. The name and address of the statutory agent of the Corporation is:

Article 7. The number of directors to constitute the board of directors is   . A director of the corporation shall not be held liable to the corporation or its shareholders for monetary damages due to a breach of fiduciary duty, unless the breach is a result of self-dealing, intentional misconduct, or illegal actions. The names and addresses of the directors are:

Article 8. All powers, duties and responsibilities of the incorporator shall cease at the time of delivery of these Articles of Incorporation to the Arizona Corporation Commission. The name and residence of the sole incorporator is:

Article 9. The Corporation shall indemnify any person who incurs expenses or liabilities by reason of the fact he or she is or was an officer, director, employee or agent of the Corporation or is or was serving at the request of the Corporation as a director, officer, employee or agent of another corporation, partnership, joint venture, trust or other enterprise. This indemnification shall be mandatory in all circumstances in which indemnification is permitted by law.

Article 10.To the fullest extent permitted by the Arizona Revised Statutes, as the same exists or may hereafter be amended, a director of the Corporation shall not be liable to the Corporation or its stockholders for monetary damages for any action taken or any failure to take any action as a director. No repeal, amendment or modification of this article, whether direct or indirect, shall eliminate or reduce its effect with respect to any act or omission of a director of the Corporation occurring prior to such repeal, amendment or modification.

In witness whereof, these Articles of Incorporation have been signed on this date:

Name of Incorporator: Telephone Number: Fax Number:

Signature of Incorporator: _____

Acceptance of Appointment by Statutory Agent:

The undersigned hereby acknowledges and accepts the appointment as statutory agent of the above-named corporation effective this _____day of _____, 19_____.

Name: Signature _____

State Information	Arizona Corporation Commission Corporation Division 1300 W. Washington, 1st floor Phoenix, AZ 85007 Arizona Corporation Commission Corporation Division 400 W. Congress Street 400 Tucson, AZ 85701	**Telephone:** **Web address:** **Filing fee:** **Office hours:**	(602) 542-3135 (520) 628-6560 800-345-5819 www.cc.state.az.us/corp/ index.htm $60 Expedited service add $35 8-5 Monday-Friday

Filing Procedure

For clarification on any step, refer to Chapter 2.

Choose a name
The name must include incorporated, corporation, association, company, limited or an abbbreviation of one of these words.

Check name availability
Call (602) 542-3230 and have them check the name for you.

File your paperwork
Complete the articles of incorporation form. Complete the certificate of disclosure. Send or take the articles and one copy, and the Certificate of Disclosure, to the Corporation Commission's office. Include a check for $60. Include the tradename application if you have one. After the articles are filed, they must be published in the newspaper three consecutive days. Within 90 days of their publication, an affidavit swearing that the articles have been published must be filed with the Corporation Commission

Organizational matters
Choose officers (at least one) and directors (at least one). When the Articles return from the state, complete the Minutes of Organizational Meeting form (appendix). Issue stock certificates to each shareholder.

Prepare corporate records
Prepare or purchase a corporate record book and corporate seal. Place all of your documents in the record book. Use the corporate seal to emboss the stock certificates and Minutes of Organizational Meeting. Review Chapter 4 for a checklist of things to do after incorporating.

Form Instructions

1. Enter the name of the corporation. Make sure it includes "Inc."

2. This statement is required by law.

3. Enter the corporation's primary business activity. A short statement is sufficient.

4. Enter the total number of shares of stock that your corporation is authorized to issue.

5. Enter the street address where your business is located.

6. Enter your name and street address. Your home address is acceptable.

7. Enter the number of directors. Also list their names and addresses.

8. Enter your name and street address in the space provided. Your home address is okay.

9. This statement is for your protection.

10. This statement is for your protection.

Complete the bottom of the form and have the incorporator and statutory agent sign the Articles with ink. You are only required to have one incorporator. The incorporator and the statutory agent can be the same person.

Notes:

To use a fictitious name, you'll need to file an application with the Corporation Commission's Office. The form you'll need is called a "Tradename Application" and is available from their office. The fee to file it is $10. Their number is (602) 542-6187.

The Certificate of Disclosure is available from the state or on the forms disk.

Stock is usually exempt from registration with the state if the number of Arizona residents purchasing the stock is 10 or fewer. Regulated by the State Securities Commission.

For information regarding publishing the articles, contact your local newspaper.

State of Arkansas
ARTICLES OF INCORPORATION

For the purpose of forming a corporation under the Arkansas Business Corporation Act (Act 958 of 1987), the undersigned natural person, being at least eighteen years of age, adopts the following Articles of Incorporation.

Article 1.   The name of the Corporation is:

Article 2.   The corporation is authorized to issue   shares of no par value, common stock, with identical rights and privileges, the transfer of which is restricted according to the bylaws of the corporation.

Article 3.   The initial registered office of this Corporation shall be located at:

Article 4.   The name of the initial registered agent of this Corporation at the above address is:

Article 5.   The name and address of the sole incorporator is:

Article 6.   The corporation is formed for the purpose of

and to engage in any legal act or activity permitted by Section 4-27-302 of the Arkansas Business Corporation Act.

In witness whereof, these Articles of Incorporation have been signed on this date:
Name of Incorporator:

Telephone Number:

Signature of Incorporator: _____

State Information	Secretary of State	**Telephone:**	(501) 682-3409
	Corporation Division		(888) 233-0325
	Suite 310 Aegon Building	**Web address:**	www.sosweb.state.ar.us/
	501 Woodlane		business.html
	Little Rock, AR 72201	**Filing fee:**	$50
		Office hours:	8-5 Monday-Friday

Filing Procedure

For clarification on any step, refer to Chapter 2.

Choose a name   The name must include incorporated, corporation, limited, company or an abbreviation of one of these words.

Check name availability   Call the telephone number above, or search for the name on their Web site.

File your paperwork   Complete the articles of incorporation form. Send or take it to the Corporation Division's office. Include a check for the filing fee.

Organizational matters   Choose officers (at least one) and directors (at least one). When the articles return from the State, complete the Minutes of Organizational Meeting form (appendix). Issue stock certificates to each shareholder.

Prepare corporate records   Prepare or purchase a corporate record book and corporate seal. Place all of your documents in the record book. Use the corporate seal to emboss the stock certificates and Minutes of Organizational Meeting. Review Chapter 4 for a checklist of things to do after incorporating.

Form Instructions

1. Enter the name of the corporation.
2. Enter the total number of shares of stock that your corporation is authorized to issue. You do not have to issue all the shares now. Authorize enough for present and future use.
3. Enter the STREET address of the initial registered office. Your home address is acceptable.
4. Enter the name of the initial registered agent at the above address. You can serve as your own registered agent.
5. Enter your name and street address in the space provided. Your home address is acceptable.
6. Enter the corporation's primary business activity in the space provided.

   Complete the bottom of the form and have the incorporator sign the Articles of Incorporation in ink. You are only required to have one incorporator. The articles should be typewritten.

Notes:

To use a fictitious name, you'll need to file an application with the Corporation Division. The form is available from their office, and the filing fee is $25. The name may also need to be registered in each county where you have an office. Call your county clerk for more information.

Stock is usually exempt from registration with the state if the number of Arkansas residents purchasing the stock is seven or fewer. Regulated by the Arkansas State Securities Commission. (501) 324-9260.

Make your check payable to the Arkansas Secretary of State.

California Stock Corporation
ARTICLES OF INCORPORATION

Pursuant to the California Corporations Code §100 et seq., the undersigned individual submits these Articles of Incorporation for the purpose of forming a domestic, for-profit corporation.

1. The name of the Corporation is:

2. The purpose of the corporation is to engage in any lawful act or activity for which corporations may be organized under the General Corporation Law of California other than the banking business, the trust company business, or the practice of a profession permitted to be incorporated by the California Corporations code.

3. The name and California street address of the corporation's initial agent for service of process is:

4. The corporation is authorized to issue   shares of no par value, common stock, with identical rights and privileges, the transfer of which is restricted according to the Bylaws of the corporation.

5. The liability of the directors of the corporation for monetary damages shall be eliminated to the fullest extent possible under California law.

6. A Director of the corporation may not be held liable to the corporation or its shareholders for monetary damages due to a breach of fiduciary duty, unless the breach is a result of self-dealing, intentional misconduct, or illegal actions.

In witness whereof, the undersigned, being all the incorporators of the corporation named above, execute these Articles of Incorporation and verify, subject to penalties of perjury, that the statements contained herein are true and that the incorporator is at least 18 years of age.

Date:

Incorporator's Name:

Incorporator's Signature _____

State Information	California Secretary of State Corporate Division 1500 11th Street Sacramento, CA 95814	**Telephone:**	(916) 657-5448
		Web address:	http://www.ss.ca.gov/business/ business.htm
		Filing fee:	$100 / Expedited add $15
		Office Hours:	8-5 Monday-Friday

Filing Procedure

For clarification on any step, refer to Chapter 2.

Choose a name — The name must include incorporated, corporation, limited, or an abbreviation of one of these words.

Check name availability — California does not offer name availability checks by phone. You can check the name in writing, or on their internet site. Some people simply go ahead and file their articles of incorporation. (See Notes.)

File your paperwork — Complete the articles of incorporation form. Send or take it and two copies to a Corporation Division office. If you file your articles in a satellite office, you'll need two originals and two copies. Include a check for the filing fee.

Organizational matters — Choose officers (at least one) and directors (see notes) When the Articles return from the State, complete the Minutes of Organizational Meeting form (appendix). Issue stock certificates to each shareholder. File a "Notice of Transaction" form with the California Department of Corporations. (See Notes.)

Prepare corporate records — Prepare or purchase a corporate record book and corporate seal. Place all of your documents in the record book. Use the corporate seal to emboss the stock certificates and Minutes of Organizational Meeting. Review Chapter 4 for a checklist of things to do after incorporating.

Form Instructions

1. Enter the name of the corporation.
2. This statement is required.
3. Enter the name and STREET address of the corporation's initial registered agent.
4. Enter the number of shares of stock that your corporation will be authorized to issue. You can authorize more shares than you plan to issue. There is no limit on the number of shares that you may have.
5. Enter your name and street address here. You're only required to have one incorporator.
6. This statement is included for your protection.

Complete the bottom of the form and have the incorporator sign and date with ink.

Notes:

The Secretary of State used to collect income tax ($800) for the upcoming year when you formed a corporation. As of January 1, 2000, they no longer do this if (1) your sales for the upcoming year are less than $1,000,000 and (2) you estimate that your corporation's tax liability for the upcoming year will not exceed $800, and (3) 50 percent or more of your corporation stock is not owned by another corporation. So, the amount collected when you form a corporation is simply the $100 fee.

If you want to check the availability of a corporate name in writing, simply write the Secretary of State and ask them to check the availability of your two or three favorite corporate names. If the name is found not to be available, you will be notified. Please note, however, that if you request expedited filing, your expedited fee will be forfeited if "your" name is found to be unavailable. (Most people simply go ahead and file their articles and hope that their name is available.)

The state maintains four satellite offices. (Documents mailed or sent by overnight courier must be sent to Sacramento.) If you file your articles in a satellite office (in person), you'll need two original articles of incorporation with original signatures. (One original is kept in the satellite office and the other is forwarded to Sacramento.)

1300 South Spring Street, Suite 12513, Los Angeles	(213) 897-3062
1355 Front Street, State Building Suite 2060, San Diego	(619) 525-4113
2497 West Shaw, Suite 101, Fresno	(209) 243-2100
455 Golden gate, Suite 7300, San Francisco	(415) 557-7047

To use a fictitious name, you'll need to file a statement with the county clerk for the county or counties in which you're doing business. This must be done within 40 days of incorporating. You also need to place a legal notice in these counties within 30 days of filing the statement with the county clerk. After this notice is published in the newspaper, you'll need to go back to the county clerk and file an affidavit stating that the notice has been published.

The "Notice of Transaction" form notifies the state that you have issued stock in your corporation. Call (916) 445-7205 and ask them to send you a "25102 (F)" package. The package includes the form and instructions.

The number of directors must be equal to the number of shareholders unless there are fewer than 3 shareholders, then the number of directors must equal the number of shareholders. One shareholder requires only one director, two shareholders requires two directors.

State of Colorado
ARTICLES OF INCORPORATION

Pursuant to the Colorado Business Corporation Act as amended, the undersigned individual submits these Articles of Incorporation for the purpose of forming a domestic, for-profit corporation.

1. The name of the corporation is:

2. The street address of the principal office of the corporation is:

3. The duration of the corporation is perpetual.

4. The corporation is authorized to issue one million shares of common stock without par value. This stock shall be of one class and shall have unlimited voting rights; identical preferences, limitations and relative rights; and shall be entitled to receive the net assets of the corporation upon dissolution. Cumulative voting is not authorized. Preemptive rights are granted to the shareholders.

5. The name of the initial registered agent of the corporation is:

   The street address of the registered office is:

   I hereby consent to the appointment as the initial registered agent of the corporation named above.

   Signature of registered agent: _____

6. A Director of the corporation may not be held liable to the corporation or its shareholders for monetary damages due to a breach of fiduciary duty, unless the breach is a result of self-dealing, intentional misconduct, or illegal actions.

The undersigned, being at least 18 years of age and acting as incorporator of a corporation under the Colorado Business Corporation Act, adopts the above articles of incorporation.

Date:

Name of Incorporator:

Signature of Incorporator: _____

State Information	Secretary of State Division of Corporations 1560 Broadway, Suite 200 Denver, CO 80202	**Telephone:**	(303) 894-2251
		Web address:	www.state.co.us/gov_dir/ sos/divinfo.html#Commercial
		Filing fee:	$50 Expedited service add $15.
		Office hours:	7:30-5 Monday-Friday

Filing Procedure

For clarification on any step, refer to Chapter 2.

Choose a name	The name must include incorporated, corporation, company, or an abbreviation of one of these words.
Check name availability	Call the telephone number above, or the "900" number listed below.
File your paperwork	Complete the articles of incorporation. Send or take the articles and one copy to the corporation division's office. Include a check for $50. Include a self-addressed stamped envelope for the return of your filing receipt.
Organizational matters	Choose officers (at least one) and directors (at least one). When the Articles return from the State, complete the Minutes of Organizational Meeting form (appendix). Issue stock certificates to each shareholder.
Prepare corporate records	Prepare or purchase a corporate record book and corporate seal. Place all of your documents in the record book. Use the corporate seal to emboss the stock certificates and Minutes of Organizational Meeting. Review Chapter 4 for a checklist of things to do after incorporating.

Form Instructions

1. Enter the name of the corporation. The corporate name must include one of the following: Incorporated, Corporation, Company or Inc., Corp., or Co.
2. Enter the name and STREET address of the corporation's principal office. Your home address is okay to use.
3. This statement is required by law.
4. This statement authorizes one million shares of common stock without par value. The other statements are required by law.
5. Enter the name and STREET address of the corporation's initial registered agent. You can serve as your corporation's own registered agent. Your home address is acceptable.
6. This statement is included for your protection.

   Complete the bottom of the form and have the incorporator sign the Articles of Incorporation with ink. You are only required to have one incorporator.

Notes:

Colorado offers a "900" telephone number for questions. It is (900) 555-1717. It usually gets a faster response, but costs $1.50 per minute.

To use a fictitious name, you'll need to file a "Certificate of Assumed or Trade Name" with the Secretary of State's office. The form must be typed and the filing fee is $10. The form is available from their office.

Make checks payable to "Colorado Secretary of State."

Stock is usually exempt from registration with the state if the number of Colorado residents purchasing the stock in the last 12 months is 10 or fewer. Registration is handled by the State Securities Commissioner, Division of Securities Office. The telephone number is (303) 894-2320.

Connecticut Stock Corporation
CERTIFICATE OF INCORPORATION

Pursuant to the provisions of the Connecticut Statutes, Section 33, the undersigned hereby adopts the following Certificate of Incorporation.

1. The name of the corporation is:

2. The corporation is authorized to issue one class of stock, that stock being   shares of no par value, common stock, with identical rights and privileges, the transfer of which is restricted according to the Bylaws of the corporation.

3. The registered agent of the corporation is:

   The business address of the registered agent is:

   The residence address of the registered agent is:

Acceptance of appointment:
   The individual named above hereby accepts the appointment as registered agent for the corporation.
   Date:

   Signature of agent:_____.

Other Provisions:
4. A director of the corporation shall not be held liable to the corporation or its shareholders for monetary damages due to a breach of fiduciary duty, unless the breach is a result of self-dealing, intentional misconduct, or illegal actions.

Execution:

Date:

Name of sole Incorporator:

Address of Incorporator:

Signature of Incorporator: _____

State Information	Connecticut Secretary of State 30 Trinity Street P.O. Box 150470 Hartford, CT 06106-0470	**Telephone:**	(860) 509-6001
		Web address:	www.sots.state.ct.us/
		Filing fee:	$200 or $275 (see notes) Expedited service add $25
		Office hours:	8:45-4: 00 Front counter closes at 3:00

Filing Procedure

For clarification on any step, refer to Chapter 2.

Choose a name
The name must include incorporated, corporation, company, limited, Society per Azion, or an abbreviation.

Check name availability
Call (860) 509-6002 and have them check the name.

File your paperwork
File the Certificate of Incorporation and one copy with the Secretary of State. You may also file the organization and first report at this time. Be sure to include the filing fees.

Organizational matters
Choose officers (See Notes) and directors (at least one). When the Certificate returns from the State, complete the Minutes of Organizational Meeting form (appendix). Issue stock certificates to each shareholder.

Prepare corporate records
Prepare or purchase a corporate record book and corporate seal. Place all of your documents in the record book. Use the corporate seal to emboss the stock certificates and Minutes of Organizational Meeting. Review Chapter 4 for a checklist of things to do after incorporating.

Form Instructions

1. Enter your corporate name.

2. Enter the number of shares of stock your corporation is authorized to issue. You can authorize up to 20,000 shares to incur the minimum organizational tax of $150. All of the shares do not need to be issued to shareholders at this time. You must have at least one share of stock.

3. Enter the name of the registered agent. You can serve as your own registered agent. Enter the complete business (street) address of the registered agent. Enter the complete residence address of the registered agent. Enter the date and sign your name.

4. This statement is for your protection.

   Complete the bottom of the form, and sign the certificate of incorporation with black ink. The certificate of incorporation should be typewritten.

Notes:

The filing fee of $275 includes $50 to file the certificate of incorporation, $150 for the minimum organizational tax, and $75 for the organization and first report. The franchise tax is calculated as:

One cent per share up to and including the first ten thousand authorized shares. One-half cent per share for each authorized share in excess of ten thousand shares up to and including one hundred thousand shares, one-quarter cent per share for each authorized share in excess of one hundred thousand shares up to and including one million shares, and one-fifth cent per share for each authorized share in excess of one million shares. So, you can authorize up to 20,000 shares and incur the minimum organization tax of $150.

The organization and first report (on the forms disk) basically contains the same information that your certificate of incorporation does. You have up to two years to file it. However, you should file it as soon as possible. If you file the report with your certificate of incorporation your filing fee will total $275. If you file the certificate without the first biennial report, your filing fee will only be $200. Make your check payable to the Connecticut Secretary Of State.

The same person can hold more than one office, however, the president and secretary cannot be the same person.

Fictitious trade names are filed in the office of the town clerk of the town where they are used in the transaction of business. For more information, contact your town clerk.

Stock is usually exempt from registration with the state if fewer than 25 Connecticut residents purchase the stock within twelve months. Regulated by the State Bank Commissioner.

State of Delaware
CERTIFICATE OF INCORPORATION
STOCK CORPORATION

Pursuant to the provisions of the Delaware Corporations Code, Title 8, the undersigned hereby adopts the following Certificate of Incorporation for the purpose of forming a stock corporation.

1. The name of this corporation is:

2. Its registered office in the State of Delaware is to be located at:

   The registered agent in charge thereof is:

3. The purpose of the corporation is to engage in any lawful act or activity for which corporations may be organized under the General Corporation Law of Delaware.

4. The corporation is authorized to issue   shares of no par value, common stock, with identical rights and privileges, the transfer of which is restricted according to the bylaws of the corporation.

5. The name and mailing address of the incorporator is:

6. A director of the corporation shall not be held liable to the corporation or its shareholders for monetary damages due to a breach of fiduciary duty, unless the breach is a result of self-dealing, intentional misconduct, or illegal actions.

I, THE UNDERSIGNED, for the purpose of forming a corporation under the laws of the State of Delaware, do make, file and record this Certificate, and do certify that the facts herein stated are true, and I have accordingly hereunto set my hand.

Date:

Incorporator:

Signature of Incorporator: _____

State Information	Delaware Secretary of State Division of Corporations P.O. Box 898 Dover, DE 19903 Hand delivered: 401 Federal Street, Suite 4 Dover, Delaware 19901	**Telephone:** (302) 739-3073 **Web address:** www.state.de.us/corp/index.htm **Filing fee:** $50 plus county fees of $24 **Office hours:** 8:45-4:00

Filing Procedure

For clarification on any step, refer to Chapter 2.

Choose a name
The name must include incorporated, corporation, company, limited, association, club, foundation, fund, institute, society, union, syndicate, or an abbreviation of one of these words.

Check name availability
Call the telephone number above and have them check the name for you.

File your paperwork
Complete the certificate of incorporation. File it and one copy with the Division of Corporations. (They both should have original signatures.) Be sure to include the filing fee of $50. When the articles return from the state, file a copy of the certificate with your county courthouse. The county will charge a filing fee of $24.

Organizational matters
Choose officers (at least one) and directors (at least one). When the Certificate returns from the State, complete the Minutes of Organizational Meeting form (appendix). Issue stock certificates to each shareholder.

Prepare corporate records
Prepare or purchase a corporate record book and corporate seal. Place all of your documents in the record book. Use the corporate seal to emboss the stock certificates and Minutes of Organizational Meeting. Review Chapter 4 for a checklist of things to do after incorporating.

Form Instructions

1. Enter your corporate name.
2. Enter the address of the corporation's registered office. Enter the name of the registered agent. You can serve as your own registered agent.
3. This is required.
4. Enter the number of shares of stock your corporation is authorized to issue. You can authorize up to 1,500 shares of stock for the minimum filing fee of $50.
5. Enter your name and mailing address.
6. Included for your protection.

   Type the date and your name, then sign the Certificate with black ink. The Certificate should be typewritten.

Notes:

Expedited service fees, $50 for 24-hour service; $100 for same day service; $500 for two-hour service.

The $50 filing fee listed above consists of a filing fee and a filing tax based on the number of shares of stock that your corporation authorizes. For this $50 fee, you can authorize up to 1,500 shares of no par value common stock. Authorize more than 1,500 shares, and your filing tax will increase.

You may also file your certificate of incorporation by fax. The fax number is (302) 739-3812. Be sure to include your credit card information. MasterCard, Visa, and Discover are accepted.

If you live outside the state of Delaware, you'll need a registered agent in the state. A list of agents is available from the Secretary of State.

The issuance of stock is usually exempt from registration if the number of shareholders purchasing the stock in the last 12 months is 25 or fewer. Regulated by the State Department of Justice.

To use a fictitious name, file a fictitious name certificate in the Office of Prothonotary.

District of Columbia
ARTICLES OF INCORPORATION

Pursuant to the provisions of the DC Code, Title 29, Chapter 3, as amended, the undersigned hereby adopts the following Articles of Incorporation for the purpose of forming a for profit corporation.

1. The name of the corporation is:

2. The registered office address of the corporation is:

3. The registered agent at the above address is:

    The individual named above hereby accepts the appointment as registered agent for the corporation.

    Signature of agent: _____

4. The purpose of the corporation is:

5. The corporation is authorized to issue   shares of no par value, common stock, with identical rights and privileges, the transfer of which is restricted according to the bylaws of the corporation.

6. The name and address of the incorporator is:

7. The name and phone number of a person to be contacted if there is a question about the filing of these articles is:

8. The period of duration for this corporation is perpetual.
9. The Corporation will not commence business until it has received at least $1000 as initial capitalization.
10. Preemptive rights to acquire additional shares of the Corporation are neither limited nor denied.
11. The number of directors constituting the initial board is   . Their names and addresses are:

I, the undersigned natural person of eighteen years or more acting as incorporator under the Business Corporation Act, adopt these Articles of Incorporation.

Date:

Signature of Incorporator:_____

State Information	Dept. of Consumer and Regulatory Affairs Corporation Division 941 North Capitol Street, NE, Washington, DC 20002	**Telephone:**	(202) 442-4430
		Web address:	www.dcra.org
		Filing fee:	$120
		Office hours:	8:15-4:15 Open until 8 PM Wednesday

Filing Procedure

For clarification on any step, refer to Chapter 2.

Choose a name — The name must include incorporated, corporation, company, limited, or an abbreviation of one of these words.

Check name availability — Call the telephone number above and have them check the name for you.

File your document — Complete the articles of incorporation. Send or take two copies of the articles, both with original signatures, to the Corporation Division. Be sure to include the filing fee.

Organizational matters — Choose officers (see notes) and directors (at least one). When the Articles return from the State, complete the Minutes of Organizational Meeting form (appendix). Issue stock certificates to each shareholder.

Prepare corporate records — Prepare or purchase a corporate record book and corporate seal. Place all of your documents in the record book. Use the corporate seal to emboss the stock certificates and Minutes of Organizational Meeting. Review Chapter 4 for a checklist of things to do after incorporating.

Form Instructions

1. Enter your corporate name.
2. Enter the mailing address of the corporation's registered office. A post office box is not acceptable.
3. Enter your name and street address.
4. Enter the corporation's primary business activity in the space provided.
5. Enter the number of shares of stock your corporation is authorized to issue. All of the shares do not need to be issued to shareholders at this time. You must have at least one share of stock.
6. Enter your name and address.
7. Enter your name and a daytime phone number.
8. This statement is required.
9. This statement is required.
10. This statement is required.
11. Entered the number, names, and street addresses of the directors.

Sign and date the Articles in black ink. The Articles should be typewritten.

Notes:

The same person may hold more than one office, except the same person cannot hold both president and secretary positions.

The filing fee of $120, consists of a $100 filing fee, and an initial license fee based on the number of shares of stock that your corporation authorizes. You can authorize up to 100,000 shares of no par value stock and incur the minimum fee of $20. Authorize more than 100,000 shares and your license fee will increase.

Stock is usually exempt from registration with the state if the number of shareholders purchasing the stock in the last 12 months is 25 or fewer.

Make your check payable to the Department of Consumer and Regulatory Affairs.

State of Florida
ARTICLES OF INCORPORATION

Pursuant to Chapter 607 of the Florida Business Corporation Act, the undersigned incorporator adopts these Articles of Incorporation for the purpose of forming a for-profit corporation.

Article 1. The name of the Corporation is:

Article 2. The principal place of business and mailing address of this corporation is:

Article 3. The corporation is authorized to issue one class of stock, that being _____ shares of no par value, common stock, with identical rights and privileges, the transfer of which is restricted according to the bylaws of the corporation.

Article 4. No Director shall be held liable to the corporation or its shareholders for monetary damages due to a breach of fiduciary duty, unless the breach is a result of self-dealing, intentional misconduct, or illegal actions.

Article 5. The effective date of this filing is   [   ] The actual date and time of filing.
                                          [   ]   /   /   at 12 o'clock PM.

Article 6. The name and address of the corporation's initial registered agent is:

Having been named as registered agent and to accept service of process for the above named corporation at the place designated in this document, I hereby accept the appointment as registered agent and agree to act in this capacity. I further agree to comply with the provisions of all statutes relating to the proper and complete performance of my duties, and I am familiar with and accept the obligations of my position as registered agent.

Signature of Registered Agent: _____   Date:

Article 7. The name and street address of the incorporator of this corporation is:

In witness whereof, the undersigned incorporator has executed these Articles of Incorporation on the date below.

Date:

Signature of Incorporator: _____

State Information	Department of State	**Telephone:**	(850) 488-9000
	Division of Corporations P.O. Box 6327 Tallahassee, FL 32314	**Web address:**	www.dos.state.fl.us/doc/ index.html
		Filing fee:	$70
	Street address: 409 E. Gaines Street Tallahassee, FL 32399	**Office hours:**	8 - 4:30 Monday-Friday Telephone hours 7:30 - 5:30

Filing Procedure

For clarification on any step, refer to Chapter 2.

Choose a name
The name must include incorporated, corporation, company, or an abbreviation of one of these words.

Check name availability
Call the telephone number above and have them check the name for you.

File your paperwork
Complete the articles of incorporation form and take it to the Division of Corporations office. Include a check for $70.

Organizational matters
Choose officers (at least one) and directors (at least one). When the Articles return from the State, complete the Minutes of Organizational Meeting form (appendix). Issue stock certificates to each shareholder. Purchase doc stamps for your certificates, and affix them to the face of the certificates.

Prepare corporate records
Prepare or purchase a corporate record book and corporate seal. Place all of your documents in the record book. Use the corporate seal to emboss the stock certificates and Minutes of Organizational Meeting. Review Chapter 4 for a checklist of things to do after incorporating.

Form Instructions

1. Enter the name of the corporation. The corporate name must include one of the following: Incorporated, Corporation, Limited or Inc., Corp., or Ltd.

2. Enter the STREET address of the corporation's principal office.

3. In the space provided, enter the total number of shares of stock that your corporation will have.

4. This statement is included for your protection.

5. Choose one. If you choose the second option, also include a date no more than 90 days in the future.

6. Enter your name and street address. Also, sign your name and enter the date in the space provided.

7. Enter your name and street address.

   Sign your name and enter the date in the space provided.

Notes:

To use a fictitious name, you'll need to file an application for registration of fictitious name with the Department of State after the articles of incorporation are filed. The form is available from the Division of Corporations office, and its filing fee is $50.

Stock is usually exempt from registration if the number of Florida residents purchasing the stock in the last 12 months is 35 or fewer. Stock registration is handled by the Florida Department of Banking and Finance. Their telephone number is (850) 410-9805 or (850) 410-9370.

Florida imposes a tax on newly issued stock certificates in a corporation. This tax is called a documentary or "doc." tax. This tax is paid by purchasing doc. stamps from the State Department of Revenue or the Clerk of Circuit Court in your county. The stamps are then affixed to your stock certificates. This tax is 35 cents on every $100 of consideration you give for your stock. Call the Department of Revenue for more information. Their number is (803) 352-3671 or (850) 488-6800.

State of Georgia
ARTICLES OF INCORPORATION

Pursuant to the Georgia Business Corporation Code, the undersigned individual submits these Articles of Incorporation for the purpose of forming a domestic, for-profit corporation.

1. The name of the Corporation is:

2. The corporation is authorized to issue   shares of no par value, common stock, with identical rights and privileges, the transfer of which is restricted according to the Bylaws of the corporation.

3. The street address of the corporation's initial registered office, the county in which the office is located, and the name of its initial registered agent at said office are as follows:

4. The street address of the corporation's principal office is:

5. A Director of the corporation may not be held liable to the corporation or its shareholders for monetary damages due to a breach of fiduciary duty, unless the breach is a result of self-dealing, intentional misconduct, or illegal actions.

In witness whereof, the undersigned incorporator has executed these Articles of Incorporation on the date below. The undersigned incorporator hereby affirms that the statements made in these Articles of Incorporation are true.

Date:

Name of Incorporator:

Address of Incorporator:

Signature of Incorporator: _____

State Information	Georgia State Corp. Commission New Corporation Filings Suite 315 West Tower 2 Martin Luther King Blvd. Atlanta, GA 30334	**Telephone:**	(404) 656-2817
		Web address:	www.sos.state.ga.us/corporations
		Filing fee:	$60
		Office hours:	8-5 Monday-Friday

Filing Procedure

For clarification on any step, refer to Chapter 2.

Choose a name — The name must include incorporated, corporation, company, limited, or an abbreviation of one of these words.

Check name availability — Call the telephone number above and have them check the name for you. Reserve the name while you have them on the phone. Request a copy of their transmittal form (Form 227). You can also check the availability of a corporate name online at their Web site.

File your paperwork — Place a legal notice of your incorporation (an ad) in your local newspaper (see below). Complete the articles of incorporation and the transmittal form. File the articles and one copy with the Secretary of State. Include the $60 filing fee, the transmittal form 227, and the name reservation certificate that was mailed to you after reserving the name.

Organizational matters — Choose officers (at least one) and directors (at least one). When the Articles return from the State, complete the Minutes of Organizational Meeting form (appendix). Issue stock certificates to each shareholder.

Prepare corporate records — Prepare or purchase a corporate record book and corporate seal. Place all of your documents in the record book. Use the corporate seal to emboss the stock certificates and Minutes of Organizational Meeting. Review Chapter 4 for a checklist of things to do after incorporating.

Form Instructions

1. Enter the name of the corporation.
2. Enter the number of shares of stock the corporation is authorized to issue.
3. Enter your name and street address. Include the name of the county.
4. Enter the street address for the corporation's principal office.
5. This statement is optional. It is added for your protection.

   Sign and date the Articles with BLACK ink. Sign your name as incorporator exactly as it appears in the Articles of Incorporation. The articles should be typewritten.

Notes:

To use a fictitious name, you'll need to file a "Trade Name Registration Statement" with the office of the Clerk of the Superior Court in each county that you conduct business (have an office). This should be done within 30 days after the articles of incorporation are filed with the state. The court clerk will charge an $8 fee to file the form.

Form 227 basically includes the same information that is on the articles of incorporation.

The legal notice of your incorporation must be in this format:

"Notice is given that articles of incorporation which incorporate (name of corporation) have been delivered to the Secretary of State for filing in accordance with the Georgia Business Corporation code. The initial registered office of the corporation is located at (your name and address) and its initial registered agent at such address is (your name)."

Stock is usually exempt from registration if the total number of Georgia citizens purchasing the stock is less than 15. The State's Securities Division handles stock registration. The following notice must be typed on all stock certificates.

"This security is issued pursuant to paragraph 13 of code section 10-5-9 of the Georgia Securities Act of 1973 and may not be sold or transferred except in a similarly exempt transaction. The shareholder acknowledges that the purchase of this security is for his/her own account and not for resale."

State of Hawaii
Articles of Incorporation

Pursuant to the provisions of Section 415-54 of the Hawaii Revised Statutes, the undersigned hereby adopts the following Articles of Incorporation for the purpose of forming a for profit corporation.

1. The name of the corporation is:

2. The street address of the initial or principal office of the corporation is:

3. The corporation is authorized to issue _____ shares of no par value, common stock, with identical rights and privileges, the transfer of which is restricted according to the bylaws of the corporation.

4. The initial Board of Directors shall consist of _____ members. The initial directors shall serve as directors until the first annual meeting of shareholders, or until their successors are duly elected and qualified as provided in the bylaws. All powers and authority of the Corporation shall be invested in and may be exercised by the Board of Directors except as otherwise provided by law, these articles of incorporation, or the bylaws of the Corporation. Their names and residence addresses are as follows.

5. The officers of the corporation shall be a president, one or more vice presidents, a secretary and a treasurer, and such other officers and assistant officers as may be deemed necessary, who shall be appointed by the Board of Directors as prescribed in the bylaws. The following individuals are the initial officers of the corporation:

Office	Name	Residence Address
President		
Vice-President		
Secretary		
Treasurer		

6. The purpose of the Corporation is:

7. The names of the shareholders, the number of shares they hold, and the consideration given for their shares are as follows:

Name	Number of shares	Consideration

We certify that we have read the above statements and that the same are true and correct to the best of our knowledge and belief.

Date:

Incorporator:

Signature of Incorporator:_____

State Information	Dept. of Commerce and Consumer Affairs Business Registration Division 1010 Richards Street P.O. Box 40 Honolulu, HI 96810	**Telephone:**	(808) 586-2727
		Web address:	www.state.hi.us/dcca/ or www.businessregistrations.com
		Filing fee:	$100 (Nonrefundable)
		Office hours:	7:45 - 4:30 Monday - Friday

Filing Procedure

For clarification on any step, refer to Chapter 2.

Choose a name   The name must include incorporated, corporation, limited, or an abbreviation of one of these words.

Check name availability   Call the telephone number above.

File your paperwork   File the Articles of Incorporation and one copy with the Business Registration Division. Be sure to include the filing fee.

Organizational matters   Choose officers (at least one) and directors (at least one). When the Articles return from the State, complete the Minutes of Organizational Meeting form (appendix). Issue stock certificates to each shareholder.

Prepare corporate records   Prepare or purchase a corporate record book and corporate seal. Place all of your documents in the record book. Use the corporate seal to emboss the stock certificates and Minutes of Organizational Meeting. Review Chapter 4 for a checklist of things to do after incorporating.

Form Instructions

1. Enter your corporate name.
2. Enter the complete street address of the initial or principal office of the corporation.
3. Enter the number of shares of stock your corporation is authorized to issue. All of the shares do not need to be issued to shareholders at this time. You must have at least one share of stock.
4. Enter the number of members of the initial Board of Directors. At least one member of the board must be a resident of the State of Hawaii. The number of directors must equal the number of shareholders, with a minimum of three. One shareholder requires one director, four shareholders requires only three. Enter the names and complete residence addresses of the initial directors of the corporation.
5. Enter the names of the initial officers of the corporation next to the respective titles. Each corporation must have a President, Vice-President, Secretary and Treasurer. The same person may hold more than one office, including that of President and Secretary. However, if the corporation has two or more directors, it must have two or more officers. Also enter the complete residence street address for each.
6. Enter the business activity of the Corporation. Be specific.
7. Enter the requested information. Consideration is the cash or property given for stock.

Enter the date and name of the incorporator (you). Then sign your name in black ink.

Notes:

Make checks payable to the "Department of Commerce and Consumer Affairs."

Stock is usually exempt from registration with the state if the number of shareholders purchasing the stock in the last 12 months is 25 or fewer.

To use a fictitious name or d.b.a., file a Form T-1 with the Department Of Commerce and Consumer Affairs. The filing fee is $50.

State of Idaho
ARTICLES OF INCORPORATION

Pursuant to the provisions of Title 30, Chapter1, of the Idaho Code, the undersigned hereby adopts the following Articles of Incorporation for the purpose of forming a for profit corporation.

1. The name of the corporation is:

2. The corporation is authorized to issue _____ shares of no par value, common stock, with identical rights and privileges, the transfer of which is restricted according to the bylaws of the corporation.

3. The street address of the registered office is:

4. The registered agent at the above address is:

5. The name and address of the sole incorporator is:

6. The mailing address of the corporation is:

7. The period of duration for this corporation is perpetual.

In witness thereof, the undersigned incorporator has executed these Articles of Incorporation on the date below. The incorporator prepared this document.

Date:

Signature of Incorporator: _____

State Information	Idaho Secretary of State 700 West Jefferson P.O. Box 83720 Boise, ID 83720-0080	**Telephone:**	(208) 334-2301
		Web address:	www.idsos.state.id.us/ corp/corindex.htm
		Filing fee:	$100 if typed. $120 if not typed. Expedited service add $20
		Office Hours:	8-5 Monday-Friday

Filing Procedure

For clarification on any step, refer to Chapter 2.

Choose a name   The name must include incorporated, corporation, company, limited, or an abbreviation of one of these words.

Check name availability   Call the telephone number above and have them check the name for you.

File your paperwork   Complete the articles of incorporation. File duplicates (two originals) with the Secretary of State. Be sure to include the filing fee. The filing fee for typed articles is $100. The filing fee for handwritten articles is $120.

Organizational matters   Choose officers (see notes) and directors (at least one). When the Articles return from the State, complete the Minutes of Organization form (appendix). Issue stock certificates to each shareholder.

Prepare corporate records   Prepare or purchase a corporate record book and corporate seal. Place all of your documents in the record book. Use the corporate seal to emboss the stock certificates and Minutes of Organizational Meeting. Review Chapter 4 for a checklist of things to do after incorporating.

Form Instructions

1. Enter your corporate name.
2. Enter the number of shares of stock your corporation is authorized to issue. All of the shares do not need to be issued to shareholders at this time. You must have at least one share of stock.
3. Enter the complete street address of the corporation's registered office.
4. Enter the name of the corporation's registered agent. You can serve as your own registered agent if you have an office within the state.
5. Enter your name and address.
6. Enter the complete mailing address of the corporation.
7. This statement is for your benefit.

   Sign and date the Articles in black ink. The Articles should be typewritten.

Notes:

The same person may hold more than one office, however, the same person cannot hold both president and secretary positions.

Expedited service offers an eight-hour turnaround time for an additional $20 fee.

Stock is usually exempt from registration if the number of shareholders purchasing the stock in the last 12 months is 25 or fewer. Regulated by the Idaho Department of Finance.

To use a fictitious name, you'll need to file an application with the Secretary of State's office.

Make your check payable to the Idaho Secretary of State.

State of Illinois
ARTICLES OF INCORPORATION

Pursuant to The Business Corporation Act of 1983, **BCA 2.10**, the undersigned individual submits the following articles of incorporation for the purpose of forming a for profit corporation. This document meets the requirements of Public Act 87-1197 as amended January 1, 1995.	State Use:	State Use: Date: Franchise Tax:$ Filing fee: $ Approved By:

1.   The name of the corporation is:

2.   The name of the corporation's registered agent is:

3.   The street address and county of the corporation's registered office is:

4.   The purpose for which the corporation is organized is the transaction of any or all lawful purposes for which corporations may be incorporated under the Illinois Business Corporation Act of 1983.

5.   The corporation is authorized to issue one class of common stock with identical rights and privileges, the transfer of which is restricted according to the bylaws of the corporation.

6.   The par value per share is $

7.   The number of shares authorized is:

8.   The number of shares proposed to be issued is:

9.   The consideration to be received therefore is $

10. The name and address of the sole incorporator of the corporation is:

The undersigned incorporator, being the sole incorporator of the corporation, hereby declares under penalties of perjury, that the statements made in the foregoing Articles of Incorporation are true.

Dated:

Name of Incorporator:

Incorporator's Signature:_____

State Information	Illinois Secretary of State	**Telephone:**	(217) 782-2201
	Corporation Division		(800) 252-8980
	Howlett Building		(312) 814-2262 in Chicago.
	Room 328		
	Springfield, IL 62756	**Web address:**	www.sos.state.il.us/depts/
			bus_serv/feature.html
	Hand delivery:		
	Suite 1137	**Filing fee:**	$75 plus franchise tax.
	17 North State Street		Expedited service add $50.
	Chicago, IL 60602		
		Office hours:	8-4:30 Monday-Friday

Filing Procedure

For clarification on any step, refer to Chapter 2.

Choose a name — The name must include incorporated, corporation, limited, company, or an abbreviation of these words.

Check name availability — Call the number above and have them check the name for you, or search for it on their Web site.

File your paperwork — File the articles of incorporation and one copy with the Springfield office. Include a check for the filing fee.

Organizational matters — Choose officers (at least one) and directors (at least one). When the Articles return from the State, complete the Minutes of Organizational Meeting form (appendix). Issue stock certificates to each shareholder.

Prepare corporate records — Prepare or purchase a corporate record book and corporate seal. Place all of your documents in the record book. Use the corporate seal to emboss the stock certificates and Minutes of Organizational Meeting. Review Chapter 4 for a checklist of things to do after incorporating.

Form Instructions

1. Enter the name of the corporation.
2. Enter your name.
3. Enter your street address and county.
4. This is required.
5. This is required.
6. Enter your stock's par value.
7. Enter the number of authorized shares.
8. Enter the number of shares that will be issued to the initial shareholders.
9. Enter the total amount of money and property that the initial shareholders will give for their stock.
10. Enter your name and street address.

   Sign and date the Articles with BLACK ink. Sign your name as incorporator exactly as it appears in the Articles of Incorporation.

Notes:

The $100 fee mentioned above actually consists of a $75 filing fee and a $25 franchise tax. The tax is based on the total amount of money that shareholders give to the corporation for their stock. The corporation can receive up to $16,667 from shareholders for its stock and pay the minimum franchise tax of $25. Give more than $16,667 for your stock and you'll pay a higher tax. The tax is calculated as .0015 multiplied by the consideration (money) received by the corporation, with a minimum of $25.

Make your check payable to the Illinois Secretary of State.

Although the Chicago office accepts your documents, they are actually forwarded to Springfield for filing. Sending your documents directly to Springfield will speed up your filing process.

To use a fictitious name, you'll need to file an "Assumed Name Statement" with the Secretary of State after the articles of incorporation are filed. Some counties required that you file a statement with them as well. Procedures vary by county, so see your county clerk for local requirements.

If you plan to issue stock to "outsiders" or more than 10 people, consider registering your stock with the Securities Division of the Secretary of State's Office.

State of Indiana
ARTICLES OF INCORPORATION

Pursuant to Indiana Business Corporation Law as amended, Indiana Code 23-1-21-2 the undersigned individual submits these Articles of Incorporation for the purpose of forming a domestic, for-profit corporation.

1. The name of the Corporation is:

2. The street address of the corporation's initial registered office, and the name of its initial registered agent at that office are as follows:

3. The post office address of the corporation's principal office is:

4. The corporation is authorized to issue   shares of no par value, common stock, with identical rights and privileges, the transfer of which is restricted according to the Bylaws of the corporation.

5. The incorporator prepared this instrument. The name and street address of the corporation's sole incorporator is:

6. A Director of the corporation may not be held liable to the corporation or its shareholders for monetary damages due to a breach of fiduciary duty, unless the breach is a result of self-dealing, intentional misconduct, or illegal actions.

In witness whereof, the undersigned, being all the incorporators of the corporation named above, execute these Articles of Incorporation and verify, subject to penalties of perjury, that the statements contained herein are true.

Date:

Incorporator's Name:

Incorporator's Signature _____

State Information	Indiana Secretary of State Division of Corporations Room E018 302 West Washington Street Indianapolis, IN 46204	**Telephone:**	(317) 232-6576
		Web address:	www.ai.org/sos/bus_service/ corps/
		Filing fee:	$90
		Office Hours:	8-5:30 Monday-Friday

Filing Procedure

For clarification on any step, refer to Chapter 2.

Choose a name	The name must include incorporated, corporation, limited, company, or an abbreviation of one of these words.
Check name availability	Call the telephone number above and have them check the name for you.
File your paperwork	Complete the articles of incorporation form for your state. Send or take it and two copies to the corporation division's office. Include a check for $90.
Organizational matters	Choose officers (at least one) and directors (at least one). When the Articles return from the State, complete the Minutes of Organizational Meeting form (appendix). Issue stock certificates to each shareholder.
Prepare corporate records	Prepare or purchase a corporate record book and corporate seal. Place all of your documents in the record book. Use the corporate seal to emboss the stock certificates and Minutes of Organizational Meeting. Review Chapter 4 for a checklist of things to do after incorporating.

Form Instructions

1. Enter the name of the corporation.
2. Enter the name and STREET address of the corporation's initial registered agent. You can serve as your corporation's own registered agent. Your home address is acceptable.
3. Enter the corporation's mailing address.
4. Enter the number of shares of stock that your corporation will be authorized to issue. You can authorize more shares than you plan to issue. There is no limit on the number of shares that you may have.
5. Enter your name and street address here. You're only required to have one incorporator.
6. This statement is included for your protection.

   Complete the bottom of the form and have the incorporator sign the Articles of Incorporation with ink. The articles should be typewritten.

Notes:

To use a fictitious name, you'll need to file a "Certificate of Assumed Business Name" with the Secretary of State and the county recorder for your county. The form is available from the corporation division. The county filing fee varies by county. The state filing fee is $30.

Stock is usually exempt from registration if the number of Indiana residents purchasing the stock in the last 12 months is 20 or fewer. Regulated by the Securities Division of the Secretary of State's office. (317) 232-6681.

You can get faster service by sending the articles by overnight carrier or hand delivering the articles yourself. Overnight or hand-delivered filings are returned in 24-48 hours. If you send the articles by overnight carrier, be sure to include a prepaid air bill for their return.

Make your check payable to the Indiana Secretary of State.

State of Iowa
ARTICLES OF INCORPORATION

Pursuant to the provisions of Chapter 490 of the Iowa Code, the undersigned hereby adopts the following Articles of Incorporation for the purpose of forming a for profit corporation.

1. The name of the corporation is:

2. The corporation is authorized to issue   shares of no par value, common stock, with identical rights and privileges, the transfer of which is restricted according to the bylaws of the corporation.

3. The street address of the registered office is:

4. The registered agent at the above address is:

5. The name and address of the sole incorporator is:

6. The mailing address of the corporation is:

7. The period of duration for this corporation is perpetual.

In witness thereof, the undersigned incorporator has executed these Articles of Incorporation on the date below. The incorporator prepared this document.

Date:

Signature of Incorporator:_____

State Information	Iowa Secretary of State	Telephone:	(515) 281-5204
	Corporations Division	Web address:	www.sos.state.ia.us
	Hoover Building, 2nd Floor	Filing fee:	$50
	Des Moines, IA 50319	Office hours:	8-4:30 Monday-Friday

Filing Procedure

For clarification on any step, refer to Chapter 2.

Choose a name — The name must include incorporated, corporation, company, limited, or an abbreviation of one of these words.

Check name availability — Call the telephone number above.

File your paperwork — File the Articles of Incorporation and one copy with the Secretary of State. Be sure to include the filing fee.

Organizational matters — Choose officers (at least one) and directors (at least one). When the Articles return from the State, complete the Minutes of Organizational Meeting form (appendix). Issue stock certificates to each shareholder.

Prepare corporate records — Prepare or purchase a corporate record book and corporate seal. Place all of your documents in the record book. Use the corporate seal to emboss the stock certificates and Minutes of Organizational Meeting. Review Chapter 4 for a checklist of things to do after incorporating.

Form Instructions

1. Enter your corporate name.
2. Enter the number of shares of stock your corporation is authorized to issue. All of the shares do not need to be issued to shareholders at this time. You must have at least one share of stock.
3. Enter the complete street address of the corporation's registered office.
4. Enter the name of the corporation's registered agent. You can serve as your own registered agent if you have an office within the state.
5. Enter your name and address.
6. Enter the complete mailing address of the corporation.
7. This statement is for your benefit.

Sign and date the Articles in black ink. The Articles should be typewritten.

Notes:

Stock is usually exempt from registration, if the number of shareholders purchasing the stock in the last 12 months is 35 or fewer.

To use a fictitious name, file a "Certificate of Assumed Business Name" with the Secretary of State's office.

Make your check payable to the Iowa Secretary of State.

State of Kansas
ARTICLES OF INCORPORATION

For the purpose of forming a corporation under the general and business Corporation Law of Kansas, the undersigned natural person, being at least 18 years of age, adopts the following articles of incorporation.

1. The name of the Corporation is:

2. The street address of the corporation's initial registered office, and the name of its initial registered agent at that office are:

3. The corporation is formed for the purpose of

   and to engage in any legal act or activity permitted by the General and Business Corporation Laws of Kansas.

4. The corporation is authorized to issue   shares of no par value, common stock, with identical rights and privileges, the transfer of which is restricted according to the Bylaws of the corporation.

5. The name and street address of the corporation's only incorporator is:

6. The number of directors to constitute the Board of Directors is
   Their names and addresses are:

7. The duration of the corporation is perpetual.

8. The corporation's tax closing date is:

9. A Director of the corporation may not be held liable to the corporation or its shareholders for monetary damages due to a breach of fiduciary duty, unless the breach is a result of self-dealing, intentional misconduct, or illegal actions.

I declare under penalty of perjury, according to the laws of Kansas, that the foregoing is true and correct.
Date:

Incorporator's Name:

Telephone number:

Incorporator's Signature _____

State Information	Secretary of State Corporation Division 120 Southwest 10th Topeka, KS 66612	**Telephone:**	(785) 296-4564
		Web address:	www.kssos.org/corpwelc.html
		Filing fee:	$75 Expedited service add $20
		Office Hours:	8-5 Monday-Friday

Filing Procedure

For clarification on any step, refer to Chapter 2.

Choose a name
The name must include incorporated, corporation, limited, company, or an abbreviation of one of these words.

Check name availability
Call the telephone number above and have them check the name for you, or check the name on their website.

File your paperwork
Complete the articles of incorporation form. Send or take it and one copy to the corporation division's office. Include a check for $75.

Organizational matters
Choose officers (at least one) and directors (at least one). When the Articles return from the State, complete the Minutes of Organizational Meeting form (appendix). Issue stock certificates to each shareholder.

Prepare corporate records
Prepare or purchase a corporate record book and corporate seal. Place all of your documents in the record book. Use the corporate seal to emboss the stock certificates and Minutes of Organizational Meeting. Review Chapter 4 for a checklist of things to do after incorporating.

Form Instructions

1. Enter the name of the corporation.
2. Enter your name and street address. Your home address is okay.
3. Enter the business of the corporation.
4. Enter the number of shares of stock that your corporation will be authorized to issue. You can authorize more shares than you plan to issue. There is no limit on the number of shares that you may have.
5. Enter your name and street address here.
6. Enter the number of directors that your corporation will have. Also, enter their names and addresses. (You're only required to have one.)
7. This statement is required.
8. Enter the month and day of your corporation's year-end. For most companies this is December 31. If you haven't decided put "unknown."
9. This is included for your protection.

   Complete the bottom of the form and have the incorporator sign the Articles with ink. (Signature must correspond exactly to the name of the incorporator listed in article 5.) The articles should be typewritten.

Notes:

To use a fictitious name, you need to register it with the county in which the business is located. Call your county registrar for more information. There is no fictitious name registration at the state level.

Stock is usually exempt from registration if the number of Kansas residents purchasing the stock is 20 or fewer. Regulated by the Kansas State Securities Commission. (785) 296-3307

Make your check payable to the Kansas Secretary of State.

State of Kentucky
ARTICLES OF INCORPORATION

For the purpose of forming a corporation under The General and Business Corporation Law of Kentucky (KRS Chapter 271B), the undersigned natural person, being at least eighteen years of age, adopts the following Articles of Incorporation.

Article 1.   The name of the corporation is:

Article 2.   The street address of the corporation's initial registered office is:

Article 3.   The name of the initial registered agent at the above office is:

Signature of Registered Agent: _____

Article 4.   The corporation is authorized to issue   shares of no par value, common stock, with identical rights and privileges, the transfer of which is restricted according to the bylaws of the corporation.

Article 5.   The mailing address of the corporation's principal office is:

Article 6.   The name and mailing address of the sole incorporator is:

In witness whereof, these Articles of Incorporation have been signed on this date:

Name of Incorporator:

Telephone Number:

Signature of Incorporator: _____

State Information	Business Filings Office of the Secretary of State 700 Capitol Avenue Room 154, State Capitol PO Box 718 Frankfort, KY 40602	**Telephone:**	(502) 564-2848
		Web address:	www.sos.state.ky.us
		Filing fee:	$40 for the filing fee and $10 for the minimum incorporation tax. ($50 total)
		Office hours:	8-4:30

Filing Procedure   For clarification on any step, refer to Chapter 2.

Choose a name
The name must include incorporated, corporation, limited, company or an abbreviation of one of these words.

Check name availability
Call the telephone number above and have them check the name.

File your paperwork
Complete the articles of incorporation form. Send or take the articles and two copies to the business filings department's office.

Organizational matters
Choose officers (at least one) and directors (at least one). When the Articles return from the State, complete the Minutes of Organizational Meeting form (appendix). Issue stock certificates to each shareholder.

Prepare corporate records
Prepare or purchase a corporate record book and corporate seal. Place all of your documents in the record book. Use the corporate seal to emboss the stock certificates and Minutes of Organizational Meeting. Review Chapter 4 for a checklist of things to do after incorporating.

Form Instructions

1. Enter the name of the corporation.
2. Enter the STREET address of the corporation's initial registered office. Your home address is acceptable.
3. Enter the name of the initial registered agent. You can serve as your own registered agent.
4. Enter the total number of shares of stock that your corporation is authorized to issue. You can authorize up to 1,000 shares of stock for the minimum filing fee of $10. Authorize more than 1,000 shares, and your filing fee will increase.
5. Enter the mailing address of the corporation's principal office. Your home address is acceptable.
6. Enter your name and mailing address here.

   Complete the bottom of the form and have the incorporator and the registered agent sign the Articles of Incorporation. You are only required to have one incorporator. You can serve as both the incorporator and the registered agent. The articles should be typewritten.

Notes:

To use a fictitious name, you'll need to file a "Certificate of Assumed Name" form with the business filings department. This fee is $20 to file this form. You also need to register your fictitious name with the county in which your business is located. Call your city or town clerk for details.

Make checks payable to the Kentucky State Treasurer.

The incorporation tax is calculated as one cent for each share up to and including 20,000; 2 cent for each share in excess of 20,000 up to and including 200,000; 1/5 cent for each share in excess of 200,000. The minimum tax is $10 for 1,000 shares or less.

Stock is usually exempt from registration if the number of Kentucky residents purchasing the stock is 25 for fewer. Securities are regulated by the Kentucky State Securities Commission (502) 573-3390.

State of Louisiana
ARTICLES OF INCORPORATION

Pursuant to the provisions of Title 12 of the Louisiana Revised Statutes, the undersigned hereby adopts the following Articles of Incorporation for the purpose of forming a for profit corporation.

1. The name of the corporation is:

2. This corporation is formed for the purpose of engaging in any lawful activity for which a corporation may be formed.

3. The period of duration for this corporation is perpetual.

4. The corporation is authorized to issue one class of stock, that stock being   shares of no par value, common stock, with identical rights and privileges, the transfer of which is restricted according to the Bylaws of the corporation.

5. The full name and street address of the sole incorporator is:

6. The name and address of the corporation's registered agent is:

7. The corporation's Federal tax identification number has been applied for.

Signature of Incorporator:_____

Sworn to and subscribed before me at:

Parish of:
State of Louisiana

On this date:

Name of notary:

My commission expires:

Signature of Notary Public _____

State Information	Louisiana Secretary of State	**Telephone:**	(225) 925-4704
	Corporations Division	**Web address:**	http://www.sec.state.la.us/
	P.O. Box 94125		
	Baton Rouge, LA 70804-9125	**Filing fee:**	$60
		Office hours:	8-4:30
	Hand delivered:		
	3851 Essen Lane		
	Baton Rouge, LA 70809		

Filing Procedure

For clarification on any step, refer to Chapter 2.

Choose a name
The name must include incorporated, corporation, company, limited, or an abbreviation of one of these words. If the designation "company" or "co." are used, it may not be preceded by the word "and" or "&".

Check name availability
Call the telephone number above and have them check the name for you.

File your paperwork
File the articles of incorporation and the Domestic Corporation Initial Report (see notes) with the Secretary of State.

When the articles of incorporation return from the state, you must file a certified copy of the articles and the Initial Report, with the office of the recorder of mortgages. This must be done within 30 days.

Organizational matters
Choose officers (at least one) and directors (see notes) Complete the Minutes of Organizational Meeting form (appendix). Issue stock certificates to each shareholder.

Prepare corporate records
Prepare or purchase a corporate record book and corporate seal. Place all of your documents in the record book. Use the corporate seal to emboss the stock certificates and Minutes of Organizational Meeting. Review Chapter 4 for a checklist of things to do after incorporating.

Form Instructions

1. Enter your corporate name.
2. This statement is required.
3. This statement is required.
4. Enter the number of shares of stock your corporation is authorized to issue.
5. Enter your full name and street address.
6. Enter your name and address. You can serve as your own registered agent if you have an office within the state of Louisiana.
7. You should apply for a Federal Tax ID number only after incorporating. Do this by filing form SS-4 with the IRS.

   Sign and date the articles in the presence of the Notary Public.
   The Articles should be typewritten.

Notes:

The number of directors must equal the number of shareholders, with a minimum of three, unless there is fewer than three shareholders, then the number of directors must equal number of shareholders. (A corporation with one shareholder requires at least one director. Two shareholders requires two directors. Three shareholders require three directors. Four shareholders only require three directors.)

Stock is usually exempt from registration if the number of shareholders purchasing the stock in the last 12 months is 25 or fewer. Regulated by the Commissioner of Financial Institutions.

To use a fictitious name, you need to file an application with the Secretary of State's office.

The Domestic Corporation Initial Report is available from the Corporations Division or on the forms disk.

State of Maine
ARTICLES OF INCORPORATION

Domestic Business Corporation

Pursuant to the provisions of 13-A MRSA §403 of the Maine Revised Statutes, the undersigned, acting as incorporator of a corporation, hereby adopts the following Articles of Incorporation for the purpose of forming a for profit corporation.

Deputy Secretary of State

A true copy when attested by signature.

Deputy Secretary of State

1. The name of the corporation is:

2. The corporation's principal business location in Maine is:

3. The name of the corporation's Clerk, who is a Maine resident is:

4. The registered office is located at:

5. The initial Board of Directors shall consist of _____ members whose names and residence addresses are as follows:

6. The board of directors is authorized to increase or decrease the number of directors.

7. If the board is so authorized, the minimum number, if any, shall be _____ directors, and the maximum number, if any, shall be _____ directors.

8. The corporation is authorized to issue one class of stock, that stock being _____ shares of no par value, common stock, with identical rights and privileges, the transfer of which is restricted according to the Bylaws of the corporation.

9. Meetings of the shareholders may be held outside of the State of Maine.

10. Preemptive rights do apply.

11. The name and address of the sole incorporator is:

In witness thereof, the undersigned incorporator has executed these Articles of Incorporation on the date below. The incorporator prepared this document.
Date:

Signature of Incorporator: _____

State Information	Maine Secretary of State	**Telephone:**	(207) 287-4195
	Corporate Examining Section		(800) 872-3838
	101 State House Station	**Web address:**	www.state.me.us/sos/cec/
	Augusta, ME 04333-0101		corp/corp.htm
		Filing fee:	$105
		Office hours:	8-4:30

Filing Procedure

For clarification on any step, refer to Chapter 2.

Choose a name
The name must include incorporated, corporation, company, or an abbreviation of one of these words.

Check name availability
Call (207) 287-4195 and have them check the name for you. You can also search the name on their website.

File your paperwork
Complete the articles of incorporation form. Send or take it and one copy, along with Form MBCA-18A (see notes), to the Secretary of State's office. Be sure to include the filing fee.

Organizational matters
Choose officers (at least one) and directors (at least one). When the Articles return from the State, complete the Minutes of Organizational Meeting form (appendix). Issue stock certificates to each shareholder.

Prepare corporate records
Prepare or purchase a corporate record book and corporate seal. Place all of your documents in the record book. Use the corporate seal to emboss the stock certificates and Minutes of Organizational Meeting. Review Chapter 4 for a checklist of things to do after incorporating.

Form Instructions

1. Enter your corporate name.
2. Enter the corporation's principal business location (street, city, state, and zip code).
3. Enter the name of the corporation's Clerk. You can serve as your own Clerk if you are a resident of Maine. The position of Clerk is referred to as a registered agent in most states.
4. Enter the complete address (street, city, state, and zip code) of the corporation's registered office. Also include mailing address, if different from physical location.
5. Enter the number of members of the initial Board of Directors. Enter their names and residence addresses.
6. This statement is required.
7. Enter the minimum and maximum number of directors allowed by the corporation.
8. Enter the number of shares of stock your corporation is authorized to issue. All of the shares do not need to be issued to shareholders at this time. You must have at least one share of stock.
9. This statement is required.
10. This statement is required.
11. Enter your name and address here.
    Sign and date the articles with black ink. The articles should be typewritten.

Notes:

If the corporation has one shareholder, you only need one or more directors. If the corporation has two shareholders, you need two or more directors. If the corporation has three or more shareholders, you need three or more directors.

Form MBCA-18A is available from the Secretary of State. It is also on the forms disk.

Stock is usually exempt from registration if the number of shareholders purchasing the stock in the last 12 months is 25 for fewer. Regulated by the State Securities Administrator.

To use a fictitious name, file an application with the Secretary of State's office.

State of Maryland
ARTICLES OF INCORPORATION

Pursuant to the laws of the State of Maryland as amended, the undersigned individual submits these Articles of Incorporation for the purpose of forming a domestic for-profit corporation.

Article 1. The name of the Corporation is:

Article 2. I,   the sole incorporator, being at least 18 years of age do hereby submit these Articles of Incorporation for the purpose of forming a corporation under the laws of the State of Maryland. My address is:

Article 3. The corporation may engage in any lawful act or activity allowed by the general laws of the State of Maryland, with the primary purpose of the corporation being:

Article 4. The complete street address of the Corporation's principal office is:

Article 5. The corporation is authorized to issue one class of stock, that stock being   shares of no par value, common stock, with identical rights and privileges, the transfer of which is restricted according to the bylaws of the corporation.

Article 6. The name(s) and address(es) of the   initial Director(s), the number of which meets the requirements of the laws of the State of Maryland as amended is/are:

Article 7. The name, street address and county of the corporation's resident agent in Maryland is:

In witness whereof, I the sole incorporator named above have executed these Articles of Incorporation and acknowledge the same to be my act.

I hereby consent to my designation in this document as resident agent for this corporation.

Date:

Name:

Signature: _____

Date:

Name:

Signature _____

State Information	Maryland Department of Assessments and Taxation Corporate Charter Division 301 West Preston street Baltimore, MD 21201	**Telephone:**	(410) 767-1350
		Web address:	www.dat.state.md.us/ sdatweb/charter.html
		Filing fee:	$20 plus tax of $20 Expedited service is an additional $30.
		Office hours:	8-3:30 Monday-Friday Telephone hours are until 4:30.

Filing Procedure

For clarification on any step, refer to Chapter 2.

Choose a name
The name must include incorporated, corporation, limited, company, or an abbreviation of one of these words.

Check name availability
Call the Corporate Charter Division (410) 767-1330 and have them check the name for you.

File your paperwork
Complete the articles of incorporation. Send or take the articles to the Corporate Charter Division's office. Include a check for $40.

Organizational matters
Choose officers (at least one) and directors (at least one). When the Articles return from the State, complete the Minutes of Organizational Meeting form (appendix). Issue stock certificates to each shareholder.

Prepare corporate records
Prepare or purchase a corporate record book and corporate seal. Place all of your documents in the record book. Use the corporate seal to emboss the stock certificates and Minutes of Organizational Meeting. Review Chapter 4 for a checklist of things to do after incorporating.

Form Instructions

1. Enter the name of the corporation.
2. Enter your name and mailing address in the spaces provided. This address must be a street address.
3. Provide a brief description of the corporation's principle business.
4. Enter the STREET address of the corporation's principle office. Your home address is okay to use.
5. Enter the number of shares of stock that your corporation will be authorized to issue. You may authorize up to 5,000 shares of no par value stock for the minimum filing fee.
6. First, enter the number of directors in the space provided, then enter their names and addresses in the space below.
7. Into your name, street address, and county in the spaces provided.

    Complete the bottom of the form and have the incorporator AND the resident agent sign the Articles of Incorporation with ink. The articles should be typewritten.

Notes:

The incorporation tax mentioned above is calculated by multiplying the number of authorized shares by the stock's par value. For the minimum tax of $20, you can authorize up to 5,000 shares of no par value stock, or up to 100,000 shares of $1 par value stock. If you authorize more than this, your filing fee (tax) will increase. Make your check payable to the Maryland State Department of Assessments and Taxation.

To use a fictitious name, you'll need to file a "Tradename Application" with the State Department of Assessments and Taxation. The form is available from the Corporate Charter Division and the filing fee is $11 plus $1 for each owner listed on the form.

Stock is usually exempt from registration if the number of Maryland residents purchasing the stock in the last 12 months is 35 or fewer. The securities division of the Maryland Attorney General's office handles stock registration. Their telephone number is (410) 576-6360.

Commonwealth of Massachusetts
ARTICLES OF ORGANIZATION

I, the undersigned person, acting as incorporator under M.G.L. Chapter 156B, adopt the following Articles of incorporation for the purpose of forming a for-profit business corporation.

1. The name of the corporation is:

2. The purpose for which the corporation is formed is to carry on any business which may be lawfully carried on by a corporation organized under M.G.L. Chapter 156B. The specific purpose of the corporation is to engage in the following business activities:

3. The corporation is authorized to issue one class of stock, that stock being   shares of no par value, common stock, with identical rights and privileges, the transfer of which is restricted according to the Bylaws of the corporation. Said shares are entitled to receive the net assets of the Corporation upon its dissolution.

4. The effective date of this filing is   [   ] The actual date and time of filing.
                                          [   ]   /   /   at 12 o'clock PM.

5. The street address of the principal office of the Corporation in Massachusetts is:

6. The name, residential address and post office address of each director and officer of the Corporation are:
   name_____title_____address_____

7. The fiscal year of the Corporation shall end on the last day of the month of

8. The name and business address of the resident agent of the corporation is:

9. A director of the corporation shall not be held liable to the corporation or its shareholders for monetary damages due to a breach of fiduciary duty, unless the breach is a result of self-dealing, intentional misconduct, or illegal actions.

Date:
Name of Incorporator:

Signature of Incorporator: _____

State Information	Massachusetts Secretary of State Corporation Division One Ashburton Place Boston, MA 02108-1512	**Telephone:**	(617) 727-9640
		Web address:	www.state.ma.us/sec/cor/
		Filing fee:	$200
		Office hours:	8:45-5 Monday-Friday

Filing Procedure

For clarification on any step, refer to Chapter 2.

Choose a name
The name should include incorporated, corporation, limited or an abbreviation of one of these words.

Check name availability
Call the telephone number above and have them check the name for you.

File your paperwork
Complete the articles of organization form. Send or take it and one copy to the Secretary of State's office. Be sure to include the filing fee.

Organizational matters
Choose officers (at least one) and directors (at least one). When the Articles return from the State, complete the Minutes of Organizational Meeting form (appendix). Issue stock certificates to each shareholder.

Prepare corporate records
Prepare or purchase a corporate record book and corporate seal. Place all of your documents in the record book. Use the corporate seal to emboss the stock certificates and Minutes of Organizational Meeting. Review Chapter 4 for a checklist of things to do after incorporating.

Form Instructions

1. Enter the corporate name.
2. Enter the corporation's business activity.
3. Enter the number of shares of stock your corporation is authorized to issue. You can authorize up to 200,000 shares of stock and incur the minimum filing fee.
4. Choose one option. If you choose the second option, enter a date that is no more than 30 days in the future.
5. Enter your name and street address.
6. Enter the names and addresses of the directors and officers. Specify next to each name the capacity in which the person serves.
7. Enter the last month of the corporation's tax year. For most companies, this is December.
8. Enter your name and street address.
9. Included for your protection.

Enter the date, and your name, then sign with black ink.

Notes:

Stock is usually exempt from registration if the number of shareholders purchasing the stock in the last 12 months is 35 or fewer. Regulated by the Massachusetts State Securities Commission. (617) 727-3548

The amount of the filing fee is based on the total amount of the corporation's capitalization. Capitalization equals the number of authorized shares of stock multiplied by the par value. You can authorize up to 200,000 shares of no par value stock and incur the minimum filing fee of $200. Authorize more stock than that, and you will incur a higher fee.

To use a fictitious name, you should file a business certificate with the city or town in which you're doing business. Call your town clerk for more information.

ARTICLES OF INCORPORATION

Date received:		Bureau use only:

Return this document to:

Effective Date:

ARTICLES OF INCORPORATION
DOMESTIC FOR PROFIT CORPORATION

Pursuant to the provisions of Act 284, Public Acts of 1972, the undersigned corporation executes the following Articles for the purpose of forming a domestic, for profit-corporation.

Article 1. The name of the corporation is:

Article 2. The purpose or purposes for which the corporation is formed is to engage in any activity within the purposes for which corporations may be formed under the Business Corporation Act of Michigan.

Article 3. The corporation is authorized to issue one class of stock, that stock being   shares of no par value, common stock, with identical rights and privileges, the transfer of which is restricted according to the bylaws of the corporation.

Article 4. The street address of the registered office, and the name of the resident agent at the registered office is:

Article 5. The name and street address of the corporation's sole incorporator is:

Article 6: A Director of the corporation shall not be held liable to the corporation or its shareholders for monetary damages due to a breach of fiduciary duty, unless the breach is a result of self-dealing, intentional misconduct, or illegal actions.

Name of person or organization remitting fees:

Preparer's name and business telephone number:

I, the sole incorporator of the corporation, sign my name on this date:

Name of Incorporator: Signature: _____

State Information	Michigan Department of Consumer and Industry Services Division of Corporations New filings 7150 Harris Drive P.O. Box 30054 Lansing, MI 48909	**Telephone:**	(517) 241-6400
		Web address:	www.commerce.state.mi.us/corp/corpinfo.htm
		Filing fee:	$60 Expedited filing add $2.50.
		Office hours:	8-5 Monday-Friday
	Hand deliver or overnight: 6546 Mercantile Way Lansing, Michigan 48910		

Filing Procedure

For clarification on any step, refer to Chapter 2.

Choose a name The name must include incorporated, corporation, company, limited, or an abbreviation of one of these words.

Check name availability Call the corporation division at (517) 334-7561 and have them check the name for you.

File your paperwork Complete the articles of incorporation and send or take it to the corporation division's office. Include a check for $60. To file by fax, obtain a "filing number" by calling (517) 334-6327, then fax the articles to this number (517) 334-8048.

Organizational matters Choose officers (at least one) and directors (at least one). When the Articles return from the State, complete the Minutes of Organizational Meeting form (appendix). Issue stock certificates to each shareholder.

Prepare corporate records Prepare or purchase a corporate record book and corporate seal. Place all of your documents in the record book. Use the corporate seal to emboss the stock certificates and Minutes of Organizational Meeting. Review Chapter 4 for a checklist of things to do after incorporating.

Form Instructions

At the top of the form, enter your name and address in the rectangle headed, "Return this document to:"

1. Enter the name of the corporation.
2. This statement is required.
3. Enter the number of shares of stock that your corporation will be authorized to issue. Up to 60,000 shares can be authorized for the minimum filing fee of $50.
4. Enter your name and street address here.
5. Enter your name and street address here
6. This is a standard statement included for your protection.

   Complete the bottom of the form and have the incorporator sign the Articles of Incorporation in ink.

Notes:

The filing fee of $60 actually consists of a filing fee of $10 and minimum organization fee of $50. You can authorize up to 60,000 shares of stock and incur the minimum organization fee of $50. Each additional 20,000 shares authorized will increase your organization fee by $30. Credit cards are accepted.

To use a fictitious name, you'll need to file a "Certificate of Assumed Name" form with the Department of Consumer and Industry Services after the articles of incorporation are filed. The form is available from the Corporation Division and its filing fee is $10.

Stock is usually exempt from registration if the number of Michigan residents purchasing the stock in the last 12 months is 15 or fewer. Regulated by the Securities Division of the Department of Consumer and Industry Services Office (517) 334-6200.

State of Minnesota
ARTICLES OF INCORPORATION

Pursuant to the provisions of Chapter 302A of the Minnesota Statutes, the undersigned person of the age of 18 years or more, acting as incorporator of a corporation, hereby adopts the following Articles of Incorporation for the purpose of forming a for-profit corporation.

1. The name of the corporation is:

2. The registered office address of the corporation is:

3. The registered agent at the above address is:

4. The corporation is authorized to issue one class of stock, that stock being   shares of no par value, common stock, with identical rights and privileges, the transfer of which is restricted according to the Bylaws of the corporation.

5. Name and phone number of person to be contacted if there is a question about the filing of these articles:

   Name:

   Phone Number:

I, the undersigned incorporator, certify that I am authorized to sign these articles and that the information in these articles is true and correct. I also understand that if any of this information is intentionally or knowingly misstated that criminal penalties will apply as if I had signed these articles under oath.

Name:

Address:

Signature:_____

State Information	Minnesota Secretary of State	**Telephone:**	(651) 296-2803
	Business Services Section	**Web address:**	www.sos.state.mn.us/business
	180 State Office Building	**Filing fee:**	$135
	100 Constitution Ave.	**Office hours:**	8-4:30 Monday - Friday
	St. Paul, MN 55155-1299		

Filing Procedure

For clarification on any step, refer to Chapter 2.

Choose a name
The name must include incorporated, corporation, limited, company, or an abbreviation of one of these words. If company or co. is used, it must not be immediately preceded by "and" or "&".

Check name availability
Call the telephone number above.

File your paperwork
File the Articles of Incorporation with the Secretary of State. Be sure to include the filing fee.

Organizational matters
Choose officers (at least one) and directors (at least one). When the Articles return from the State, complete the Minutes of Organizational Meeting form (appendix). Issue stock certificates to each shareholder.

Prepare corporate records
Prepare or purchase a corporate record book and corporate seal. Place all of your documents in the record book. Use the corporate seal to emboss the stock certificates and Minutes of Organizational Meeting. Review Chapter 4 for a checklist of things to do after incorporating.

Form Instructions

1. Enter your corporate name.
2. Enter the complete street address or rural route and rural route box number for the registered office address. Post office box numbers are not acceptable.
3. Enter the name of the registered agent at the above address. You can serve as your own registered agent.
4. Enter the number of shares of stock your corporation is authorized to issue. All of the shares do not need to be issued to shareholders at this time. You must have at least one share of stock.
5. Enter your name and phone number.

   Enter your name and complete address. Sign your name in black ink. The articles should be typewritten.

Notes:

The stock is usually exempt from registration with the state if the number of shareholders purchasing the stock in the last 12 months is 25 for fewer. Regulated by the State Department of Commerce.

To use a fictitious name, file an application with the Secretary of State's office. The fee is $25.

State of Mississippi
ARTICLES OF INCORPORATION

Pursuant to the provisions of Title 79 of the Mississippi Code of 1972, the undersigned person, acting as incorporator of a corporation, hereby adopts the following Articles of Incorporation:

1. This corporation shall be a for-profit corporation.

2. The name of the corporation is:

3. This filing will be effective as of the actual date filed.

4. The corporation is authorized to issue one class of stock, that stock being   shares of no par value, common stock, with identical rights and privileges, the transfer of which is restricted according to the Bylaws of the corporation.

5. The name and street address of the Registered Agent and Registered Office is:

6. The name and complete address of the sole incorporator is:

In witness thereof, the undersigned incorporator has executed these Articles of Incorporation on the date below. The incorporator prepared this document.

Date:

Signature of Incorporator: _____

State Information	Mississippi Secretary of State	**Telephone:**	(601) 359-1633
	Business Services Division		(800) 256-3494
	P.O. Box 136		Fax: (601) 359-1499
	Jackson, MS 39205-0136		
		Web address:	www.sos.state.ms.us/
	Hand delivered:	**Filing fee:**	$50
	401 Mississippi Street	**Office hours:**	8-5 Monday - Friday
	Jackson, MS 39201		

Filing Procedure

For clarification on any step, refer to Chapter 2.

Choose a name

The name must include incorporated, corporation, limited, company, or an abbreviation of one of these words.

Check name availability

Call the telephone number above and have them check the name for you, or search the name on their website with "CorpSnap."

File your paperwork

File the Articles of Incorporation and one exact copy with the Secretary of State. Be sure to include the filing fee.

Organizational matters

Choose officers (at least one) and directors (at least one). When the Articles return from the State, complete the Minutes of Organizational Meeting form (appendix). Issue stock certificates to each shareholder.

Prepare corporate records

Prepare or purchase a corporate record book and corporate seal. Place all of your documents in the record book. Use the corporate seal to emboss the stock certificates and Minutes of Organizational Meeting. Review Chapter 4 for a checklist of things to do after incorporating.

Form Instructions

1. This statement is required.
2. Enter your corporate name.
3. This statement is required.
4. Enter the number of shares of stock your corporation is authorized to issue. All of the shares do not need to be issued to shareholders at this time. You must have at least one share of stock.
5. Enter the name and complete address of the registered agent and office. You can serve as your own registered agent.
6. Enter your name and complete address.

   Sign and date the Articles in black ink. The Articles should be typewritten.

Notes:

Mississippi prefers that you use their special computer readable form. This form is available from their office, their website, or on the forms disk. (There is an additional charge for not using their form.)

Stock is usually exempt from registration if the number of shareholders purchasing the stock in the last 12 months is 11 or fewer. Regulated by the Secretary of State.

Make your check payable to the Mississippi Secretary of State.

State of Missouri
ARTICLES OF INCORPORATION

For the purpose of forming a corporation under The General and Business Corporation Law of Missouri, the undersigned natural person, being at least eighteen years of age, adopts the following Articles of Incorporation.

Article 1.   The name of the Corporation is:

Article 2.   The name and address of the company's registered agent in Missouri is:

Article 3.   The corporation is authorized to issue   shares of no par value, common stock, with identical rights and privileges, the transfer of which is restricted according to the bylaws of the corporation.

Article 4.   Preemptive rights are neither limited nor denied.

Article 5.   The name and place of residence of the sole incorporator is:

Article 6.   The number of directors to constitute the board of directors is   . A director of the corporation shall not be held liable to the corporation or its shareholders for monetary damages due to a breach of fiduciary duty, unless the breach is a result of self-dealing, intentional misconduct, or illegal actions.

Article 7.   The duration of the corporation is perpetual.

Article 8.   The corporation is formed for the purpose of

and to engage in any legal act or activity permitted by The General and Business Corporation Laws Of Missouri.

In witness whereof, these Articles of Incorporation have been signed on this date:

Name of Incorporator: Telephone Number:

Signature of Incorporator: _____

State of Missouri
County of _____.
I,   , a Notary Public, do hereby certify that on this   day
of   , 20   ,   , personally appeared before
me,   who being by me first duly sworn, declared that he/she is the person
who signed the forgoing document as incorporator, and that the statements therein contained are true.

Notary Public _____   My commission expires:

State Information	Secretary of State Corporation Division P.O. Box 778 600 W. Main and 208 State Capitol Jefferson City, MO 65102	**Telephone:**	(573) 751-2359, or 751-4544
		Web address:	http://mosl.sos.state.mo.us/ bus-ser/soscor.html
		Filing fee:	$58 for 30,000 shares or fewer
		Office hours:	8-5 Monday-Friday

Filing Procedure

For clarification on a step, refer to Chapter 2.

Choose a name
The name must include incorporated, corporation, limited, company, or an abbreviation of one of these words.

Check name availability
Call (573) 751-3317 and have them check the name.

File your paperwork
Complete the articles of incorporation. Send or take the articles and one copy to the Corporation Division's office. Include a check for $58. (see notes)

Organizational matters
Choose officers (at least one) and directors (at least one). When the Articles return from the State, complete the Minutes of Organizational Meeting form (appendix). Issue stock certificates to each shareholder.

Prepare corporate records
Prepare or purchase a corporate record book and corporate seal. Place all of your documents in the record book. Use the corporate seal to emboss the stock certificates and Minutes of Organizational Meeting. Review Chapter 4 for a checklist of things to do after incorporating.

Form Instructions

1. Enter the name of the corporation.
2. Enter the name and STREET address of the corporation's initial registered agent. You can serve as your company's own registered agent. Your home address is acceptable.
3. Enter the total number of shares of stock that your corporation is authorized to issue.
4. This statement is required.
5. Enter your name and street address in the space provided. Your home address is acceptable.
6. Enter the number of directors in the space provided.
7. This statement is required.
8. Enter the corporation's primary business activity in the space provided.

   Complete the bottom of the form and have the incorporator sign the Articles of Incorporation in the presence of a notary. You are only required to have one incorporator.

Notes:

To use a fictitious name, you'll need to file an application with the Corporation Division. The form is available from their office, and the fee to file it is $7. Make your check payable to the Missouri Director of Revenue.

Stock is usually exempt from registration if the total number of Missouri residents purchasing the stock is 25 or fewer, or the number of Missouri residents purchasing the stock in the last 12 months is 15 or fewer. Choose whichever applies. For questions regarding stock registration, contact the Missouri State Securities Commission at (573) 751-4136.

The filing fee is based on the number of shares that your corporation authorizes. You can authorize up to 30,000 shares of stock for the minimum filing fee of $58. If you authorize more than that, your filing fee will increase $5 for each additional 10,000 shares. (40,000 shares of stock will cost $63; 50,000 shares of stock will cost $68, etc.)

Branch offices are maintained in
    Kansas City (816) 889-2925
    Springfield (417) 895-6330
    St. Louis (314) 340-7490

[   ] Priority Filing Add $20

State of Montana
ARTICLES OF INCORPORATION
Domestic for Profit Corporation

Pursuant to the provisions of Title 35 of the Montana Code, the undersigned person, hereby adopts the following Articles of Incorporation for the purpose of forming a Montana corporation.

1. The name of the corporation is:

2. The name and address of the corporation's registered agent and office in Montana is:

   Signature of Agent _____

3. The corporation is authorized to issue one class of stock, that stock being   shares of no par value, common stock, with identical rights and privileges, the transfer of which is restricted according to the Bylaws of the corporation.

4. The name and complete address of the sole incorporator is:

In witness thereof, the undersigned incorporator has executed these Articles of Incorporation on the date below. The incorporator prepared this document.

Date:

Signature of Incorporator: _____

State Information	Montana Secretary of State Business Service Bureau P.O. Box 202801 Helena, MT 59620-2801 Hand delivery: State Capital Building Room 225 Helena, MT 59620	**Telephone:**	(406) 444-3665
		Web address:	www.state.mt.us/sos/biz.htm
		Filing fee:	$70
		Office hours:	8-5 Monday-Friday

Filing Procedure

For clarification on any step, refer to Chapter 2.

Choose a name
The name must include incorporated, corporation, limited, company, or an abbreviation of one of these words.

Check name availability
Call the telephone number above.

File your paperwork
File the Articles of Incorporation and one exact copy with the Secretary of State. Be sure to include the filing fee.

To request priority filing of your document, simply mark the "priority filing" blank on your Articles and include an additional $20. Priority filing ensures that your application will be handled within 24 hours of receipt.

Organizational matters
Choose officers (at least one) and directors (at least one). When the Articles return from the State, complete the Minutes of Organizational Meeting form (appendix). Issue stock certificates to each shareholder.

Prepare corporate records
Prepare or purchase a corporate record book and corporate seal. Place all of your documents in the record book. Use the corporate seal to emboss the stock certificates and Minutes of Organizational Meeting. Review Chapter 4 for a checklist of things to do after incorporating.

Form Instructions

1. Enter your corporate name.
2. Enter the name and address of the corporation's registered agent and office in Montana. You can serve as your own registered agent. Sign your name in the "Signature of Agent" blank in black ink.
3. Enter the number of shares of stock your corporation is authorized to issue. You can authorize up to 50,000 shares of stock and incur the minimum license fee of $50. (see notes)
4. Enter your name and complete address here.

   Sign and date the Articles in black ink. The Articles should be typewritten.

Notes:

The filing fee of $70 consists of a $20 filing fee and a license fee based on the number of shares of stock that your corporation authorizes. For the minimum fee of $50, you can authorize up to 50,000 shares of stock. Authorize more than this, and you will incur a higher license fee.

Stock is usually exempt from registration if the number of shareholders purchasing the stock in the last 12 months is 10 or fewer. Regulated by the State Auditor/Securities Commissioner.

To use a fictitious name, or d.b.a., file an application with the Secretary of State's office.

State of Nebraska
ARTICLES OF INCORPORATION
A Business/Stock Corporation

Pursuant to the provisions of Chapter 21 of the Revised Nebraska Statutes, the undersigned person, hereby adopts the following Articles of Incorporation for the purpose of forming a Nebraska corporation.

1. The name of the corporation is:

2. The name and address of the corporation's registered agent and office in Nebraska is:

    Signature of Agent _____

3. The corporation is authorized to issue one class of stock, that stock being _____ shares of no par value, common stock, with identical rights and privileges, the transfer of which is restricted according to the Bylaws of the corporation.

4. The business and mailing address of the corporation is:

5. The duration of the corporation is perpetual.

6. The corporation has been organized to transact any and all lawful business for which corporations may be incorporated in this state.

7. The initial Board of Directors shall consist of _____ members whose names and residence addresses are:

8. The name and complete address of the sole incorporator is:

In witness thereof, the undersigned incorporator has executed these Articles of Incorporation on the date below. The incorporator prepared this document.

Date:

Signature of Incorporator: _____

State Information	Nebraska Secretary of State	**Telephone:**	(402) 471-4079
	Suite 1305	**Web address:**	www.nol.org/home/SOS/ corps/corpform.htm
	State Capitol		
	Lincoln, NE 68509	**Filing fee:**	$65 Expedited service add $20
		Office hours:	8-5 Monday-Friday

Filing Procedure

For clarification on any step, refer to Chapter 2.

Choose a name	The name must include incorporated, corporation, limited, company, or an abbreviation of one of these words.
Check name availability	Call the telephone number above, and have them check the name for you.
File your paperwork	File the Articles of Incorporation and one duplicate copy with the Secretary of State. Be sure to include the filing fee.
Organizational matters	Choose officers (at least one) and directors (at least one). When the Articles return from the State, record the duplicate copy with the county clerk of the county where the registered office of the corporation is located. Complete the Minutes of Organizational Meeting form (appendix). Issue stock certificates to each shareholder.
Prepare corporate records	Prepare or purchase a corporate record book and corporate seal. Place all of your documents in the record book. Use the corporate seal to emboss the stock certificates and Minutes of Organizational Meeting. Review Chapter 4 for a checklist of things to do after incorporating.

Form Instructions

1. Enter your corporate name.
2. Enter the name and address of the corporation's registered agent and office in Nebraska. You can serve as your own registered agent. Sign your name in the "Signature of Agent" blank in black ink.
3. Enter the number of shares of stock your corporation is authorized to issue. All of the shares do not need to be issued to shareholders at this time. You must have at least one share of stock.
4. Enter the corporation's business and mailing address here.
5. This statement is required.
6. This statement is required.
7. Enter the number of members of the initial Board of Directors. Enter their names and residence addresses.
8. Enter your name and complete address here.

   Sign and date the Articles in black ink. The Articles should be typewritten.

Notes:

Make check payable to the Nebraska Secretary of State.

Stock is usually exempt from registration if the number of shareholders purchasing the stock in the last twelve months is 15 or fewer. Regulated by the Director of Banking and Finance.

To use a fictitious name, file an application with the Secretary of State's office. The filing fee is $100.

State of Nevada
ARTICLES OF INCORPORATION

Pursuant to Nevada Revised Statutes, NRS '78, the undersigned incorporator hereby files these articles for the purpose of forming a for-profit, business corporation in Nevada.

Article 1. The name of the corporation is:

Article 2. The corporation is authorized to issue one class of stock, that being _____ shares of no par value, common stock, with identical rights and privileges, the transfer of which is restricted according to the corporation bylaws. Preemptive rights to acquire additional shares are neither limited nor denied.

Article 3. The members of the corporation's governing board are styled as directors. The name(s) and address(es) of the First Board of Directors, consisting of _____ individuals are:

Resident Agent:
   The name of the corporation's Resident Agent and the street address in Nevada for service of process is:

   Acceptance of appointment:

   I, _____ hereby accept appointment as Resident agent for the above named corporation.

   Signature: _____   Date of signature: _____/_____/_____

Incorporator:
   The name and address of the corporation's only incorporator is:

   Incorporator's Signature: _____ Date of signature: _____

Notary Public:
   State of:
   County of:

   This instrument was acknowledged before me on:
   by _____ as the incorporator of the above named corporation.

   Notary Public Signature: _____ Seal:

   My commission expires: _____

State Information	Secretary of State Commercial Recording Division Capitol Complex Carson City, NV 89710	**Telephone:**	(775) 684-5708 (800) 992-0900
		Web address:	http://sos.state.nv.us/ comm_rec/index.htm
	Secretary of State Commercial Recording Division 555 E. Washington Ave. # 2900 Las Vegas, NV 89101	**Filing fee:**	Based on the number of authorized shares and par value, a minimum of $125.
		Office hours:	8-5 Monday-Friday

Filing Procedure

For clarification on any step, refer to Chapter 2.

Choose a name   You're not required to use incorporated, corporation or other corporate designators with the name.

Check name availability   Nevada does not offer name checks by phone. They do offer name checks on their Web site.

File your paperwork   Complete the articles of incorporation form. Have the form notarized. File the form with the Secretary of State. Include the filing fee of $125.

Organizational matters   Choose officers (at least one) and directors (at least one). When the Articles return from the State, complete the Minutes of Organizational Meeting form (appendix). Complete the business license application (see notes) and the "List of Officers and Directors." Return them to the addresses listed on the forms. Issue stock certificates to each shareholder.

Prepare corporate records   Prepare or purchase a corporate record book and corporate seal. Place all of your documents in the record book. Use the corporate seal to emboss the stock certificates and Minutes of Organizational Meeting. Review Chapter 4 for a checklist of things to do after incorporating.

Form Instructions

1. Enter the name of the corporation. The name does not have to include incorporated, corporation or similar wording. You should, however, add one of these corporate designators if you plan on doing business in another state. They will require it.

2. Enter the total number of shares that your corporation will authorize. The filing fee is based on the number of authorized shares multiplied by their par value. You can authorize up to 25,000 shares of no par value stock and incur the minimum filing fee of $125. By changing the par value to one mil ($.001), you can authorize up to 25 million shares. See the main text for discussion on par value.

3. Enter the number of directors your corporation will have, their names and addresses.

   In the resident agent section, put your name and Nevada street address. Sign and date the acceptance. This does not have to be notarized. If you are outside Nevada, obtain a list of resident agent services from the Secretary of State's office.

   In the incorporator section, list your name and address, then sign and date in the presence of a Notary Public. This should be a local notary from your own county.

   In the Notary Public section, have a Notary Public witness the incorporator's signature. The notary will complete this section.

Notes:

To use a fictitious name, file a form called "Certificate of Business: Fictitious Firm Named" with the county clerk for the county where the offices are located. If outside Nevada, you may have to register with your own Secretary of State's office.

When your articles are filed and returned from the state, they will come with two forms that you'll need to complete and send back with additional fees; the "List of Officers and Directors" $85, and a state of Nevada business license application $25.

Stock is usually exempt from registration if the total number of sales to Nevada residents in the last 12-month period, is 25 or fewer. Stock registration is overseen by the Secretary of State's Securities Division (702) 486-2440.

Make your check payable to the Nevada Secretary of State.

State of New Hampshire
ARTICLES OF INCORPORATION

A Business/Stock Corporation

Pursuant to the provisions of Chapter 293-A of the New Hampshire Revised Statutes, the undersigned person, hereby adopts the following Articles of Incorporation for the purpose of forming a New Hampshire corporation.

1. The name of the corporation is:

2. The name and address of the corporation's registered agent and office in New Hampshire is:

    Signature of Agent _____

3. The corporation is authorized to issue one class of stock, that stock being _____ shares of no par value, common stock, with identical rights and privileges, the transfer of which is restricted according to the Bylaws of the corporation.

4. The business and mailing address of the corporation is:

5. The duration of the corporation is perpetual.

6. The corporation has been organized to transact any and all lawful business for which corporations may be incorporated in this state.

7. The initial Board of Directors shall consist of _____ members whose names and residence addresses are as follows:

8. The name and complete address of the only incorporator is:

In witness thereof, the undersigned incorporator has executed these Articles of Incorporation on the date below. The incorporator prepared this document.

Date:

Signature of Incorporator: _____

State Information	New Hampshire Secretary of State State House Annex, Room 204 107 N. Main St. Concord, NH 03301-4989	**Telephone:**	(603) 271-3246 (603) 271-3244
		Web address:	www.state.nh.us/sos/ corporate/index.htm
		Filing fee:	$85
		Office hours:	8-4 Monday - Friday (Closed from 12-1)

Filing Procedure	For clarification on any step, refer to Chapter 2.	
	Choose a name	The name must include incorporated, corporation, limited, or an abbreviation of one of these words.
	Check name availability	Call the telephone number above and have them check the name for you.
	File your paperwork	Complete the articles of incorporation form. Send or take the original articles and one copy, along with form 11-A (see notes) to the Secretary of State. Be sure to include the filing fee.
	Organizational matters	Choose officers (at least one) and directors (at least one). When the Articles return from the State, complete the Minutes of Organizational Meeting form (appendix). Issue stock certificates to each shareholder.
	Prepare corporate records	Prepare or purchase a corporate record book and corporate seal. Place all of your documents in the record book. Use the corporate seal to emboss the stock certificates and Minutes of Organizational Meeting. Review Chapter 4 for a checklist of things to do after incorporating.

Form Instructions

1. Enter your corporate name.

2. Enter the name and address of the corporation's registered agent and office in New Hampshire. You can serve as your own registered agent. The registered agent and the secretary must be the same person. Sign your name in the "Signature of Agent" blank in black ink.

3. Enter the number of shares of stock your corporation is authorized to issue. All of the shares do not need to be issued to shareholders at this time. You must have at least one share of stock.

4. Enter the corporation's business and mailing address here.

5. This statement is required.

6. This statement is required.

7. Enter the number of members of the initial Board of Directors. Enter their names and residence addresses.

8. Enter your name and complete address here.

Sign and date the Articles in black ink. The Articles should be typewritten.

Notes:

New Hampshire requires that a special form, Form 11-A, be filed along with the articles of incorporation. This form is available from their office, their website, or the forms disk. Form 11-A is used to notify the state that stock in your corporation is being issued subject to an exemption, and therefore does not need to be registered with the state. To complete the form, enter your name and address and corporate name in the spaces provided at the top of the form. Next, place a check on the line underneath statement No. 1). Enter your name and date at the bottom, then sign.

The filing fee of $85, consists of $50 to file form 11-A, and $35 to file the articles of incorporation.

Stock is usually exempt from registration if the number of shareholders purchasing the stock in the last 12 months is 10 or fewer. Regulated by the Secretary of State's office.

State of New Jersey
CERTIFICATE OF INCORPORATION

Pursuant to the provisions of Title 14A:2-7 of the New Jersey Business Corporation Act, the undersigned individual submits this Certificate of Incorporation for the purpose of forming a corporation.

Article 1. The name of the Corporation is:

Article 2. The purpose for which this corporation is organized is to engage in any activity within the purposes for which corporations may be organized under NJSA 14A 1-1 et seq.:

Article 3. The name of the corporation's registered agent is:

Article 4. The street address of the corporation's registered office is:

Article 5. The corporation is authorized to issue   shares of no par value, common stock, with identical rights and privileges, the transfer of which is restricted according to the Bylaws of the corporation.

Article 6. The number of directors constituting the initial board of directors is:

Article 7. The names and street addresses of the initial Directors are as follows:

Article 8. The corporation's period of duration is perpetual.

Article 9. The name and street address of the sole incorporator of this corporation is:

Optional Provisions:
Article 10. A director of the corporation may not be held liable to the corporation or its shareholders for monetary damages due to a breach of fiduciary duty, unless the breach is a result of self-dealing, intentional misconduct, or illegal actions.

In witness whereof, the incorporator of this corporation, with authority to do so, has signed this certificate of incorporation on the date below. The incorporator is at least eighteen years of age.

Date:

Name of incorporator:

Signature of Incorporator: _____

State Information	New Jersey Division of Revenue Division of Commercial Recording P. O. Box 308 Trenton, NJ 08625-0308	**Telephone:**	(609) 292-9292
		Web address:	www.state.nj.us/ njbgs/services.html
	Hand delivered: Third floor 225 West State Street	**Filing fee:**	$100 Add $10 for next day service. Add $50 for same day service.
		Office hours:	8:30-5 Monday-Friday

Filing Procedure

For clarification on any step, refer to Chapter 2.

Choose a name — The name must include incorporated, corporation, limited or abbreviation of these words.

Check name availability — Call the telephone number above and have them check the name for you. There is a charge for this service, $15 to check one name, $20 for two, and $25 for three names. Credit cards are accepted for payment.

File your paperwork — Complete the certificate of incorporation form. File it with the Division of Commercial Recording. Include the fee.

Organizational matters — Choose officers (at least one) and directors (at least one). When the certificate returns from the State, complete the Minutes of Organizational Meeting form (appendix). Issue stock certificates to each shareholder.

Prepare corporate records — Prepare or purchase a corporate record book and corporate seal. Place all of your documents in the record book. Use the corporate seal to emboss the stock certificates and Minutes of Organizational Meeting. Review Chapter 4 for a checklist of things to do next.

Form Instructions

1. Enter the name of the corporation.
2. This statement is required.
3. Enter the name of the corporation's registered agent.
4. Enter your name and street address. Your home address is okay to use.
5. Enter the number of shares of stock your corporation is authorized to issue.
6. Enter the number of directors that the corporation will initially have.
7. Enter the names and street addresses of the corporation's initial directors.
8. This statement means that the corporation will exist until you decide to terminate it.
9. Enter your name and address here. You are only required to have one incorporator.
10. This statement is optional. It has been added for your protection

Sign and date the Certificate with BLACK ink. Sign your name as incorporator exactly as it appears in the Certificate of Incorporation.

Notes:

Three levels of service are offered, regular, expedited, and same day. Expedited service is only available for hand delivered documents. It costs an additional $10. Same day service is only available by fax. It costs an additional $50. Documents faxed before noon will be filed that day. Documents faxed after noon will be received the next business day.

To use a fictitious name (alternate name), file an alternate name registration form with the Division of Commercial Recording after the Certificate of Incorporation is filed. There is a $50 filing fee.

Faxed filings must include a cover letter entitled "Facsimile Filing Service Request." The cover sheet must include the name of the individual submitting the request, the date of submission, credit card number and expiration date, description of the service requested i.e. "Filing of Certificate of Incorporation", the type of service requested - expedited or same day, the proposed corporate name, the total number of faxed pages including the cover letter, your return fax number. Fax the form to this number (609) 984-6851. Do not fax these instructions.

Stock is usually exempt from registration if the number of New Jersey shareholders does not exceed 35. Regulated by the Bureau of Securities, (973) 504-3600.

State of New Mexico
ARTICLES OF INCORPORATION
A Business/Stock Corporation

Pursuant to the provisions of Chapter 53 of the New Mexico Business Corporation Act, the undersigned person, hereby adopts the following Articles of Incorporation for the purpose of forming a New Mexico corporation.

1. The name of the corporation is:

2. The duration of the corporation is perpetual.

3. The corporation has been organized to transact any and all lawful business for which corporations may be incorporated in this state.

4. The corporation is authorized to issue one class of stock, that stock being   shares of no par value, common stock, with identical rights and privileges, the transfer of which is restricted according to the Bylaws of the corporation.

5. Preemptive rights are neither limited nor denied.

6. The name of the initial registered agent of the corporation is:

7. The initial Board of Directors shall consist of   members whose names and residence addresses are as follows:

8. The name and complete address of the sole incorporator is:

In witness thereof, the undersigned incorporator has executed these Articles of Incorporation on the date below. The incorporator prepared this document.

Date:

Signature of Incorporator: _____

State Information	State Corporation Commission Corporation Department P.O. Drawer 1269 Santa Fe, NM 87504-1269	**Telephone:**	(505) 827-4511 (505) 827-4504
		Web address:	http://www.sos.state.nm.us/
		Filing fee:	$100
		Office hours:	8-5 Monday-Friday (Closed from 12-1)

Filing Procedure   For clarification on any step, refer to Chapter 2.

Choose a name   The name must include incorporated, corporation, company, limited, or an abbreviation of one of these words.

Check name availability   Call the telephone number above.

File your paperwork   File duplicate originals of the Articles of Incorporation with the State Corporation Commission.. Be sure to include the filing fee.

Organizational matters   Choose officers (at least one) and directors (at least one). When the Articles return from the State, complete the Minutes of Organizational Meeting form (appendix). Issue stock certificates to each shareholder.

Prepare corporate records   Prepare or purchase a corporate record book and corporate seal. Place all of your documents in the record book. Use the corporate seal to emboss the stock certificates and Minutes of Organizational Meeting. Review Chapter 4 for a checklist of things to do after incorporating.

Form Instructions

1. Enter your corporate name.
2. This statement is required.
3. This statement is required.
4. Enter the number of shares of stock your corporation is authorized to issue. All of the shares do not need to be issued to shareholders at this time. You must have at least one share of stock.
5. This statement is required.
6. Enter the name of the corporation's initial registered agent. You can serve as your own registered agent if you have an office within the state.
7. Enter the number of members of the initial Board of Directors. Enter their names and residence addresses.
8. Enter your name and complete address here.

   Sign and date the Articles in black ink. The Articles should be typewritten.

Notes:

You are allowed to authorize up to 100,000 shares of stock for the minimum filing fee of $100. Authorize more than this and you will incur a higher filing fee.

Make check payable to the State Corporation Commission.

Stock is usually exempt from registration if the number of shareholders purchasing the stock in the last 12 months is 25 or fewer. Regulated by the Regulation and Licensing Department.

To use a fictitious name or d.b.a., file an application with the Secretary of State's office. The filing fee is $25.

State of New York
CERTIFICATE OF INCORPORATION

Pursuant to Section 402 of the New York State Business Corporation Law, the undersigned individual submits this Certificate of Incorporation for the purpose of forming a for-profit corporation.

1. The name of the Corporation is:

2. The corporation is formed to engage in any lawful act or activity allowed by New York State Business Corporation Law. The corporation is not formed to engage in any act or activity requiring the consent or approval of any State official, department, board, or other body without such consent or approval first being obtained.

3. The office of the corporation is located in New York, County of

4. The corporation is authorized to issue one class of stock, that stock being
   shares of no par value, common stock, with identical rights and privileges, the transfer of which is restricted according to the bylaws of the corporation.

5. The corporation hereby designates the Secretary of State of New York as its agent for service of process. The mailing address to which the Secretary of State may forward any process served or other documents is:

6. No Director shall be held liable to the corporation or its shareholders for monetary damages due to a breach of fiduciary duty, unless the breach is a result of self-dealing, intentional misconduct, or illegal actions.

7. The effective date of this filing is   [   ] The actual date and time of filing.
                                             [   ]   /   /   at 12 o'clock PM.

IN WITNESS WHEREOF, this certificate has been subscribed on the date below, by the undersigned who affirms that the statements made herein are true under the penalties of perjury.

Date:

Name of Incorporator:

Address of Incorporator:

Signature of Incorporator: _____

State Information	Department of State Division of Corporations 41 State Street Albany, NY 12231-0001	**Telephone:**	(518) 473-2492
		Web address:	www.dos.state.ny.us/corp/ corpwww.html
		Filing fee:	$125 plus $10 tax. Add $25 for expedited service.
		Office hours:	8-4:30 Monday-Friday

Filing Procedure

For clarification on any step, refer to Chapter 2.

Choose a name
The name must include incorporated, corporation, limited, or an abbreviation of one of these words.

Check name availability
New York does not offer name checks by telephone. You may check a name's availability in writing. There is a $5 fee for each name submitted. Most people simply file the articles and hope the name is available. If your name is not available you will be notified.

File your paperwork
Complete the certificate of incorporation form. Send or take it to the corporation division. Include a check for $135. Within ten days of this filing, you must file form MT-610.1 with the Department of Taxation and Finance. They will send you one in the mail after incorporating.

Organizational matters
Choose officers (see notes) and directors (at least one). When the certificate returns from the State, complete the Minutes of Organizational Meeting form (appendix). Issue stock certificates to each shareholder.

Prepare corporate records
Prepare or purchase a corporate record book and corporate seal. Place all of your documents in the record book. Use the corporate seal to emboss the stock certificates and Minutes of Organizational Meeting. Review Chapter 4 for a checklist of things to do after incorporating.

Form Instructions

1. Enter the name of the corporation.
2. This statement is required.
3. Enter the county in which your corporate office is located.
4. Enter the total number of authorized shares.
5. Enter your mailing address here. Your PO Box is acceptable.
6. This statement is included for your protection.
7. Choose one. If you choose the second option, also include a date no more than 60 days in the future.

Complete the bottom of the form and have the incorporator sign the certificate of incorporation in BLACK ink. The articles should be typewritten.

Notes:

The incorporation tax is five cents for each share of no par value stock that you're corporation authorizes, with a $10 minimum. You can authorize up to 200 shares of stock for $10. If you authorize more than 200 shares, the incorporation tax will increase. If you want to authorize more than 200 shares, change the par value to $1. You can authorize up to 20,000 shares of $1 par stock and incur the minimum filing fee of $10. Make checks payable to "New York Department of State."

One way to check your corporate name's availability is to call the Department of State's corporate status line at 1(900) 835-2677. This service allows you to check the status of up to 5 corporations. If you have them check the status of a corporation using your proposed name and they say that the corporation does not exist, then you know the name is available for your use. A fee of $4 will appear on your telephone bill if you use this service.

For expedited service, include an additional fee of $25. This must be paid with a second, separate check. Be sure to mark your package "Expedited Handling." This $25 fee is forfeited if your corporate name is unavailable.

The corporation president and secretary may not be the same person, unless there's only one shareholder.

To use a fictitious name, file an assumed name statement with the Department of State after the certificate of incorporation is filed. The form is available from their office and the filing fee is $25. You'll also need to file a notice with your county clerk. Most counties charge a $25 filing fee. New York City boroughs charge $100.

Stock is usually exempt from registration if the number of New York residents purchasing the stock in the last 12 months is 40 or fewer. Regulated by the Bureau of Securities, in the Attorney General's office. Telephone (212) 416-8200.

State of North Carolina
ARTICLES OF INCORPORATION

Pursuant to §55-2-02 of the General Statutes of North Carolina, the undersigned does hereby submit these Articles of Incorporation for the purpose of forming a business corporation.

1. The name of the Corporation is:

2. The corporation is authorized to issue one class of stock, that stock being   shares of no par value, common stock, with identical rights and privileges, the transfer of which is restricted according to the bylaws of the corporation.

3. The name of the corporation's initial registered agent is:

4. The street address and county of the corporation's initial registered office is:

5. The name and street address of the incorporator is:

6. A Director of the corporation shall not be held liable to the corporation or its shareholders for monetary damages due to a breach of fiduciary duty, unless the breach is a result of self-dealing, intentional misconduct, or illegal actions.

7. The effective date of this filing is   [   ] The actual date and time of filing.
                                 [   ]   /   /   at 12 o'clock PM.

In witness whereof, the undersigned incorporator has executed these Articles of Incorporation on the date below. The undersigned incorporator hereby affirms, under penalty of perjury, that the statements made in the forgoing Articles of Incorporation are true.

Date:

Name of Incorporator:

Signature of Incorporator: _____

State Information	Secretary of State Division of Corporations P.O. Box 29622 Raleigh, NC 27626-0525	Telephone:	(919) 733-4201 (888) 246-7636
		Web address:	www.secretary.state.nc.us/ corp/indxfees.asp
	Hand delivered: 300 N. Salisbury Street Raleigh, NC 27603-5905	Filing fee:	$125
		Office hours:	8-5 Monday-Friday

Filing Procedure

For clarification on any step, refer to Chapter 2.

Choose a name The name must include incorporated, corporation, company, limited, or an abbreviation of one of these words.

Check name availability Call the telephone number above and have them check the name for you, or search it on their website.

File your paperwork Complete the articles of incorporation form. Send or take it to the corporation division's office. Include a check for $125. If you request expedited service, be sure to mark your envelope "EXPEDITED SERVICE."

Organizational matters Choose officers (at least one) and directors (at least one). When the Articles return from the State, complete the Minutes of Organizational Meeting form (appendix). Issue stock certificates to each shareholder.

Prepare corporate records Prepare or purchase a corporate record book and corporate seal. Place all of your documents in the record book. Use the corporate seal to emboss the stock certificates and Minutes of Organizational Meeting. Review Chapter 4 for a checklist of things to do after incorporating.

Form Instructions

1. Enter the name of the corporation. The corporate name must include one of the following: Incorporated, Corporation, Company, Limited, or Inc., Corp., Co., or Ltd.
2. Enter the number of shares that your corporation is authorized to issue.
3. Enter your name.
4. Enter your street address.
5. Enter the name and address of the corporation's incorporator. The incorporator is the person who files the articles of incorporation.
6. This is included for your protection.
7. Check one. If you choose to specify a filing date other than the actual filing date, chose the second option and enter a date not more than 90 days in the future.

   Complete the bottom of the form and have the incorporator sign the Articles of Incorporation with BLACK ink. The article should be typewritten.

Notes:

To use a fictitious name, file an "assumed name certificate" with the Register of Deeds in your county after the articles of incorporation are filed. There is a small filing fee for the service. See your Register of Deeds for information.

Stock is usually exempt from registration if the number of North Carolina residents purchasing the stock in the last 12 months is 25 or fewer. Regulated by the Securities Division of the Secretary of State's office. (919) 733-3924.

Expedited service is an additional $100 for 24-hour turnaround, and an additional $200 for same day service.

Make your check payable to the North Carolina Secretary of State.

State of North Dakota
ARTICLES OF INCORPORATION

[} Business Corporation   [   ] Farming Corporation

I, the undersigned natural person of the age of eighteen years or more, acting as incorporator of a corporation organized under the North Dakota Business Corporation Act, adopt the following Articles of Incorporation.

1. The name of the corporation is:

2. The duration of the corporation is perpetual.

3. The corporation has been organized to transact any and all lawful business for which corporations may be incorporated in this state.

4. The corporation is authorized to issue one class of stock, that stock being   shares of no par value, common stock, with identical rights and privileges, the transfer of which is restricted according to the Bylaws of the corporation.

5. The name and address of the corporation's registered agent and office in North Dakota is:

    Social Security number or Federal ID number of Registered Agent:

    Signature of Agent _____

6. The name and complete address of the sole incorporator is:

I, the above named incorporator, have read the foregoing Articles of Incorporation, know the contents, and believe the statements made therein to be true.

Date:

Signature of Incorporator: _____

State Information	North Dakota Secretary of State	**Telephone:**	(701) 328-4284
	Corporations Division		(800) 352-0867 Ext. 4284
	Capitol Building	**Web address:**	www.state.nd.us/sec/
	600 E. Boulevard Avenue		
	Bismarck, ND 58505-0500	**Filing fee:**	$90
		Office hours:	8-5 Monday-Friday

Filing Procedure

For clarification on any step, refer to Chapter 2.

Choose a name — The name must include incorporated, corporation, company, limited, or an abbreviation of one of these words, but that word or abbreviation may not be immediately preceded by "and" or "&".

Check name availability — Call the telephone number above.

File your paperwork — File duplicate originals of the Articles of Incorporation with the Secretary of State. Be sure to include the filing fee.

Organizational matters — Choose officers (at least one) and directors (at least one). When the Articles return from the State, complete the Minutes of Organizational Meeting form (appendix). Issue stock certificates to each shareholder.

Prepare corporate records — Prepare or purchase a corporate record book and corporate seal. Place all of your documents in the record book. Use the corporate seal to emboss the stock certificates and Minutes of Organizational Meeting. Review Chapter 4 for a checklist of things to do after incorporating.

Form Instructions

At the top of the form, check whether the business is a farming corporation or a business corporation.

1. Enter your corporate name.
2. This statement is required.
3. This statement is required.
4. Enter the number of shares of stock your corporation is authorized to issue. All of the shares do not need to be issued to shareholders at this time. You must have at least one share of stock.
5. Enter your name, address, and Social Security Number in the spaces provided. Also, sign your name in the space provided.
6. Enter your name and street address.

Sign and date the Articles in black ink. The Articles should be typewritten.

Notes:

The filing fee of $90 consists of a $30 filing fee, a $10 consent of agent filing fee, and the minimum license fee of $50. The minimum license fee is based on the number of shares of stock that you authorize, multiplied by the par value. You can authorize up to 50,000 shares of $1 par or 500,000 shares of no par value stock and incur the minimum license fee. Authorize more stock than this and you will incur a higher license fee.

Stock is usually exempt from registration if the number of shareholders purchasing the stock in the last 12 months is 25 or fewer. Regulated by the State Securities Commissioner.

To use a fictitious name or d.b.a., file an application with the Secretary of State's office. The filing fee is $25.

State of Ohio
ARTICLES OF INCORPORATION

Pursuant to Section 1701 of the Ohio Revised Code, the undersigned individual submits these Articles of Incorporation for the purpose of forming a for-profit corporation.

1. The name of the Corporation is:

2. The principal office of the corporation is located in Ohio, in the city of
    and in the county of

3. The corporation is formed to engage in any lawful act or activity allowed by laws of the state of Ohio. The corporation is not formed to engage in any act or activity requiring the consent or approval of any State official, department, board, or other body without such consent or approval first being obtained.

4. The corporation is authorized to issue one class of stock, that stock being   shares of no par value, common stock, with identical rights and privileges, the transfer of which is restricted according to the bylaws of the corporation.

5. No Director shall be held liable to the corporation or its shareholders for monetary damages due to a breach of fiduciary duty, unless the breach is a result of self-dealing, intentional misconduct, or illegal actions.

IN WITNESS WHEREOF, this certificate has been subscribed by the undersigned incorporator on the date below:

Date:

Name of Incorporator:

Address of Incorporator:

Signature of Incorporator: _____

State Information	Secretary of State Division of Corporations P.O. Box 1329 Columbus, OH 43216 Hand delivered 30 East Broad Street, 14th Floor Columbus, OH 43266-0418	**Telephone:**	(614) 466-3910
		Web address:	www.state.oh.us/sos/ formcorp.html
		Filing fee:	Based on the number of autho-rized shares with an $85 mini-mum. (see notes)
		Office hours:	8-5 Monday-Friday

Filing Procedure

For clarification on any step, refer to Chapter 2.

Choose a name

The name must include incorporated, corporation, company or an abbreviation of one of these words.

Check name availability

Call the telephone number above and have them check the name for you.

File your paperwork

Complete the articles of incorporation. Also complete the "Original Appointment of Statutory Agent" form. (see notes) Send or take both forms to the Corporation Division's office. Include a check for $85.

Organizational matters

Choose officers (at least one) and directors (at least one). When the Articles return from the State, complete the Minutes of Organizational Meeting form (appendix). Issue stock certificates to each shareholder.

Prepare corporate records

Prepare or purchase a corporate record book and corporate seal. Place all of your documents in the record book. Use the corporate seal to emboss the stock certificates and Minutes of Organizational Meeting. Review Chapter 4 for a checklist of things to do after incorporating.

Form Instructions

1. Enter the name of the corporation. The corporate name must include one of the follow-ing: Incorporated, Corporation, Company or Inc., Corp., or Co.
2. Enter the city and county in which your corporate office is located.
3. This statement is required.
4. Enter the number of shares of stock that your corporation will be authorized to issue. Up to 850 shares can be authorized for the minimum fee of $85.
5. This statement is included for your protection.

   Complete the bottom of the form and have the incorporator sign the Articles of Incorpora-tion with BLACK ink. The articles should be typewritten.

Notes:

To use a fictitious name (d.b.a.), file a "Fictitious Name Report" with the Secretary of State after the articles of incorpo-ration are filed. The form is available from the Corporation Division and the filing fee is $10.

The filing fee is based on the total number of authorized shares of stock that your corporation has. Up to 850 shares of stock can be authorized for the minimum fee of $85. If you authorize more than 850 shares of stock, your filing fee will increase.

The Original Appointment of Statutory Agent form is for appointing the corporation's registered agent. This form is available on the Secretary of State's web site, and on our forms disc.

Stock offerings are usually exempt from registration if the number of Ohio residents purchasing the stock in the last 12 months is 10 or fewer. Regulated by the Secretary of State's Securities Division (614) 466-3440.

Make your check payable to the Ohio Secretary of State.

State of Oklahoma
CERTIFICATE OF INCORPORATION

For the purpose of forming an Oklahoma profit corporation pursuant to the provisions of Title 18, Section 1001, the undersigned natural person, being at least eighteen years of age, adopts the following Certificate of Incorporation.

Article 1. The name of the Corporation is:

Article 2. The name of the registered agent and the street address of the registered office in the State of Oklahoma is:

Article 3. The duration of the corporation is perpetual.

Article 4. The corporation is formed for the purpose of
and to engage in any legal act or activity permitted by The General and Business Corporation Laws of Oklahoma.

Article 5. The corporation is authorized to issue   shares of no par value, common stock, with identical rights and privileges, the transfer of which is restricted according to the bylaws of the corporation.

Article 6. The name and mailing address of the undersigned incorporator is:

In witness whereof, this Certificate of Incorporation has been signed on:

Telephone Number:

Name of Incorporator:

Signature of Incorporator: _____

State Information	Oklahoma Secretary of State	**Telephone:**	(405) 522-4560
	Room 101	**Web address:**	www.state.ok.us/~sos
	State Capitol Building	**Filing fee:**	$50
	2300 N. Lincoln Blvd.,	**Office hours:**	8-4 Monday-Friday
	Oklahoma City, OK 73105-4897		

Filing Procedure

For clarification on any step, refer to Chapter 2.

Choose a name
The name must include incorporated, corporation, limited, company, or an abbreviation of one of these words.

Check name availability
Call 1-900-555-2424 and have them check the name. There is a $5 fee for this service. (see notes)

File your paperwork
Complete the certificate of incorporation form. Send or take the certificate and one copy to the business filings division of the Secretary of State's office. Include a check for $50. This fee allows up to 1,000 shares of no par value stock.

Organizational matters
Choose officers (at least one) and directors (at least one). When the certificate of incorporation returns from the State, complete the Minutes of Organizational Meeting form (appendix). Issue stock certificates to each shareholder.

Prepare corporate records
Prepare or purchase a corporate record book and corporate seal. Place all of your documents in the record book. Use the corporate seal to emboss the stock certificates and Minutes of Organizational Meeting. Review Chapter 4 for a checklist of things to do after incorporating.

Form Instructions

1. Enter the name of the corporation.
2. Enter the name of the registered agent and the STREET address of the registered office. You can serve as your company's own registered agent. PO Boxes are not acceptable.
3. This statement is required by law.
4. Enter the corporation's primary business activity in the space provided.
5. Enter the total number of shares of stock that your corporation is authorized to issue. You do not have to issue all the shares now. Authorize enough for present and future use.
6. Enter your name and mailing address here.

   Complete the bottom of the form and have the incorporator sign the Certificate of Incorporation in ink. You are only required to have one incorporator. The certificate should be typewritten.

Notes:

To use a fictitious name, you'll need to file an application with the business filings division of the Secretary of State's office. The form is called a "tradename report" and is available from their office. The fee to file it is $25. You may also need to register the name with your local County clerk. Call their office for details.

Stock transactions are usually exempt from registration with the state if the number of Oklahoma residents purchasing the stock is 25 for fewer. Regulated by the Oklahoma State Securities Commission, (405) 280-7700

Make checks payable to the Oklahoma Secretary of State.

You can also check availability of a corporate name in writing, or by using online terminals in their office, both at no charge. You can also call the main office number to have a name searched, and bill the $5 fee to your Discover card.

The wavy character in the internet address is a "tilde." It is located above the tab key.

State of Oregon
ARTICLES OF INCORPORATION

Pursuant to the Oregon Business Corporation Act as amended, the undersigned individual submits these Articles of Incorporation for the purpose of forming a domestic, for-profit, business corporation.

1. The name of the Corporation is:

2. The name of the corporation's initial registered agent is:

3. Being identical to the registered agent's business office, the street address of the corporation's initial registered office is:

4. The mailing address of the corporation's registered agent is:

5. The address for mailing notices to the corporation is:

6. The corporation is authorized to issue one class of stock, that stock being   shares of no par value, common stock, with identical rights and privileges, the transfer of which is restricted according to the bylaws of the corporation.

7. A Director of the corporation shall not be held liable to the corporation or its shareholders for monetary damages due to a breach of fiduciary duty, unless the breach is a result of self-dealing, intentional misconduct, or illegal actions.

In witness whereof, the undersigned incorporator has executed these Articles of Incorporation on the date below. The undersigned incorporator hereby affirms, under penalty of perjury, that the statements made in the forgoing Articles of Incorporation are true.

Date:

Telephone Number:

Name of Incorporator:

Signature of Incorporator: _____

State Information	Secretary of State Corporation Division 255 Capital Street NE Suite 151 Salem, OR 97310-1327	**Telephone:**	(503) 986-2200
		Web address:	www.sos.state.or.us/ corporation/corphp.htm
		Filing fee:	$50
		Office hours:	8-5 Monday-Friday

Filing Procedure

For clarification on any step, refer to Chapter 2.

Choose a name The name must include incorporated, corporation, limited, company, or an abbreviation of one of these words.

Check name availability Call the telephone number above.

File your paperwork File the articles of incorporation with the judge of probate in your county. Be sure to include the filing fee.

Organizational matters Choose officers (at least one) and directors (at least one). When the Articles return from the State, complete the Minutes of Organizational Meeting form (appendix). Issue stock certificates to each shareholder.

Prepare corporate records Prepare or purchase a corporate record book and corporate seal. Place all of your documents in the record book. Use the corporate seal to emboss the stock certificates and Minutes of Organizational Meeting. Review Chapter 4 for a checklist of things to do after incorporating.

Form Instructions

1. Enter the name of the corporation. The corporate name must include one of the following: Incorporated, Corporation, Company, Limited, Inc., Corp., Ltd., or Co.

2. Enter the name of the corporation's initial registered agent. You can serve as your company's own registered agent.

3. Enter the STREET address of the corporation's registered office. Your home address is acceptable.

4. Enter the mailing address for the registered agent. A post office box is okay. Your home address is acceptable.

5. Enter the address for mailing notices to the corporation. This includes correspondence other than service of process to the registered agent. A post office box is okay. Your home address is acceptable.

6. Enter the total number of shares of stock that your corporation is authorized to issue. You do not have to issue all the shares now. Authorize enough for present and future use.

7. This statement is included for your protection.

   Complete the bottom of the form and have the incorporator sign the Articles of Incorporation with ink. You are only required to have one incorporator. The articles should be type-written.

Notes:

To use a fictitious name, you'll need to file an application with the Corporation Division. The form is available from their office and the filing fee is $10 plus $2 for each county registered. (The name must be registered in each county where you have an office. They do this for you.)

You can file your articles by fax. Fax the articles of incorporation and a cover letter to this fax number (503) 378-4381. The cover letter must include your credit card number, the expiration date, and your signature.

Stock is usually exempt from registration if the number of Oregon residents purchasing the stock in the last 12 months is 10 or fewer. Regulated by the Oregon Department of Consumer & Business Services (503) 378-4387.

Make your check payable to the Oregon Secretary of State.

Microfilm Number _____   Filed with the Dept. of State on _____

Entity Number _____   _____
                                            Secretary of the Commonwealth

State of Pennsylvania
ARTICLES OF INCORPORATION - FOR PROFIT

In compliance with the requirements of the applicable provisions of 15 Pa.C.S. §1306 relating to for-profit domestic business stock corporations, the undersigned, desiring to form such a corporation hereby states that:

1. The name of the Corporation is:

2. The street address and county of the corporation's initial registered office in the Commonwealth of Pennsylvania and the name of its initial registered agent at that office are:

3. The corporation is incorporated under the provisions of the Business Corporation Law of 1988.

4. The corporation is authorized to issue   shares of no par value, common stock, with identical rights and privileges, the transfer of which is restricted according to the Bylaws of the corporation.

5. The name and street address of the corporation's sole incorporator is:

Optional Items:
6. The effective date of this filing is   [   ] The actual date and time of filing.
                                            [   ]   /   /   at 12 o'clock p.m.

7. A Director of the corporation may not be held liable to the corporation or its shareholders for monetary damages due to a breach of fiduciary duty, unless the breach is a result of self-dealing, intentional misconduct, or illegal actions.

In testimony whereof, the undersigned incorporator has executed these Articles of Incorporation on the date below. The undersigned incorporator hereby affirms, under penalty of perjury, that the statements made in the forgoing Articles of Incorporation are true.

Date of signature:

Name of Incorporator:

Signature of Incorporator: _____

State Information	Pennsylvania Department of State Corporation Bureau P.O. Box 8722 Harrisburg, PA 17105B8722 308 North Office Building Harrisburg, PA 17120	**Telephone:** **Web address:** **Filing fee:** **Office Hours:**	(717) 787-1057 www.dos.state.pa.us/corp/corp.htm $100 8-5 Monday-Friday

Filing Procedure

For clarification on any step, refer to Chapter 2.

Choose a name
The name must include incorporated, corporation, company, limited, or an abbreviation of one of these words.

Check name availability
Call the telephone number above and have them check the name.

File your paperwork
Complete the articles of incorporation and docketing statement (docketing statement available from their office or the forms disk). Send the original articles and three copies of the docketing statement to the Dept. of State. Include the $100 filing fee. Place an ad in your local newspaper notifying the public of your incorporation. (see notes)

Organizational matters
Choose officers (at least one) and directors (at least one). When the Articles return from the State, complete the Minutes of Organizational Meeting form (appendix). Issue stock certificates to each shareholder.

Prepare corporate records
Prepare or purchase a corporate record book and corporate seal. Place all of your documents in the record book. Use the corporate seal to emboss the stock certificates and Minutes of Organizational Meeting. Review Chapter 4 for a checklist of things to do after incorporating.

Form Instructions

1. Enter the name of the corporation. The corporate name must include one of the following: Incorporated, Corporation, Company or Inc., Corp., or Co.
2. Enter your name and street address.
3. This statement is required.
4. Enter the number of shares of stock that the corporation is authorized to issue.
5. Enter the name and STREET address of the incorporator. The incorporator is the person who files the Articles of Incorporation.
6. Choose one. If you choose the second option, also include a date in the future, 1/1/01 for example.
7. This is included for your protection.

   Sign and date the Articles with BLACK ink. Sign your name exactly as it appears in the Articles of Incorporation.

Notes:

To use a fictitious name, you'll need to file an "assumed name statement" with the Dept. of State after the articles of incorporation are filed. Ask for form No. DSCB:54-311. The filing fee for this form is $52.

After you receive the certified copy of your articles from the state, you're required to place a notice of your incorporation in two newspapers. The notice must state that your corporation has been formed under A1988 BCL." See your local newspaper for details.

To receive the certified copy of your articles faster, included an extra copy of the articles, and a self-addressed stamped envelope.

Stock is usually exempt from registration if the number of Pennsylvania residents purchasing the stock in the last 12 months is 25 or fewer. Regulated by the Pennsylvania Securities Commission (717) 787-8061.

State of Rhode Island and Providence Plantations
ARTICLES OF INCORPORATION
Business Corporation

ID Number:_____

The undersigned acting as incorporator of a corporation under Chapter 7-1.1 of the General Laws, 1956, as amended, adopt the following Articles of Incorporation for such corporation:

1. The name of the corporation is:

2. The duration of the corporation is perpetual.

3. The specific purpose or purposes for which the corporation is organized are:

4. The corporation is authorized to issue one class of stock, that stock being   shares of no par value, common stock, with identical rights and privileges, the transfer of which is restricted according to the Bylaws of the corporation.

5. Preemptive rights are neither limited nor denied.

6. The address of the initial registered office of the corporation is

    The name of its initial registered agent at such address is

7. The initial Board of Directors shall consist of   members whose names and residence addresses are:

8. The name and complete address of the sole incorporator is:

9. Date when corporate existence is to begin:

Date:

Signature of Incorporator: _____

State of Rhode Island
County of _____

In_____, on this_____day of_____, 20___, personally appeared before
me_____, known to me and known by me to be the person
executing the foregoing instrument, and does acknowledge said instrument to be a free act and deed.

My Commission Expires:

Notary Public:_____

State Information	Rhode Island Secretary of State	**Telephone:**	(401) 222-3040
	Corporations Division	**Web address:**	www.state.ri.us/corporations
	First floor	**Filing fee:**	$150
	100 North Main Street		
	Providence, RI 02903-1335		

Filing Procedure	For clarification on any step, refer to Chapter 2.	
	Choose a name	The name must include incorporated, corporation, company, limited, or an abbreviation of one of these words.
	Check name availability	Call the telephone number above.
	File your paperwork	Complete the articles of incorporation form. Send or take two originals, with original signatures, to the Secretary of State's office. Be sure to include the filing fee.
	Organizational matters	Choose officers (at least one) and directors (see notes). When the Articles return from the State, complete the Minutes of Organizational Meeting form (appendix). Issue stock certificates to each shareholder.
	Prepare corporate records	Prepare or purchase a corporate record book and corporate seal. Place all of your documents in the record book. Use the corporate seal to emboss the stock certificates and Minutes of Organizational Meeting. Review Chapter 4 for a checklist of things to do after incorporating.

Form Instructions

1. Enter your corporate name.
2. This statement is required.
3. Enter the corporation's primary business activity or activities.
4. Enter the number of shares of stock your corporation is authorized to issue. All of the shares do not need to be issued to shareholders at this time. You must have at least one share of stock.
5. This statement is required.
6. Enter the street address of the initial registered office of the corporation. Enter the city and zip code. Enter the name of the initial registered agent at this address. You can serve as your own registered agent if you have an office within the state.
7. Enter the number of members of the initial Board of Directors. Enter their names and residence addresses.
8. Enter your name and complete address.
9. Enter the date when you want your corporate existence to begin, not more than 30 days after filing the articles.

   Sign and date the Articles in black ink. The Articles should be typewritten. Complete the last paragraph and have the Articles signed by a Notary.

Notes:

If you want to authorize more than 8,000 shares of stock, the Corporation's Division can help you calculate the correct filing fee.

The number of directors must equal the number of shareholders, with a minimum of three, unless there are fewer than three shareholders, then the number of directors must be equal to the number of shareholders.

Stock is usually exempt from registration if the number of shareholders purchasing the stock in the last 12 months is 25 or fewer. Regulated by the Department of Business Registration.

To use a fictitious name, file an application with the Secretary of State's office. The filing fee is $50.

State of South Carolina
ARTICLES OF INCORPORATION
Business/Stock Corporation

Pursuant to the provisions of Title 33 of the Code of Laws of South Carolina, the undersigned person, hereby adopts the following Articles of Incorporation for the purpose of forming a South Carolina corporation.

1. The name of the proposed Corporation is:

2. The street address of the initial registered office of the Corporation is:

    Located in the county of:

    The initial registered agent at this address is:

    I hereby consent to the appointment as registered agent of the Corporation:

    Agent's signature: _____

3. The corporation is authorized to issue one class of stock, that stock being _____ shares of no par value, common stock, with identical rights and privileges, the transfer of which is restricted according to the Bylaws of the corporation.

4. The existence of the Corporation shall begin   [   ] as of the filing date with the Secretary of State
                                                   [   ] as of this date   /   /

5. The name and complete address of the only incorporator is:

In witness thereof, the undersigned incorporator has executed these Articles of Incorporation on the date below.

Date:

Signature of Incorporator: _____

I, _____ an attorney licensed to practice in the State of South Carolina, certify that the Corporation, to whose articles of incorporation this certificate is attached, has complied with the requirements of Chapter 2, Title 33 of the South Carolina Code of Laws, as amended, relating to articles of incorporation.

            Date:
Name of attorney:
        Address:
      Telephone:

        Signature: _____

State Information	South Carolina Secretary of State Division of Business Filings P.O. Box 11350 Columbia, SC 29211	**Telephone:**	(803) 734-2158
		Web address:	www.scsos.com/ corporations.htm
		Filing fee:	$135
	Hand delivered: Wade Hampton Building 1205 Pendleton Street Columbia, SC 29201	**Office hours:**	8:30-5 Monday-Friday

Filing Procedure

For clarification on any step, refer to Chapter 2.

Choose a name — The name must include incorporated, corporation, limited, company, or an abbreviation of one of these words.

Check name availability — Call the telephone number above and have them check the name for you. Also, request a forms packet that includes the "Initial Annual Report" form, also known as form CL-1.

File your paperwork — Complete the articles of incorporation form and the form CL-1. Have the articles reviewed and signed by a South Carolina attorney (see notes) Send or take the original articles and one copy along with the form CL-1 to the Secretary of State. Include a check for the filing fee.

Organizational matters — Choose officers (at least one) and directors (at least one). When the Articles return from the State, complete the Minutes of Organizational Meeting form (appendix). Issue stock certificates to each shareholder.

Prepare corporate records — Prepare or purchase a corporate record book and corporate seal. Place all of your documents in the record book. Use the corporate seal to emboss the stock certificates and Minutes of Organizational Meeting. Review Chapter 4 for a checklist of things to do after incorporating.

Form Instructions

1. Enter the corporate name.
2. Enter your name, address, and county. Also, sign your name in the space provided.
3. Enter the number of shares of stock your corporation is authorized to issue. All of the shares do not need to be issued to shareholders at this time. You must have at least one share of stock.
4. Choose an option. If you choose a future effective date, it should not be more than 30 days from the actual filing date.
5. Enter your name and street address.

   Sign and date the articles in black ink. Also, have a South Carolina attorney review and sign the articles. The Articles should be typewritten.

Notes:

The Articles must be reviewed and signed by a South Carolina attorney. You can save a lot of money by checking the name and doing the paperwork yourself and simply having an attorney sign off on your work. Call the bar association in your town for a listing of attorneys specializing in corporations. Tell the attorney that you've done the work yourself and simply need an attorney to sign off on the work. You should be able to have this done for $100 or less.

The Initial Annual Report, form CL-1, is only available from the Secretary of State's office. It is a basic form that includes essentially the same information as your articles of incorporation. This form does not need to be signed by an attorney.

Stock is usually exempt from registration if the number of shareholders purchasing the stock in the last 12 months is 25 or fewer. Regulated by the Secretary of State.

State of South Dakota
ARTICLES OF INCORPORATION

Pursuant to the provisions of Chapter 47 of SDCL, the undersigned person, hereby adopts the following Articles of Incorporation for the purpose of forming a South Dakota Business Corporation.

1. The name of the corporation is:

2. The duration of the corporation is perpetual.

3. The corporation has been organized to transact any and all lawful business for which corporations may be incorporated in this state.

4. The corporation is authorized to issue one class of stock, that stock being   shares of   par value, common stock, with identical rights and privileges, the transfer of which is restricted according to the Bylaws of the corporation.

5. The corporation will not commence business until consideration of the value of at least one thousand dollars ($1,000) has been received for the issuance of shares.

6. The name and address of the corporation's registered agent and office in South Dakota is:

Consent of Appointment by the Registered Agent

I,_____, hereby give my consent to serve as the registered agent for the above named corporation.
Date:
Signature of Registered Agent: _____

7. The initial Board of Directors shall consist of   members whose names and residence addresses are:

8. The name and complete address of the sole incorporator is:

In witness thereof, the undersigned incorporator has executed these Articles of Incorporation on the date below. The incorporator prepared this document.

Date: Signature of Incorporator: _____

State of South Dakota
County of:

On_____, the above person appeared before me, a notary public and is personally known or proved to me to be the person whose name is subscribed to the above instrument who acknowledged that he/she executed the instrument.

Name of Notary

Signature _____   (Notary Stamp or Seal)

State Information	South Dakota Secretary of State	**Telephone:**	(605) 773-4845
	State Capitol	**Web address:**	www.state.sd.us/sos/
	500 E. Capitol Ave.		Corpadmn.htm
	Pierre, SD 57501		
		Filing fee	$90

Filing Procedure   For clarification on any step, refer to Chapter 2.

Choose a name   The name must include incorporated, corporation, limited, company, or an abbreviation of one of these words.

Check name availability   Call the telephone number above and have them check the name for you.

File your paperwork   Complete the articles of incorporation form. Sign it in the presence of a Notary Public. Send or take the articles and one copy to the Secretary of State's office. Be sure to include the filing fee.

Organizational matters   Choose officers (at least one) and directors (at least one). When the Articles return from the State, complete the Minutes of Organizational Meeting form (appendix). Issue stock certificates to each shareholder.

Prepare corporate records   Prepare or purchase a corporate record book and corporate seal. Place all of your documents in the record book. Use the corporate seal to emboss the stock certificates and Minutes of Organizational Meeting. Review Chapter 4 for a checklist of things to do after incorporating.

Form Instructions

1. Enter your corporate name.
2. This statement is required.
3. This statement is required.
4. Enter the number of shares of stock your corporation is authorized to issue and the stock's par value.
5. This statement is required. The $1,000 in consideration can be cash, property, or labor or services given to the corporation in exchange for its stock.
6. Enter the name and address of the corporation's registered agent and office in South Dakota. Also, sign your name in the space provided, and enter the date.
7. Enter the number of members of the initial Board of Directors. Enter their names and residence addresses.
8. Enter your name and complete address here.

   Sign and date the Articles in black ink in the presence of a Notary. The Articles should be typewritten.

Notes:

The filing fee is based on the number of authorized shares multiplied by the par value. For the minimum filing fee of $90, you can have up to $25,000 of stock. That's 25,000 shares of $1 par stock, or 250 shares of no par value stock. Authorize more shares than this, and you will incur a higher filing fee. Make check payable to the Secretary of State.

Any corporation engaged in farming must comply with the Family Farm Act of 1974 by filing an additional qualification form available upon request from the Secretary of State's office.

Stock is usually exempt from registration if the number of shareholders purchasing the stock in the last 12 months as 25 or fewer.

State of Tennessee
CHARTER

Pursuant to the Tennessee Business Corporation Act as amended, the undersigned individual submits this Charter for the purpose of forming a domestic, for-profit corporation.

1. The name of the Corporation is:

2. The street address and county of the corporation's initial registered office, and the name of its initial registered agent at that office are:

3. The street address of the corporation's principal office is:

4. The corporation is authorized to issue   shares of no par value, common stock, with identical rights and privileges, the transfer of which is restricted according to the Bylaws of the corporation.

5. The incorporator prepared this instrument. The name and street address of the corporation's sole incorporator is:

6. A Director of the corporation may not be held liable to the corporation or its shareholders for monetary damages due to a breach of fiduciary duty, unless the breach is a result of self-dealing, intentional misconduct, or illegal actions.

7. The corporation is for-profit.

In witness whereof, the undersigned, being all the incorporators of the corporation named above, execute these Articles of Incorporation and verify, subject to penalties of perjury, that the statements contained herein are true.

Date:

Incorporator's Name:

Incorporator's Signature _____

State Information	Tennessee Secretary of State	**Telephone:**	(615) 741-0537
	Business Services	**Web address:**	www.state.tn.us/sos/
	18th Floor	**Filing fee:**	$100
	James K. Polk Building	**Office Hours**	8-4:30 Monday-Friday (CST)
	Nashville, TN 37243-0306		

Filing Procedure

For clarification on any step, refer to Chapter 2.

Choose a name The name must include incorporated, corporation, limited, company, or an abbreviation of one of these words.

Check name availability Call the telephone number above and have them check the name for you.

File your paperwork Complete the articles of incorporation form. Send or take it and one copy to the Secretary Of State's office. Include a check for $100. After it comes back from the state, file a copy with the register of deeds in your county. The county will charge a small fee.

Organizational matters Choose officers (at least one) and directors (at least one). When the Articles return from the State, complete the Minutes of Organizational Meeting form (appendix). Issue stock certificates to each shareholder.

Prepare corporate records Prepare or purchase a corporate record book and corporate seal. Place all of your documents in the record book. Use the corporate seal to emboss the stock certificates and Minutes of Organizational Meeting. Review Chapter 4 for a checklist of things to do after incorporating.

Form Instructions

1. Enter the name of the corporation.
2. Enter the name and STREET address of the corporation's initial registered agent. You can serve as your corporation's own registered agent. Your home address is acceptable.
3. Enter your name and street address or business street address.
4. Enter the number of shares of stock that your corporation will be authorized to issue. You can authorize more shares than you plan to issue. There is no limit on the number of shares that you may have.
5. Enter your name and street address here. You're only required to have one incorporator.
6. This statement is included for your protection.
7. This statement is required.

   Complete the bottom of the form and have the incorporator sign the Articles of Incorporation with ink. The articles should be typewritten.

Notes:

To use a fictitious name, file an "Assumed Name Statement" with the Secretary of State after the articles of incorporation are filed. The form is available from the Secretary Of State. There is a $20 fee for this filing. By the way, you don't have to use "Inc." with an assumed name.

Stock is usually exempt from registration if the number of Tennessee residents purchasing the stock in the last 12 months is 15 or fewer. Regulated by the Securities Division of the Commissioner of Commerce and Insurance. (615) 741-5911.

Documents sent by overnight courier receive priority handling at no additional charge.

The fee listed above, is actually a $50 filing fee and a $50 filing tax, totaling $100. Make your check payable to the Tennessee Secretary of State.

State of Texas
ARTICLES OF INCORPORATION

Pursuant to Article 3.02 of the Texas Business Corporation Act, the undersigned incorporator submits these Articles of Incorporation for the purpose of forming a for-profit corporation.

1. The name of the Corporation is:

2. The corporation's period of duration is perpetual.

3. The purpose or purposes for which the corporation is organized is to engage in any lawful act or activity allowed by The Texas Business Corporation Act.

4. The corporation is authorized to issue one class of stock, that stock being
   shares of no par value, common stock, with identical rights and privileges, the transfer of which is restricted according to the bylaws of the corporation.

5. The corporation will not commence business until it has received for the issuance of its shares consideration of the value of at least one thousand dollars ($1,000).

6. The name of the corporation's registered agent, and the street address of the corporation's registered office is:

7. The number of directors constituting the initial board of directors is:
   The names and street addresses of the initial Directors are:

8. The name and street address of the sole incorporator of this corporation is:

9. No Director shall be held liable to the corporation or its shareholders for monetary damages due to a breach of fiduciary duty, unless the breach is a result of self-dealing, intentional misconduct, or illegal actions.

In witness whereof, the undersigned incorporator has executed these Articles of Incorporation on the date below. The undersigned incorporator hereby declares, under penalty of perjury, that the statements made in the forgoing Articles of Incorporation are true, and that the incorporator is at least eighteen years of age.

Date:

Signature of Incorporator: _____

State Information	Secretary of State Business Services/Corporations P.O. Box 13697 Austin, Texas 78711-3697	**Telephone:**	(512) 463-5555
		Web address:	www.sos.state.tx.us/function/ forms/index.html
	Hand delivered: 1019 Brazos Austin, Texas 78701	**Filing fee:**	$300 Expedited service add $10.
		Office Hours	8-5 Monday-Friday

Filing Procedure

For clarification on any step, refer to Chapter 2.

Choose a name
The name must include incorporated, corporation, company, or an abbreviation of one of these words.

Check name availability
Call the telephone number above and have them check the name for you.

File your paperwork
Complete the articles of incorporation form. File it and two copies with the Secretary of State. Include the filing fee.

Organizational matters
Choose officers (at least one) and directors (at least one). When the Articles return from the State, complete the Minutes of Organizational Meeting form (appendix). Issue stock certificates to each shareholder.

Prepare corporate records
Prepare or purchase a corporate record book and corporate seal. Place all of your documents in the record book. Use the corporate seal to emboss the stock certificates and Minutes of Organizational Meeting. Review Chapter 4 for a checklist of things to do after incorporating.

Form Instructions

1. Enter the name of the corporation.
2. This statement is required
3. This statement is required.
4. Enter the number of shares of stock that the corporation is authorized to issue.
5. Texas requires this statement.
6. Enter the name and STREET address of the corporation's registered agent.
7. Enter the number of directors comprising the initial board of directors. The corporation is only required to have one director. Also, enter the names and STREET addresses of the director(s).
8. Enter the name and STREET address of the corporation's incorporator. The incorporator is simply the person who files the articles of incorporation. Only one incorporator is required. The incorporator must be of legal age. There are no citizenship or shareholder requirements for the incorporator.
9. This is an optional item added for your protection.

   Sign and date the Articles with BLACK ink. Sign your name as incorporator exactly as it appears in the Articles of Incorporation. The articles should be typewritten.

Notes:

To use a fictitious name, you'll need to file an Assumed Name Statement with the Secretary of State and the county clerk for the county where the registered office is located. The Secretary of State has the form you'll need.

Credit cards are excepted, but are charged an additional fee to cover the State's credit card processing fees.

Stock is usually exempt from registration if the number of Texas shareholders does not exceed 35. Regulated by the State Securities Board (512) 305-8300.

With expedited service, your documents will be filed by the end of the next business day. It will, however, take them from 5-7 days to return the paperwork to you.

Texas is unusual in that it requires a corporation to have at least $1,000 of consideration received for the corporate stock before operations may begin. This means that the initial shareholders must give at least $1,000 in money, work done, or property for their stock.

State of Utah
ARTICLES OF INCORPORATION

I, the undersigned person, acting as incorporator under the Utah Revised Business Corporation Act, adopt the following Articles of Incorporation for such Corporation:

1. The name of the corporation is:

2. The corporation has been organized to transact any and all lawful business for which corporations may be incorporated in this state.

3. The corporation is authorized to issue one class of stock, that stock being _____ shares of no par value, common stock, with identical rights and privileges, the transfer of which is restricted according to the Bylaws of the corporation.

4. The name and street address of the corporation's registered agent and office in Utah is:

    I hereby acknowledge and accept appointment as corporation registered agent:

    Signature of Agent _____

5. The name and complete address of the only incorporator is:

In witness whereof, I _____, the only incorporator, have executed these Articles of Incorporation in duplicate this_____day of _____, 20_____, and say that I am the only incorporator of the corporation and that I have read the above and foregoing Articles of Incorporation; know the contents thereof and that the same is true to the best of my knowledge and belief, excepting as to matters herein alleged upon information and belief and as to those matters I believe to be true.

Signature of Incorporator: _____

State Information	Utah Department of Commerce	**Telephone:**	(801) 530-4849
	Division of Corporations and Commercial Code	**Web address:**	www.commerce.state.ut.us/
	160 East 300 South	**Filing fee:**	$50
	Box 146705	**Office hours:**	8-5 Monday-Friday
	Salt Lake City, UT 84114-6705		

Filing Procedure For clarification on any step, refer to Chapter 2.

Choose a name	The name must include incorporated, corporation, company, or an abbreviation of one of these words.
Check name availability	Call the telephone number above and have them search the name for you, or search the name on their website.
File your paperwork	File the Articles of Incorporation and one copy with the Department of Commerce. Be sure to include the filing fee.
Organizational matters	Choose officers and directors (see notes) When the Articles return from the State, complete the Minutes of Organizational Meeting form (appendix). Issue stock certificates to each shareholder.
Prepare corporate records	Prepare or purchase a corporate record book and corporate seal. Place all of your documents in the record book. Use the corporate seal to emboss the stock certificates and Minutes of Organizational Meeting. Review Chapter 4 for a checklist of things to do after incorporating.

Form Instructions

1. Enter your corporate name.
2. This statement is required.
3. Enter the number of shares of stock your corporation is authorized to issue. All of the shares do not need to be issued to shareholders at this time. You must have at least one share of stock.
4. Enter your name and street address. Also, sign your name in the space provided.
5. Enter your name and complete address here.

   At the bottom, enter your name and date in the spaces provided, and then sign the articles with black ink. The Articles should be typewritten.

Notes:

Make checks payable to the State of Utah.

The same person may hold more than one office, except for the offices of president and secretary.

The number of directors must be equal to the number of shareholders with a minimum of three, unless there are fewer than three shareholders, then the number of directors must be equal to the number of shareholders. For example, if the corporation has one shareholder, you only need one director. If the Corporation has four shareholders, you only need three directors.

Stock is usually exempt from registration with the state if the number of shareholders purchasing the stock in the last 12 months is 15 or fewer. Regulated by the State Division of Securities.

To use a fictitious name, file an application with the Division of Corporations.

State of Vermont
ARTICLES OF INCORPORATION
General Corporation (T.11, Ch.3)

I, the undersigned person, acting as incorporator under Title 11A, 2.02 of the Vermont Statutes, adopt the following Articles of Incorporation for the purpose of forming a for-profit corporation.

1. The name of the corporation is:

2. The name and address of the corporation's registered agent and office in Vermont is:

3. The fiscal year ends the month of:

4. The corporation is authorized to issue one class of stock, that stock being _____ shares of no par value, common stock, with identical rights and privileges, the transfer of which is restricted according to the Bylaws of the corporation.

5. The corporation has been organized to transact any and all lawful business for which corporations may be incorporated in this state. The specific purpose of this corporation is:

6. The name and complete address of the sole incorporator is:

In witness thereof, the undersigned incorporator has executed these Articles of Incorporation on the date below. The incorporator prepared this document.

Date:

Signature of Incorporator:_____

State Information	Vermont Secretary of State	**Telephone:**	(802) 828-2386
	Heritage I Building	**Web address:**	www.sec.state.vt.us
	81 River Street	**Filing fee:**	$75
	Drawer 09		
	Montpelier, VT 05609-1104	**Office hours:**	7:45-4:30 Monday - Friday

---

Filing Procedure

For clarification on any step, refer to Chapter 2.

Choose a name — The name must include incorporated, corporation, company, limited or an abbreviation of one of these words.

Check name availability — Call the telephone number above and have them check the name for you, or search the name on their website.

File your paperwork — File the Articles of Incorporation in duplicate with the Secretary of State. Be sure to include the filing fee.

Organizational matters — Choose officers and directors (see notes). When the Articles return from the State, complete the Minutes of Organizational Meeting form (appendix). Issue stock certificates to each shareholder.

Prepare corporate records — Prepare or purchase a corporate record book and corporate seal. Place all of your documents in the record book. Use the corporate seal to emboss the stock certificates and Minutes of Organizational Meeting. Review Chapter 4 for a checklist of things to do after incorporating.

Form Instructions

1. Enter your corporate name.
2. Enter the name and address of the corporation's registered agent and office in Vermont. You can serve as your own registered agent if you have an office within the state.
3. Enter the month in which the corporation's fiscal year ends.
4. Enter the number of shares of stock your corporation is authorized to issue. All of the shares do not need to be issued to shareholders at this time. You must have at least one share of stock.
5. Enter the corporation's primary business activity.
6. Enter your name and complete address here.

   Sign and date the Articles in black ink. The Articles should be typewritten.

Notes:

The same person may hold more than one office, except for the offices of president and secretary.

The number of directors must equal the number of shareholders, with a minimum of three, unless there are fewer than three shareholders, then the number of directors must equal the number of shareholders. If the corporation has one shareholder, you only need one director. If the corporation has two shareholders, you only need two directors. If the corporation has three or more shareholders, you need three or more directors.

Stock is usually exempt from registration if the number of shareholders purchasing the stock in the last 12 months is 10 or fewer. Regulated by the Commissioner of Banking, Insurance and Securities.

To use a fictitious name, file an application with the Commissioner of Taxes and your local town clerk.

Commonwealth of Virginia
ARTICLES OF INCORPORATION

Pursuant to Chapter 9 of Title 13.1 of the Code of Virginia, the undersigned individual submits these Articles of Incorporation for the purpose of forming a for-profit, stock corporation.

1. The name of the Corporation is:

2. The corporation is authorized to issue   shares of no par value, common stock, with identical rights and privileges, the transfer of which is restricted according to the Bylaws of the corporation.

3. The corporation's initial registered agent is an individual, a resident of the State of Virginia and an initial director of the corporation. The name of the corporation's initial registered agent, whose business office is identical to the initial registered office below, is:

   The corporation's initial registered office address is:

   The corporation's initial registered office address is located in

   the County of
   and the City of

4. The name(s) and address(es) of the initial Directors, consisting of   individual(s) is (are):

5. A director of the corporation shall not be held liable to the corporation or its shareholders for monetary damages due to a breach of fiduciary duty, unless the breach is a result of self-dealing, intentional misconduct, or illegal actions.

In witness whereof, the undersigned incorporator has executed these Articles of Incorporation on the date below. The undersigned incorporator hereby affirms, that the statements made in the forgoing Articles of Incorporation are true.

Date:

Name of Incorporator:

Address of Incorporator:

Signature of Incorporator: _____

State Information	Virginia State Corporation Commission Corporations Division P.O. Box 1197 Richmond, Virginia 23218-1197 Hand delivered: 1300 East Main Street Richmond, VA 23219	**Telephone:** **Web address:** **Filing fee:** **Office Hours:**	(804) 371-9733 http://dit1.state.va.us/scc/ division/clk/index.htm $75 (see notes) Expedited service add $10. 8-5 Monday-Friday

Filing Procedure

For clarification on any step, refer to Chapter 2.

Choose a name
The name must include incorporated, corporation, company, limited, or an abbreviation of one of these words.

Check name availability
Call the telephone number above and have them check the name for you.

File your paperwork
Complete the articles of incorporation form. File it with the Secretary of State. Include a check for the filing fee.

Organizational matters
Choose officers (at least one) and directors (at least one). When the Articles return from the State, complete the Minutes of Organizational Meeting form (appendix). Issue stock certificates to each shareholder.

Prepare corporate records
Prepare or purchase a corporate record book and corporate seal. Place all of your documents in the record book. Use the corporate seal to emboss the stock certificates and Minutes of Organizational Meeting. Review Chapter 4 for a checklist of things to do after incorporating.

Form Instructions

1. Enter the name of the corporation. The corporate name must include one of the following: Incorporated, Corporation, Company or Inc., Corp., or Co.

2. Enter the number of shares of stock the corporation is authorized to issue.

3. Enter your name and street address. Also include the name of your city and county.

4. Enter the number of directors comprising the initial board of directors. The corporation is only required to have one director. Also, enter the names and STREET addresses of the director(s).

5. This is an optional item added for your protection.

Sign and date the Articles with BLACK ink. Sign your name as incorporator exactly as it appears in the Articles of Incorporation.

Notes:

The charter fee is $50 for each 25,000 shares of stock. So, if you authorize more than 25,000 shares of stock, your fee will increase. A $25 filing fee plus the $50 charter fee makes the total fee $75. Make your check payable to the Virginia Corporation Commission.

To use a fictitious name, you'll need to file a Fictitious Name Certificate with the State Corporation Commission as well as the Clerk of the Circuit Court in each county or city that you conduct business. The county will charge a $10 fee and the State Corporation Commission will charge a $10 fee to file this document.

Stock is usually exempt from registration if the number of Virginia shareholders purchasing the stock in the last 12 months is 35 or fewer. Regulated by the Corporation Commission's Securities Division (804) 371-9276.

State of Washington
ARTICLES OF INCORPORATION

Pursuant to Chapter 23B.02 RCW, the undersigned individual submits these Articles of Incorporation for the purpose of forming a domestic, for-profit corporation.

The person to contact regarding this filing is:
Daytime telephone number: (   )

1. The name of the Corporation is:

2. The corporation is authorized to issue   shares of no par value, common stock, with identical rights and privileges, the transfer of which is restricted according to the Bylaws of the corporation.

3. The effective date of this filing is   [   ] The actual date and time of filing.
                                             [   ]   /   /   at 12 o'clock PM.

4. The name and street address of the corporation's registered agent, located in the state of Washington is:

   Registered agent's consent:

   I consent to serve as registered agent in the state of Washington for the above name corporation. I understand it will be my responsibility to accept service of process on behalf of the corporation; to forward mail to the corporation; and to immediately notify the office of the Secretary of State if I resign or change the registered office address.

   Date
   Printed name: Signature of agent _____

5.   The name and address of the corporation's only incorporator is:

6.   A Director of the corporation may not be held liable to the corporation or its shareholders for monetary damages due to a breach of fiduciary duty, unless the breach is a result of self-dealing, intentional misconduct, or illegal actions.

This document is hereby executed under penalties of perjury, and is, to the best my knowledge, true and correct.

Date:

Name of Incorporator:

Address of Incorporator:

Signature of Incorporator: _____

State Information	Secretary of State Corporations Division 505 E. Union P.O. Box 40234 Olympia, WA 98504-0234	**Telephone:**	(360) 753-7115 TTD (360) 753-1485
		Web address:	www.secstate.wa.gov/corps/ default.htm
		Filing fee:	$175 Expedited service add $20.
		Office hours:	8-5 Monday-Friday Front counter hours are 8-4.

Filing Procedure

For clarification on any step, refer to Chapter 2.

Choose a name
The name must include incorporated, corporation, limited, or an abbreviation of one of these words.

Check name availability
Call the telephone number above and have them check the name for you, or search for it on their Web site.

File your paperwork
Complete the articles of incorporation. File the articles and one copy with the Secretary of State. Include the filing fee of $175.

Organizational matters
Choose officers (at least one) and directors (at least one). When the Articles return from the State, complete the Minutes of Organizational Meeting form (appendix). Issue stock certificates to each shareholder.

Prepare corporate records
Prepare or purchase a corporate record book and corporate seal. Place all of your documents in the record book. Use the corporate seal to emboss the stock certificates and Minutes of Organizational Meeting. Review Chapter 4 for a checklist of things to do after incorporating.

Form Instructions

In the space provided at the top of the form, put your name and daytime telephone number.

1. Enter the name of the corporation. The corporate name must include one of the following: Incorporated, Corporation, Company, Limited or Inc., Corp., Ltd., or Co.
2. Enter the number of shares of stock the corporation is authorized to issue.
3. Select an option. Specifying a date is a convenient way to begin your new corporation at some point in the future, January 1st of the next year, for example.
4. Enter the registered agent's name and street address. You may serve as your own registered agent. Have the agent sign and date the registered agent's consent.
5. Enter your name and address here.
6. This statement is optional. It is added for your protection.

   Sign and date the Articles with BLACK ink. Sign your name as incorporator exactly as it appears in the Articles of Incorporation. The articles should be typewritten.

Notes:

A fictitious name or "d.b.a." is registered with the Washington Department of Licensing on their "Master Application". All new businesses are required to file this application. The registration of a fictitious name is simply included as a part of this master application form. The filing fee is $5 for each fictitious tradename listed plus $15 to file the master application. To get this form, call (360) 664-1400. It is also available on the forms disk.

If you request expedited service, be sure to mark your envelope "EXPEDITED SERVICE REQUESTED."

Make your check payable to Washington Secretary of State.

Stock is usually exempt from registration if the number of Washington residents purchasing the stock in the last 12 months is 10 or fewer, and the offering is less than $500,000. Securities registration is handled by the Washington Department of Financial Institutions, Securities Division.

State of West Virginia
ARTICLES OF INCORPORATION

I, the undersigned person, acting as incorporator according to West Virginia Code 31-1-27, adopt the following Articles of Incorporation for a West Virginia Domestic Corporation, which shall be perpetual:

1. The name of the corporation is:

2. The physical address of the principal office and the principal place of business of the corporation will be:

    The mailing address of the above location, if different, will be:

3. The name and address of the person to whom notice of process may be sent is:

4. This corporation is organized as a for-profit corporation.

5. The corporation is authorized to issue one class of stock, that stock being _____ shares of no par value, common stock, with identical rights and privileges, the transfer of which is restricted according to the Bylaws of the corporation. Preemptive rights to acquire additional shares of the corporation's stock are neither limited nor denied.

6. The corporation has been organized to transact any and all lawful business for which corporations may be incorporated in this state. The specific purpose of this corporation is:

7. The provisions for the regulation of the internal affairs of the corporation are set forth in the bylaws of the corporation.

8. The initial Board of Directors shall consist of _____ members whose names and residence addresses are as follows:

9. The name and complete address of the sole incorporator is:

The Articles were prepared by the incorporator who resides at the above address.
I, the undersigned, for the purpose of forming a corporation under the laws of the State of West Virginia, do make and file these Articles of Incorporation. In witness whereof, I have accordingly set my hand.

Date:

Signature of Incorporator: _____

State of West Virginia
County of _____

I, _____, a Notary Public,

hereby certify that _____, whose name is signed to the foregoing Articles of

Incorporation, this day personally appeared before me and acknowledged his/her signature.

Notary _____   Seal

Sate Information	West Virginia Secretary of State Corporations Division Bldg. 1, Suite 157-K 1900 Kanawha Blvd. East Charleston, WV 25305-0770	**Telephone:**	(304) 558-8000
		Web address:	www.state.wv.us/sos/
		Filing fee:	See notes
		Office hours:	8:30-4:30 Monday-Friday

Filing Procedure

For clarification on any step, refer to Chapter 2.

Choose a name
The name must include incorporated, corporation, company, limited or an abbreviation of one of these words.

Check name availability
Call the telephone number above.

File your paperwork
Complete the articles of incorporation form. Send or take two originals with original signatures to the Secretary of State's office for filing. Your signature on both documents must be witnessed by a Notary Public. Be sure to include the fee.

After filing with the state, file one copy of the articles with the county clerk in your county.

Organizational matters
Choose officers (see notes) and directors (at least one). When the Articles return from the State, complete the Minutes of Organizational Meeting form (appendix). Issue stock certificates to each shareholder.

Prepare corporate records
Prepare or purchase a corporate record book and corporate seal. Place all of your documents in the record book. Use the corporate seal to emboss the stock certificates and Minutes of Organizational Meeting. Review Chapter 4 for a checklist of things to do after incorporating.

Form Instructions

1. Enter your corporate name.
2. Enter the complete address of the principal office and the principal place of business of the corporation. Enter the name of the county in which it is located.
3. Enter your name and address.
4. This statement is required.
5. Enter the number of shares of stock your corporation is authorized to issue.
6. Enter the corporation's primary business activity.
7. This statement is for your protection.
8. Enter the number of members of the initial Board of Directors. Enter their names and residence addresses.
9. Enter your name and complete address here.

Sign and date the Articles in black ink in the presence of a Notary. The articles should be typewritten.

Notes:

The filing fee is actually comprised of three fees, a registration fee, an attorney-in-fact fee, and a license tax fee. The registration fee is fixed at $50. The attorney in-fact-fee changes depending on the month in which your articles are filed. It varies from $6-$12. The license fee is calculated based on the total value of your stock—its par value multiplied by the number of authorized shares. This fee varies from $10-$30 depending on the month in which you file your articles. You may authorize up to 5,000 shares of $1 par stock and incur the minimum fee, or you may authorize up to 200 shares of no-par value stock and incur the minimum fee. The fee schedule is available on their website or on our forms disk. Call the Secretary of State if you need help calculating the fee.

The same person may hold more than one office, except for the offices of president and secretary, which must be held by two different people.

Stock is usually exempt from registration if the number of shareholders purchasing the stock in the last 12 months is 25 for fewer. Regulated by the Commissioner of Securities.

To use a fictitious name, file an application with the Secretary of State's office. The filing fee is $25.

State of Wisconsin
ARTICLES OF INCORPORATION

For the purpose of forming a Wisconsin for-profit corporation under Ch.180 of the Wisconsin Statutes, the undersigned natural person, being at least eighteen years of age, adopts the following Articles of Incorporation.

Article 1.   The name of the Corporation is:

Article 2.   The corporation is organized under Chapter 180 of the Wisconsin Statutes.

Article 3.   The corporation is authorized to issue   shares of no par value, common stock, with identical rights and privileges, the transfer of which is restricted according to the bylaws of the corporation.

Article 4.   The name of the initial registered agent is:

Article 5.   The street address of the initial registered office is:

Article 6.   The name and place of residence of the sole incorporator is:

In witness whereof, these Articles of Incorporation have been signed on this date:

Name of Incorporator:

Telephone Number:

Signature of Incorporator: _____

State Information	Corporation Section Department of Financial Institutions 345 W. Washington Ave. 3rd Floor Madison, WI 53703	**Telephone:**	(608) 261-7577
		Web address:	http://badger.state.wi.us/
		Filing fee:	$90 plus one cent for each share in excess of 9,000. Expedited service fee is $25.
	Mailing Address: PO Box 7846 Madison WI 53707	**Office hours:**	8-4 Monday-Friday

---

Filing Procedure   For clarification on any step, refer to Chapter 2.

Choose a name   The name must include incorporated, corporation, limited, company or an abbreviation of one of these words.

Check name availability   Call the telephone number above and have them check the name.

File your paperwork   Complete the articles of incorporation. Send or take the articles and one copy to the corporation section of the Department of Financial Institutions. Include a check for $90.

Organizational matters   Choose officers (at least one) and directors (at least one). When the Articles return from the State, complete the Minutes of Organizational Meeting form (appendix). Issue stock certificates to each shareholder.

Prepare corporate records   Prepare or purchase a corporate record book and corporate seal. Place all of your documents in the record book. Use the corporate seal to emboss the stock certificates and Minutes of Organizational Meeting. Review Chapter 4 for a checklist of things to do after incorporating.

Form Instructions

1. Enter the name of the corporation.

2. This statement is required by law.

3. Enter the total number of shares of stock that your corporation is authorized to issue. You do not have to issue all the shares now. Authorize enough for present and future use. You can authorize up to 9,000 shares of stock and incur the minimum filing fee of $90. Authorize more than 9,000 shares, and your filing fee will increase by one cent for each share, with a $10,000 maximum fee.

4. Enter the name of the initial registered agent. You can serve as your own registered agent.

5. Enter the complete address of the initial registered office, including street and number, and zip code. PO Box address may be included as part of the address, but is insufficient alone.

6. Enter your name and street address here.

   Complete the bottom of the form and have the incorporator sign the Articles of Incorporation in ink. You are only required to have one incorporator. The articles should be typewritten.

Notes:

To use a fictitious name, you'll need to file an application with the Department of Trade Names. The telephone number is (608) 266-5653. The form is called "Application for Registration of Marks." The filing fee is $15.

Make checks payable to the Department of Financial Institutions.

The filing fee of $90 allows you to authorize up to 9,000 shares of stock. If you need to authorize more than 9,000 shares, you will pay an additional filing fee equal to one cent for each additional share over 9,000.

Stock is usually exempt from registration if the number of Wisconsin residents purchasing the stock is 10 or fewer. Stock registration is handled by the Department of Financial Institutions. Their telephone number is (608) 266-3431.

State of Wyoming
ARTICLES OF INCORPORATION

I, the undersigned person, acting as incorporator under Title 17 of the Wyoming Statutes, adopt the following Articles of Incorporation for the purpose of forming a for-profit corporation.

1. The name of the corporation is:

2. The name and address of the corporation's registered agent and office in Wyoming is:

3. The corporation is authorized to issue one class of stock, that stock being _____ shares of no par value, common stock, with identical rights and privileges, the transfer of which is restricted according to the Bylaws of the corporation. Said shares are entitled to receive the net assets of the Corporation upon its dissolution.

4. The address for mailing the annual report form is:

5. The name and complete address of the sole incorporator is:

Date:

Contact Name / Name of Incorporator:

Daytime telephone:

Signature of Incorporator: _____

Consent to Appointment by Registered Agent

I, _____, voluntarily consent to serve as the registered agent for the above named Corporation on the date shown below. I certify that I am an individual who resides in this state and whose business office is identical to the registered office.

Date:

Signature of Registered Agent: _____

State Information	Wyoming Secretary of State Corporation Division The State Capitol Cheyenne, WY 82002-0020	**Telephone:**	(307) 777-7311 (307) 777-7312
		Web address:	http://soswy.state.wy.us/ corporat/corporat.htm
		Filing fee:	$100
		Office hours:	8-5 Monday-Friday

Form Instructions

For clarification on any step, refer to Chapter 2.

Choose a name — The name should include incorporated, corporation, company, limited, or an abbreviation of one of these words.

Check name availability — Call the telephone number above and have them check the name for you, or search the name on their website.

File your paperwork — File the Articles of Incorporation and one exact copy with the Secretary of State. Be sure to include the filing fee.

Organizational matters — Choose officers (at least one) and directors (at least one). When the Articles return from the State, complete the Minutes of Organizational Meeting form (appendix). Issue stock certificates to each shareholder.

Prepare corporate records — Prepare or purchase a corporate record book and corporate seal. Place all of your documents in the record book. Use the corporate seal to emboss the stock certificates and Minutes of Organizational Meeting. Review Chapter 4 for a checklist of things to do after incorporating.

Form Instructions

1. Enter your corporate name.

2. Enter the name and address of the corporation's registered agent and office in Wyoming. You can serve as your own registered agent if you have an office within the state.

3. Enter the number of shares of stock your corporation is authorized to issue. All of the shares do not need to be issued to shareholders at this time. You must have at least one share of stock.

4. Enter the address that you want the annual report form mailed to.

5. Enter your name and complete address here.

   Enter the date, your name, and daytime telephone number, then sign with black ink.

   At the bottom of the form, complete the Consent to Appointment by Registered Agent section. Sign your name and the date in black ink. The Articles should be typewritten.

Notes:

To use a fictitious name, file an application with the Secretary of State's office. The filing fee is $25.

Stock is usually exempt from registration if the number of shareholders purchasing the stock in the last 12 months is 25 or fewer. Regulated by the Secretary of State.

MINUTES OF THE ORGANIZATIONAL MEETING OF THE BOARD OF DIRECTORS
of

Pursuant to State Law, a meeting was held to complete the organization of the corporation. The meeting was held on the _____ day of _____ , at _____ o'clock _____ M, 20 _____ at the principal office of the corporation.

Present at the meeting were the incorporator, and the director(s), officer(s) and shareholder(s) named herein. As evidenced by their attendance and their signatures on the reverse, all directors, officers, and shareholders hereby waive any notice of the meeting that may be required by law. The incorporator duly called the meeting to order and the following items of business were resolved.

DIRECTORS

The incorporator, being all of the incorporators of the corporation, elected the person(s) named below to be director(s) of the corporation until the first annual shareholders meeting at which directors are elected or until new or replacement directors are elected. With the duties of the incorporator being completed, the incorporator resigned. A motion was duly made and seconded that the corporation adopt all pre-incorporation transactions entered into by the incorporator. The Chairperson of the Board presided over the remainder of the meeting.

_____	_____
Director - Chairperson	Director
_____	_____
Director	Director

OFFICERS

As their duties are outlined in the corporation bylaws, the Board unanimously elected the following individuals to be officers of the corporation—their respective titles below their name, and their annual salary to the right. These individuals will be officers until which time officers are either reelected or replaced. The president of the corporation was unanimously elected to serve as chairperson of the board of directors. Each person elected to an office accepted their appointment. The president noted that being an officer of the corporation did not preclude officers from holding other salaried positions within the corporation.

_____	_____
President / Chairperson of the Board of Directors	Pres. Salary
_____	_____
Vice-President	V.P. Salary
_____	_____
Secretary	Sec. Salary
_____	_____
Treasurer	Treas. Salary

ARTICLES OF INCORPORATION

A copy of the Articles of Incorporation filed with the State on _____ was presented at the meeting. The articles were approved by the directors of the corporation, and it was agreed that the corporate secretary shall place the articles in the corporate records book.

CORPORATE SEAL

The secretary presented at the meeting a proposed corporate seal. After a short discussion, a motion was made and duly seconded that the seal presented at the meeting be adopted as the seal of the corporation. The president noted that the seal shall remain in the custody of the corporate secretary along with the record book of the corporation.

The corporate secretary was directed to place an impression of the seal in the space to the right of this paragraph.

BYLAWS

A copy of the proposed bylaws for the corporation was presented at the meeting and was considered by the board. Upon motion duly made and seconded it was resolved that the bylaws presented at the meeting shall be the bylaws of the corporation. It was further agreed that the corporate secretary shall include a copy of the bylaws in the corporate records book.

BANK ACCOUNT

The authority by which a bank account may be opened for the corporation is granted by a separate resolution. The corporate secretary was asked to include a copy of that resolution with the corporate records book.

ACCOUNTING PERIOD

Upon motion duly made and seconded it is hereby resolved that the accounting period of the corporation shall end on the last day of the month of _____. It was noted by the president that the corporation must have a December 31 year end to elect IRS Subchapter S status.

ORGANIZATIONAL EXPENSES

After motion duly made and seconded, is was unanimously approved for the corporation to incur, pay, and reimburse any reasonable expenses related to the formation of the corporation. The president noted that organizational expenses of the corporation must be amortized over a period of 60 months.

STOCK

The stock of the corporation was issued under the direction of the Board of Directors. The members of the Board stated that they believe all State and Federal requirements relating to the issuance of the stock of the corporation have been met. Accordingly, a notice that the stock of the corporation is unregistered shall be placed on the certificates. The Board further stated that the stock shall be offered as Section 1244 stock and the issuance shall meet the requirements of IRS Section 1244. The president noted that by meeting the qualifications of IRS Section 1244, shareholders will receive preferential tax treatment in the event of a loss in the value of their stock. Verbal offers to purchase stock in the corporation were made by the individuals listed below and accepted by the Board of Directors. The individuals stated that the shares of stock were purchased for their own account and would not be traded publicly. The corporate secretary presented a stock certificate form at the meeting and it was approved by the board. The secretary will issue certificates to each shareholder and impress the corporate seal on the face of each certificate. Certificates will be signed by the President and Secretary of the Corporation.

Name	No. of Shares	% Ownership	Payment Given *
Name	No. of Shares	% Ownership	Payment Given *
Name	No. of Shares	% Ownership	Payment Given *
Name	No. of Shares	% Ownership	Payment Given *

* If needed, payment may be listed on a separate sheet of paper.

_____
Signature of Corporate Secretary

_____
Date

BYLAWS
of

The following shall be known as the Bylaws of the Corporation, the Bylaws being rules of self government of the Corporation. These bylaws are the set of rules by which the Corporation operates on a daily basis and settles disputes that may arise from time to time; and they are binding on all those associated with the Corporation either now, or in the future. If the Bylaws are found to be inconsistent with State Law, then State Law will override. The Bylaws may be amended by the Directors provided there is a majority of Directors votes favoring the amendments.

Article One: Purpose

The Corporation may take advantage of the rights granted to it by State law, and engage in any business allowed by State Business Corporation Law.

Article Two: Duration

The Corporation has perpetual duration and succession in its corporate name and will exist until such time that the Board of Directors elects to end its existence.

Article Three: Powers

The Corporation has the powers given by State Business Corporation Law, to do all things necessary or practical to carry out its business and affairs including without limitation, the power to sue, make contracts, deal in property of any kind, make investments, borrow or lend money, be a part of another entity, or conduct its business in any way allowed by the laws of this State.

Article Four: Stock

The shares of the Corporation will be common stock, with full voting rights and identical rights and privileges, with no par value. The issuance of shares will be governed by the Board of Directors, as will be the consideration to be paid for the shares, which will meet the requirements of State Business Corporation Law. The Corporation through its Board of Directors may issue fractional shares, acquire its own shares, declare and pay cash or stock dividends, or issue certificates.

In order to insure the continued existence of the Corporation, the transfer of shares of the Corporation to any individual or other entity will be restricted in the manner described herein. No shares may be transferred on the books of the Corporation unless the number of shares are first offered to the Corporation, and then to the other shareholders on a right of first refusal basis, the corporation having first option. This option to purchase the stock will expire in thirty (30) days from when offered. If the option is not exercised within the stated period, the Shareholder may dispose of the shares in any manner he wishes. The share certificates shall bear the following notice: RESTRICTED STOCK

Article Five: Meetings

Regular Meetings

The Corporation may hold any number of meetings to conduct its business. At a minimum, it will hold an annual Shareholders' meeting at which the Directors will review with the Shareholders the operating results of the Corporation for the prior year, hold elections for Directors, and conduct any other business that may be necessary at that time. Unless decided otherwise at the time, the place and time for the annual Shareholders' meeting will be at the offices of the Corporation on the day of at o'clock am/PM, each year. The Secretary will give proper notice to the Shareholders as may be required by law, however that notice may be waived by the Shareholder by submitting a signed waiver either before or after the meeting, or by his attendance at the meeting. Meetings may be held in or out of this State. Minutes must be taken by the Secretary for inclusion in the Corporate Records.

Special Meetings

The Corporation may hold meetings from time to time at such times and places that may be convenient. These meetings may be Directors meetings or Shareholder meetings or combined Director and Shareholder meetings. Special Shareholder meetings may be called by The Board of Directors or demanded in writing by the holders of ten percent or more shares. Special Director meetings may be called by the Chairman, the President, or any two Directors. The Corporate Secretary will give proper notice as may be required by law, however that notice may be waived by the individual by submitting a signed waiver either before or after the meeting, or by his attendance at the meeting. Meetings may be held in or out of this State. Minutes must be taken by the Secretary for inclusion in the Corporate Records.

Article Six: Voting

From time to time it may be necessary for a Director or Shareholder to vote on issues brought before a meeting. No voting may take place at a meeting unless there is a quorum present. That is, a quorum of Directors must be present at a meeting before any Director may vote, and likewise a quorum of Shareholders must be present at a meeting before any Shareholder may vote. A quorum of Directors at a meeting is defined as a majority of the number of Directors. A quorum of Shareholders at a meeting is defined as a majority of the shares entitled to vote. If a quorum is present at a meeting, action on a matter may be passed if the number of votes favoring the action is cast by a majority. For voting purposes, a Director may cast one vote, and a Shareholder may cast one vote for each share held except in the case of director elections when voting is cumulative. A Shareholder may vote in person or by proxy.

Article Seven: Action Without Meeting

Directors or Shareholders may approve actions without a formal meeting if all entitled to vote on a matter consent to taking such action without a meeting. A majority still is required to pass actions without a meeting. The action must be evidenced by a written consent describing the action taken, signed by the Directors or Shareholders (depending on which group is taking the action) indicating each signer's vote or abstention on the matter, and it must be delivered to the Corporate Secretary for inclusion with the Corporate Records.

Article Eight: Directors

All corporate powers will be exercised by, or under the authority of, and the business affairs of the Corporation managed under the direction of, its Board of Directors. The Board may consist of one or more individuals, who need not need be Shareholders or residents of this state. The terms of the initial Directors or subsequently elected Directors will end at the next Shareholders' meeting following their election, at which time new Directors will be elected or the current Directors will be reelected.

A director may resign at any time by delivering a written notice to the Corporation. A Director may be removed at any time with or without cause if the number of votes cast to remove him exceeds the number of votes cast not to remove him. Vacancies on the Board will be filled by the Shareholders in the manner described above.

The Directors of the Corporation are not liable to either the Corporation or its Shareholders for monetary damages for a breach of fiduciary duties unless the breach involves disloyalty to the Corporation or its Shareholders, acts or omissions not in good faith, or self dealing. The Corporation may indemnify the Directors or Officers who are named as defendants in litigation relating to Corporate affairs and the Directors or Officers role therein.

Article Nine: Officers

The officers of the Corporation will be initially appointed by the Board of Directors. The officers of the Corporation will be at least those required by State law, and any other officers that the Board of Directors may deem necessary. The duties and responsibilities of the Officers will be set by, and will be under the continued direction of, the Directors. Officers may be removed at any time with or without cause, and may resign at any time by delivering written notice to the Board of Directors. If allowed by state law, one person may hold more than one officer position.

President

The President is the principal executive officer of the Corporation and in general supervises and directs the daily business operations of the Corporation, subject to the direction of the Board of Directors. The President is also the proper official to execute contracts, share certificates, and any other document that may be required on behalf of the Corporation. The President shall also preside at all meetings of Directors or meetings of Shareholders.

Secretary

The Corporate Secretary will in general be responsible for the records of the Corporation which generally includes keeping minutes at any meeting, giving proper notice of any meeting, maintaining the Director and Shareholder registers and transfer records; and along with the President, sign stock certificates of the Corporation.

Vice President

The Corporate Vice-President if appointed will be responsible for duties to be assigned by the Board of Directors.

Treasurer

The Corporate treasurer if appointed will be responsible for duties to be assigned by the Board of Directors.

Other Officers

The directors may appoint other officers as they deem necessary.

Number of Shares

Certificate Number

Certificate of Stock

This Certifies that

is the registered holder of

shares of the above named corporation.

This certificate is transferable on the books of the corporation only by the shareholder named herein or by the shareholder's duly appointed representative upon surrender of the certificate properly endorsed. This series is designated as Class   and its total authorized issue is   shares with   par value.

This stock has not been registered with any State or Federal agency and its transfer is subject to restriction.

The Corporation is organized in the State of

In Witness Whereof, said corporation has caused this certificate to be signed by its duly authorized officers and its seal to be hereunto affixed this   day of   20

_____
President

_____
Secretary

For value received,   *hereby sell, assign, and transfer unto*

                              shares of stock represented by this certificate, and do hereby irrevocably

constitute and appoint   *Corporate Secretary as Agent to transfer said*

shares on the books of the within named Corporation with full power of substitution in the premises.

Dated:

Signature of Shareholder:

Signature of Witness:

The following abbreviations, when used in the inscription on the face of the certificate, shall be construed as though they were written out in full according to applicable laws or regulations:

TEN COM   as tenants in common

TEN ENT   as tenants by the entirety

JT TEN   as joint tenants with right of survivorship and not as tenants in common

UNIF GIFT MIN ACT (name of custodian) as custodian for (name of minor) under the (name of state) Uniform Gifts to Minors Act

Certificate of Stock

Number of Shares

Certificate Number

This Certifies that

is the registered holder of

shares of the above named corporation.

This certificate is transferable on the books of the corporation only by the shareholder named herein or by the shareholder's duly appointed representative upon surrender of the certificate properly endorsed. This series is designated as Class   and its total authorized issue is   shares with   par value.

This stock has not been registered with any State or Federal agency and its transfer is subject to restriction.

The Corporation is organized in the State of

In Witness Whereof, said corporation has caused this certificate to be signed by its duly authorized officers and its seal to be hereunto affixed this   day of   20

_____
President

_____
Secretary

For value received, _____ *hereby sell, assign, and transfer unto*

_____ *shares of stock represented by this certificate, and do hereby irrevocably*

constitute and appoint _____ *Corporate Secretary as Agent to transfer said*

shares on the books of the within named Corporation with full power of substitution in the premises.

Dated:

Signature of Shareholder:

Signature of Witness:

The following abbreviations, when used in the inscription on the face of the certificate, shall be construed as though they were written out in full according to applicable laws or regulations:

TEN COM   as tenants in common
TEN ENT   as tenants by the entirety
JT TEN   as joint tenants with right of survivorship and not as tenants in common
UNIF GIFT MIN ACT (name of custodian) as custodian for (name of minor) under the (name of state) Uniform Gifts to Minors Act

Number of Shares

Certificate Number

Certificate of Stock

This Certifies that

is the registered holder of

shares of the above named corporation.

This certificate is transferable on the books of the corporation only by the shareholder named herein or by the shareholder's duly appointed representative upon surrender of the certificate properly endorsed. This series is designated as Class _____ and its total authorized issue is _____ shares with _____ par value.

This stock has not been registered with any State or Federal agency and its transfer is subject to restriction.

The corporation is organized in the State of

In Witness Whereof, said corporation has caused this certificate to be signed by its duly authorized officers and its Seal to be hereunto affixed this _____ day of _____ 20____

_____
President

_____
Secretary

For value received, _____ *hereby sell, assign, and transfer unto*

_____ *shares of stock represented by this certificate, and do hereby irrevocably*

constitute and appoint _____ *Corporate Secretary as Agent to transfer said*

shares on the books of the within named Corporation with full power of substitution in the premises.

Dated:

Signature of Shareholder:

Signature of Witness:

The following abbreviations, when used in the inscription on the face of the certificate, shall be construed as though they were written out in full according to applicable laws or regulations:

TEN COM   as tenants in common
TEN ENT   as tenants by the entirety
JT TEN   as joint tenants with right of survivorship and not as tenants in common
UNIF GIFT MIN ACT (name of custodian) as custodian for (name of minor) under the (name of state) Uniform Gifts to Minors Act

Certificate of Stock

Number of Shares

Certificate Number

_____ is the registered holder of _____ shares of the above named corporation.

This Certifies that

This certificate is transferable on the books of the corporation only by the shareholder named herein or by the shareholder's duly appointed representative upon surrender of the certificate properly endorsed. This series is designated as Class _____ and its total authorized issue is _____ shares with _____ par value. This stock has not been registered with any State or Federal agency and its transfer is subject to restriction. The corporation is organized in the State of _____

In Witness Whereof, said corporation has caused this certificate to be signed by its duly authorized officers and its Seal to be hereunto affixed this _____ day of _____ 20 _____

_____
Secretary

_____
President

For value received, _____ *hereby sell, assign, and transfer unto*

_____ *shares of stock represented by this certificate, and do hereby irrevocably*

constitute and appoint _____ *Corporate Secretary as Agent to transfer said*

shares on the books of the within named Corporation with full power of substitution in the premises.

Dated:

Signature of Shareholder:

Signature of Witness:

The following abbreviations, when used in the inscription on the face of the certificate, shall be construed as though they were written out in full according to applicable laws or regulations:

TEN COM   as tenants in common
TEN ENT   as tenants by the entirety
JT TEN   as joint tenants with right of survivorship and not as tenants in common
UNIF GIFT MIN ACT (name of custodian) as custodian for (name of minor) under the (name of state) Uniform Gifts to Minors Act

Number of Shares

Certificate Number

Certificate of Stock

This Certifies that

is the registered holder of

shares of the above named corporation.

This certificate is transferable on the books of the corporation only by the shareholder named herein or by the shareholder's duly appointed representative upon surrender of the certificate properly endorsed. This series is designated as Class _____ and its total authorized issue is _____ shares with _____ par value. This stock has not been registered with any State or Federal agency and its transfer is subject to restriction. The Corporation is organized in the State of

In Witness Whereof, said corporation has caused this certificate to be signed by its duly authorized officers and its Seal to be hereunto affixed this _____ day of _____

20 ____

_____
President

_____
Secretary

For value received, _____ *hereby sell, assign, and transfer unto*

_____ *shares of stock represented by this certificate, and do hereby irrevocably*

constitute and appoint _____ *Corporate Secretary as Agent to transfer said*

shares on the books of the within named Corporation with full power of substitution in the premises.

Dated:

Signature of Shareholder:

Signature of Witness:

The following abbreviations, when used in the inscription on the face of the certificate, shall be construed as though they were written out in full according to applicable laws or regulations:

TEN COM   as tenants in common
TEN ENT   as tenants by the entirety
JT TEN   as joint tenants with right of survivorship and not as tenants in common
UNIF GIFT MIN ACT (name of custodian) as custodian for (name of minor) under the (name of state) Uniform Gifts to Minors Act

Number of Shares

Certificate Number

Certificate of Stock

is the registered holder of

shares of the above named corporation.

This Certifies that

This certificate is transferable on the books of the corporation only by the shareholder named herein or by the shareholder's duly appointed representative upon surrender of the certificate properly endorsed. This series is designated as Class _____ and its total authorized issue is _____ shares with _____ par value.

This stock has not been registered with any State or Federal agency and its transfer is subject to restriction.

The Corporation is organized in the State of

In Witness Whereof, said corporation has caused this certificate to be signed by its duly authorized officers and its Seal to be hereunto affixed this _____ day of _____ 20_____

_____
Secretary

_____
President

For value received, _____ *hereby sell, assign, and transfer unto*

_____ *shares of stock represented by this certificate, and do hereby irrevocably*

constitute and appoint _____ *Corporate Secretary as Agent to transfer said*

shares on the books of the within named Corporation with full power of substitution in the premises.

Dated:

Signature of Shareholder:

Signature of Witness:

The following abbreviations, when used in the inscription on the face of the certificate, shall be construed as though they were written out in full according to applicable laws or regulations:

TEN COM   as tenants in common
TEN ENT   as tenants by the entirety
JT TEN   as joint tenants with right of survivorship and not as tenants in common
UNIF GIFT MIN ACT (name of custodian) as custodian for (name of minor) under the (name of state) Uniform Gifts to Minors Act

Form **SS-4**

(Rev. February 1998)

Department of the Treasury
Internal Revenue Service

Application for Employer Identification Number

(For use by employers, corporations, partnerships, trusts, estates, churches, government agencies, certain individuals, and others. See instructions.)

▶ **Keep a copy for your records.**

EIN

OMB No. 1545-0003

Please type or print clearly.

1 Name of applicant (legal name) (see instructions)	

2 Trade name of business (if different from name on line 1)	**3** Executor, trustee, "care of" name

4a Mailing address (street address) (room, apt., or suite no.)	**5a** Business address (if different from address on lines 4a and 4b)
4b City, state, and ZIP code	**5b** City, state, and ZIP code

6 County and state where principal business is located

7 Name of principal officer, general partner, grantor, owner, or trustor—SSN or ITIN may be required (see instructions) ▶ _____

8a Type of entity (Check only one box.) (see instructions)

Caution: *If applicant is a limited liability company, see the instructions for line 8a.*

- ☐ Sole proprietor (SSN) _____
- ☐ Partnership ☐ Personal service corp.
- ☐ REMIC ☐ National Guard
- ☐ State/local government ☐ Farmers' cooperative
- ☐ Church or church-controlled organization
- ☐ Other nonprofit organization (specify) ▶ _____
- ☐ Other (specify) ▶ _____

- ☐ Estate (SSN of decedent) _____
- ☐ Plan administrator (SSN) _____
- ☐ Other corporation (specify) ▶ _____
- ☐ Trust
- ☐ Federal government/military
  (enter GEN if applicable) _____

8b If a corporation, name the state or foreign country (if applicable) where incorporated

State	Foreign country

9 Reason for applying (Check only one box.) (see instructions)
- ☐ Started new business (specify type) ▶ _____
- ☐ Hired employees (Check the box and see line 12.)
- ☐ Created a pension plan (specify type) ▶ _____
- ☐ Banking purpose (specify purpose) ▶ _____
- ☐ Changed type of organization (specify new type) ▶ _____
- ☐ Purchased going business
- ☐ Created a trust (specify type) ▶ _____
- ☐ Other (specify) ▶ _____

10 Date business started or acquired (month, day, year) (see instructions)

11 Closing month of accounting year (see instructions)

12 First date wages or annuities were paid or will be paid (month, day, year). **Note:** *If applicant is a withholding agent, enter date income will first be paid to nonresident alien. (month, day, year)* . . . . ▶

13 Highest number of employees expected in the next 12 months. **Note:** *If the applicant does not expect to have any employees during the period, enter -0-. (see instructions)* . . . . ▶	Nonagricultural	Agricultural	Household

14 Principal activity (see instructions) ▶

15 Is the principal business activity manufacturing? . . . . ☐ **Yes** ☐ **No**
If "Yes," principal product and raw material used ▶

16 To whom are most of the products or services sold? Please check one box. ☐ Business (wholesale)
☐ Public (retail) ☐ Other (specify) ▶ ☐ N/A

17a Has the applicant ever applied for an employer identification number for this or any other business? . . . . ☐ **Yes** ☐ **No**
Note: *If "Yes," please complete lines 17b and 17c.*

17b If you checked "Yes" on line 17a, give applicant's legal name and trade name shown on prior application, if different from line 1 or 2 above.
Legal name ▶ Trade name ▶

17c Approximate date when and city and state where the application was filed. Enter previous employer identification number if known.

Approximate date when filed (mo., day, year)	City and state where filed	Previous EIN

Under penalties of perjury, I declare that I have examined this application, and to the best of my knowledge and belief, it is true, correct, and complete.

Business telephone number (include area code)

Fax telephone number (include area code)

Name and title (Please type or print clearly.) ▶

Signature ▶ Date ▶

Note: *Do not write below this line. For official use only.*

Please leave blank ▶	Geo.	Ind.	Class	Size	Reason for applying

For Paperwork Reduction Act Notice, see page 4.

Cat. No. 16055N

Form **SS-4** (Rev. 2-98)

General Instructions

Section references are to the Internal Revenue Code unless otherwise noted.

Purpose of Form

Use Form SS-4 to apply for an employer identification number (EIN). An EIN is a nine-digit number (for example, 12-3456789) assigned to sole proprietors, corporations, partnerships, estates, trusts, and other entities for tax filing and reporting purposes. The information you provide on this form will establish your business tax account.

Caution: *An EIN is for use in connection with your business activities only. Do **NOT** use your EIN in place of your social security number (SSN).*

Who Must File

You must file this form if you have not been assigned an EIN before and:

• You pay wages to one or more employees including household employees.

• You are required to have an EIN to use on any return, statement, or other document, even if you are not an employer.

• You are a withholding agent required to withhold taxes on income, other than wages, paid to a nonresident alien (individual, corporation, partnership, etc.). A withholding agent may be an agent, broker, fiduciary, manager, tenant, or spouse, and is required to file **Form 1042,** Annual Withholding Tax Return for U.S. Source Income of Foreign Persons.

• You file **Schedule C,** Profit or Loss From Business, **Schedule C-EZ,** Net Profit From Business, or **Schedule F,** Profit or Loss From Farming, of **Form 1040,** U.S. Individual Income Tax Return, **and** have a Keogh plan or are required to file excise, employment, or alcohol, tobacco, or firearms returns.

The following must use EINs even if they do not have any employees:

• State and local agencies who serve as tax reporting agents for public assistance recipients, under Rev. Proc. 80-4, 1980-1 C.B. 581, should obtain a separate EIN for this reporting. See **Household employer** on page 3.

• Trusts, except the following:

   1. Certain grantor-owned trusts. (See the **Instructions for Form 1041.**)

   2. Individual Retirement Arrangement (IRA) trusts, unless the trust has to file **Form 990-T,** Exempt Organization Business Income Tax Return. (See the **Instructions for Form 990-T.**)

• Estates

• Partnerships

• REMICs (real estate mortgage investment conduits) (See the **Instructions for Form 1066,** U.S. Real Estate Mortgage Investment Conduit Income Tax Return.)

• Corporations

• Nonprofit organizations (churches, clubs, etc.)

• Farmers' cooperatives

• Plan administrators (A plan administrator is the person or group of persons specified as the administrator by the instrument under which the plan is operated.)

When To Apply for a New EIN

New Business. If you become the new owner of an existing business, **do not** use the EIN of the former owner. IF YOU ALREADY HAVE AN EIN, USE THAT NUMBER. If you do not have an EIN, apply for one on this form. If you become the "owner" of a corporation by acquiring its stock, use the corporation's EIN.

Changes in Organization or Ownership. If you already have an EIN, you may need to get a new one if either the organization or ownership of your business changes. If you incorporate a sole proprietorship or form a partnership, you must get a new EIN. However, **do not** apply for a new EIN if:

• You change only the name of your business,

• You elected on **Form 8832,** Entity Classification Election, to change the way the entity is taxed, or

• A partnership terminates because at least 50% of the total interests in partnership capital and profits were sold or exchanged within a 12-month period. (See Regulations section 301.6109-1(d)(2)(iii).) The EIN for the terminated partnership should continue to be used. This rule applies to terminations occurring after May 8, 1997. If the termination took place after May 8, 1996, and before May 9, 1997, a new EIN must be obtained for the new partnership unless the partnership and its partners are consistent in using the old EIN.

Note: *If you are electing to be an "S corporation," be sure you file **Form 2553,** Election by a Small Business Corporation.*

File Only One Form SS-4. File only one Form SS-4, regardless of the number of businesses operated or trade names under which a business operates. However, each corporation in an affiliated group must file a separate application.

EIN Applied for, But Not Received. If you do not have an EIN by the time a return is due, write "Applied for" and the date you applied in the space shown for the number. **Do not** show your social security number (SSN) as an EIN on returns.

If you do not have an EIN by the time a tax deposit is due, send your payment to the Internal Revenue Service Center for your filing area. (See **Where To Apply** below.) Make your check or money order payable to Internal Revenue Service and show your name (as shown on Form SS-4), address, type of tax, period covered, and date you applied for an EIN. Send an explanation with the deposit.

For more information about EINs, see **Pub. 583,** Starting a Business and Keeping Records, and **Pub. 1635,** Understanding your EIN.

How To Apply

You can apply for an EIN either by mail or by telephone. You can get an EIN immediately by calling the Tele-TIN number for the service center for your state, or you can send the completed Form SS-4 directly to the service center to receive your EIN by mail.

Application by Tele-TIN. Under the Tele-TIN program, you can receive your EIN by telephone and use it immediately to file a return or make a payment. To receive an EIN by telephone, complete Form SS-4, then call the Tele-TIN number listed for your state under **Where To Apply.** The person making the call must be authorized to sign the form. (See **Signature** on page 4.)

An IRS representative will use the information from the Form SS-4 to establish your account and assign you an EIN. Write the number you are given on the upper right corner of the form and sign and date it.

*Mail or fax (facsimile) the signed SS-4 **within 24 hours** to the Tele-TIN Unit at the service center address for your state.* The IRS representative will give you the fax number. The fax numbers are also listed in Pub. 1635.

Taxpayer representatives can receive their client's EIN by telephone if they first send a fax of a completed **Form 2848,** Power of Attorney and Declaration of Representative, or **Form 8821,** Tax Information Authorization, to the Tele-TIN unit. The Form 2848 or Form 8821 will be used solely to release the EIN to the representative authorized on the form.

Application by Mail. Complete Form SS-4 at least 4 to 5 weeks before you will need an EIN. Sign and date the application and mail it to the service center address for your state. You will receive your EIN in the mail in approximately 4 weeks.

Where To Apply

The Tele-TIN numbers listed below will involve a long-distance charge to callers outside of the local calling area and can be used only to apply for an EIN. THE NUMBERS MAY CHANGE WITHOUT NOTICE. Call 1-800-829-1040 to verify a number or to ask about the status of an application by mail.

If your principal business, office or agency, or legal residence in the case of an individual, is located in: ▼	Call the Tele-TIN number shown or file with the Internal Revenue Service Center at: ▼
Florida, Georgia, South Carolina	Attn: Entity Control Atlanta, GA 39901 770-455-2360
New Jersey, New York City and counties of Nassau, Rockland, Suffolk, and Westchester	Attn: Entity Control Holtsville, NY 00501 516-447-4955
New York (all other counties), Connecticut, Maine, Massachusetts, New Hampshire, Rhode Island, Vermont	Attn: Entity Control Andover, MA 05501 978-474-9717
Illinois, Iowa, Minnesota, Missouri, Wisconsin	Attn: Entity Control Stop 6800 2306 E. Bannister Rd. Kansas City, MO 64999 816-926-5999
Delaware, District of Columbia, Maryland, Pennsylvania, Virginia	Attn: Entity Control Philadelphia, PA 19255 215-516-6999
Indiana, Kentucky, Michigan, Ohio, West Virginia	Attn: Entity Control Cincinnati, OH 45999 606-292-5467

Kansas, New Mexico, Oklahoma, Texas	Attn: Entity Control Austin, TX 73301 512-460-7843
Alaska, Arizona, California (counties of Alpine, Amador, Butte, Calaveras, Colusa, Contra Costa, Del Norte, El Dorado, Glenn, Humboldt, Lake, Lassen, Marin, Mendocino, Modoc, Napa, Nevada, Placer, Plumas, Sacramento, San Joaquin, Shasta, Sierra, Siskiyou, Solano, Sonoma, Sutter, Tehama, Trinity, Yolo, and Yuba), Colorado, Idaho, Montana, Nebraska, Nevada, North Dakota, Oregon, South Dakota, Utah, Washington, Wyoming	Attn: Entity Control Mail Stop 6271 P.O. Box 9941 Ogden, UT 84201 801-620-7645
California (all other counties), Hawaii	Attn: Entity Control Fresno, CA 93888 209-452-4010
Alabama, Arkansas, Louisiana, Mississippi, North Carolina, Tennessee	Attn: Entity Control Memphis, TN 37501 901-546-3920
If you have no legal residence, principal place of business, or principal office or agency in any state	Attn: Entity Control Philadelphia, PA 19255 215-516-6999

Specific Instructions

The instructions that follow are for those items that are not self-explanatory. Enter N/A (nonapplicable) on the lines that do not apply.

Line 1. Enter the legal name of the entity applying for the EIN exactly as it appears on the social security card, charter, or other applicable legal document.

Individuals. Enter your first name, middle initial, and last name. If you are a sole proprietor, enter your individual name, not your business name. Enter your business name on line 2. Do not use abbreviations or nicknames on line 1.

Trusts. Enter the name of the trust.

Estate of a decedent. Enter the name of the estate.

Partnerships. Enter the legal name of the partnership as it appears in the partnership agreement. **Do not** list the names of the partners on line 1. See the specific instructions for line 7.

Corporations. Enter the corporate name as it appears in the corporation charter or other legal document creating it.

Plan administrators. Enter the name of the plan administrator. A plan administrator who already has an EIN should use that number.

Line 2. Enter the trade name of the business if different from the legal name. The trade name is the "doing business as" name.

Note: *Use the full legal name on line 1 on all tax returns filed for the entity. However, if you enter a trade name on line 2 and choose to use the trade name instead of the legal name, enter the trade name on all returns you file. To prevent processing delays and errors, **always** use either the legal name only or the trade name only on all tax returns.*

Line 3. Trusts enter the name of the trustee. Estates enter the name of the executor, administrator, or other fiduciary. If the entity applying has a designated person to receive tax information, enter that person's name as the "care of" person. Print or type the first name, middle initial, and last name.

Line 7. Enter the first name, middle initial, last name, and SSN of a principal officer if the business is a corporation; of a general partner if a partnership; of the owner of a single member entity that is disregarded as an entity separate from its owner; or of a grantor, owner, or trustor if a trust. If the person in question is an alien individual with a previously assigned individual taxpayer identification number (ITIN), enter the ITIN in the space provided, instead of an SSN. You are not required to enter an SSN or ITIN if the reason you are applying for an EIN is to make an entity classification election (see Regulations section 301.7701-1 through 301.7701-3), and you are a nonresident alien with no effectively connected income from sources within the United States.

Line 8a. Check the box that best describes the type of entity applying for the EIN. If you are an alien individual with an ITIN previously assigned to you, enter the ITIN in place of a requested SSN.

Caution: *This is not an election for a tax classification of an entity. See "Limited liability company" below.*

If not specifically mentioned, check the "Other" box, enter the type of entity and the type of return that will be filed (for example, common trust fund, Form 1065). Do not enter N/A. If you are an alien individual applying for an EIN, see the **Line 7** instructions above.

Sole proprietor. Check this box if you file Schedule C, C-EZ, or F (Form 1040) and have a Keogh plan, or are required to file excise, employment, or alcohol, tobacco, or firearms returns, or are a payer of gambling winnings. Enter your SSN (or ITIN) in the space provided. If you are a nonresident alien with no effectively connected income from sources within the United States, you do not need to enter an SSN or ITIN.

REMIC. Check this box if the entity has elected to be treated as a real estate mortgage investment conduit (REMIC). See the **Instructions for Form 1066** for more information.

Other nonprofit organization. Check this box if the nonprofit organization is other than a church or church-controlled organization and specify the type of nonprofit organization (for example, an educational organization).

If the organization also seeks tax-exempt status, you must file either **Package 1023,** Application for Recognition of Exemption, or **Package 1024,** Application for Recognition of Exemption Under Section 501(a). Get **Pub. 557,** Tax Exempt Status for Your Organization, for more information.

Group exemption number (GEN). If the organization is covered by a group exemption letter, enter the four-digit GEN. (Do not confuse the GEN with the nine-digit EIN.) If you do not know the GEN, contact the parent organization. Get Pub. 557 for more information about group exemption numbers.

Withholding agent. If you are a withholding agent required to file Form 1042, check the "Other" box and enter "Withholding agent."

Personal service corporation. Check this box if the entity is a personal service corporation. An entity is a personal service corporation for a tax year only if:

● The principal activity of the entity during the testing period (prior tax year) for the tax year is the performance of personal services substantially by employee-owners, and

● The employee-owners own at least 10% of the fair market value of the outstanding stock in the entity on the last day of the testing period.

Personal services include performance of services in such fields as health, law, accounting, or consulting. For more information about personal service corporations, see the **Instructions for Form 1120,** U.S. Corporation Income Tax Return, and **Pub. 542,** Corporations.

Limited liability company (LLC). See the definition of limited liability company in the **Instructions for Form 1065.** An LLC with two or more members can be a partnership or an association taxable as a corporation. An LLC with a single owner can be an association taxable as a corporation or an entity disregarded as an entity separate from its owner. See Form 8832 for more details.

● If the entity is classified as a partnership for Federal income tax purposes, check the "partnership" box.

● If the entity is classified as a corporation for Federal income tax purposes, mark the "Other corporation" box and write "limited liability co." in the space provided.

● If the entity is disregarded as an entity separate from its owner, check the "Other" box and write in "disregarded entity" in the space provided.

Plan administrator. If the plan administrator is an individual, enter the plan administrator's SSN in the space provided.

Other corporation. This box is for any corporation other than a personal service corporation. If you check this box, enter the type of corporation (such as insurance company) in the space provided.

Household employer. If you are an individual, check the "Other" box and enter "Household employer" and your SSN. If you are a state or local agency serving as a tax reporting agent for public assistance recipients who become household employers, check the "Other" box and enter "Household employer agent." If you are a trust that qualifies as a household employer, you do not need a separate EIN for reporting tax information relating to household employees; use the EIN of the trust.

QSSS. For a qualified subchapter S subsidiary (QSSS) check the "Other" box and specify "QSSS."

Line 9. Check only **one** box. Do not enter N/A.

Started new business. Check this box if you are starting a new business that requires an EIN. If you check this box, enter the type of business being started. **Do not** apply if you already have an EIN and are only adding another place of business.

Hired employees. Check this box if the existing business is requesting an EIN because it has hired or is hiring employees and is therefore required to file employment tax returns. **Do not** apply if you already have an EIN and are only hiring employees. For information on the applicable employment taxes for family members, see **Circular E,** Employer's Tax Guide (Publication 15).

Created a pension plan. Check this box if you have created a pension plan and need this number for reporting purposes. Also, enter the type of plan created.

Note: *Check this box if you are applying for a trust EIN when a new pension plan is established.*

Banking purpose. Check this box if you are requesting an EIN for banking purposes only, and enter the banking purpose (for example, a bowling league for depositing dues or an investment club for dividend and interest reporting).

Changed type of organization. Check this box if the business is changing its type of organization, for example, if the business was a sole proprietorship and has been incorporated or has become a partnership. If you check this box, specify in the space provided the type of change made, for example, "from sole proprietorship to partnership."

Purchased going business. Check this box if you purchased an existing business. **Do not** use the former owner's EIN. **Do not** apply for a new EIN if you already have one. Use your own EIN.

Created a trust. Check this box if you created a trust, and enter the type of trust created. For example, indicate if the trust is a nonexempt charitable trust or a split-interest trust.

Note: *Do not check this box if you are applying for a trust EIN when a new pension plan is established. Check "Created a pension plan."*

Exception. Do **not** file this form for certain grantor-type trusts. The trustee does not need an EIN for the trust if the trustee furnishes the name and TIN of the grantor/owner and the address of the trust to all payors. See the Instructions for Form 1041 for more information.

Other (specify). Check this box if you are requesting an EIN for any reason other than those for which there are checkboxes, and enter the reason.

Line 10. If you are starting a new business, enter the starting date of the business. If the business you acquired is already operating, enter the date you acquired the business. Trusts should enter the date the trust was legally created. Estates should enter the date of death of the decedent whose name appears on line 1 or the date when the estate was legally funded.

Line 11. Enter the last month of your accounting year or tax year. An accounting or tax year is usually 12 consecutive months, either a calendar year or a fiscal year (including a period of 52 or 53 weeks). A calendar year is 12 consecutive months ending on December 31. A fiscal year is either 12 consecutive months ending on the last day of any month other than December or a 52-53 week year. For more information on accounting periods, see **Pub. 538,** Accounting Periods and Methods.

Individuals. Your tax year generally will be a calendar year.

Partnerships. Partnerships generally must adopt one of the following tax years:
• The tax year of the majority of its partners,
• The tax year common to all of its principal partners,
• The tax year that results in the least aggregate deferral of income, or
• In certain cases, some other tax year.
See the **Instructions for Form 1065,** U.S. Partnership Return of Income, for more information.

REMIC. REMICs must have a calendar year as their tax year.

Personal service corporations. A personal service corporation generally must adopt a calendar year unless:
• It can establish a business purpose for having a different tax year, or
• It elects under section 444 to have a tax year other than a calendar year.

Trusts. Generally, a trust must adopt a calendar year except for the following:
• Tax-exempt trusts,
• Charitable trusts, and
• Grantor-owned trusts.

Line 12. If the business has or will have employees, enter the date on which the business began or will begin to pay wages. If the business does not plan to have employees, enter N/A.

Withholding agent. Enter the date you began or will begin to pay income to a nonresident alien. This also applies to individuals who are required to file Form 1042 to report alimony paid to a nonresident alien.

Line 13. For a definition of agricultural labor (farmwork), see **Circular A,** Agricultural Employer's Tax Guide (Publication 51).

Line 14. Generally, enter the exact type of business being operated (for example, advertising agency, farm, food or beverage establishment, labor union, real estate agency, steam laundry, rental of coin-operated vending machine, or investment club). Also state if the business will involve the sale or distribution of alcoholic beverages.

Governmental. Enter the type of organization (state, county, school district, municipality, etc.).

Nonprofit organization (other than governmental). Enter whether organized for religious, educational, or humane purposes, and the principal activity (for example, religious organization—hospital, charitable).

Mining and quarrying. Specify the process and the principal product (for example, mining bituminous coal, contract drilling for oil, or quarrying dimension stone).

Contract construction. Specify whether general contracting or special trade contracting. Also, show the type of work normally performed (for example, general contractor for residential buildings or electrical subcontractor).

Food or beverage establishments. Specify the type of establishment and state whether you employ workers who receive tips (for example, lounge—yes).

Trade. Specify the type of sales and the principal line of goods sold (for example, wholesale dairy products, manufacturer's representative for mining machinery, or retail hardware).

Manufacturing. Specify the type of establishment operated (for example, sawmill or vegetable cannery).

Signature. The application must be signed by (a) the individual, if the applicant is an individual, (b) the president, vice president, or other principal officer, if the applicant is a corporation, (c) a responsible and duly authorized member or officer having knowledge of its affairs, if the applicant is a partnership or other unincorporated organization, or (d) the fiduciary, if the applicant is a trust or an estate.

How To Get Forms and Publications

Phone. You can order forms, instructions, and publications by phone. Just call 1-800-TAX-FORM (1-800-829-3676). You should receive your order or notification of its status within 7 to 15 workdays.

Personal computer. With your personal computer and modem, you can get the forms and information you need using:
• IRS's Internet Web Site at **www.irs.ustreas.gov**
• Telnet at **iris.irs.ustreas.gov**
• File Transfer Protocol at **ftp.irs.ustreas.gov**

You can also dial direct (by modem) to the Internal Revenue Information Services (IRIS) at 703-321-8020. IRIS is an on-line information service on FedWorld.

For small businesses, return preparers, or others who may frequently need tax forms or publications, a CD-ROM containing over 2,000 tax products (including many prior year forms) can be purchased from the Government Printing Office.

CD-ROM. To order the CD-ROM call the Superintendent of Documents at 202-512-1800 or connect to **www.access.gpo.gov/su_docs**

Privacy Act and Paperwork Reduction Act Notice. We ask for the information on this form to carry out the Internal Revenue laws of the United States. We need it to comply with section 6109 and the regulations thereunder which generally require the inclusion of an employer identification number (EIN) on certain returns, statements, or other documents filed with the Internal Revenue Service. Information on this form may be used to determine which Federal tax returns you are required to file and to provide you with related forms and publications. We disclose this form to the Social Security Administration for their use in determining compliance with applicable laws. We will be unable to issue an EIN to you unless you provide all of the requested information which applies to your entity.

You are not required to provide the information requested on a form that is subject to the Paperwork Reduction Act unless the form displays a valid OMB control number. Books or records relating to a form or its instructions must be retained as long as their contents may become material in the administration of any Internal Revenue law. Generally, tax returns and return information are confidential, as required by section 6103.

The time needed to complete and file this form will vary depending on individual circumstances. The estimated average time is:

Recordkeeping . . . . 7 min.
Learning about the law or the form . . . . 19 min.
Preparing the form . . . . 45 min.
Copying, assembling, and sending the form to the IRS . . 20 min.

If you have comments concerning the accuracy of these time estimates or suggestions for making this form simpler, we would be happy to hear from you. You can write to the Tax Forms Committee, Western Area Distribution Center, Rancho Cordova, CA 95743-0001. **Do not** send this form to this address. Instead, see **Where To Apply** on page 2.

Form **2553**
(Rev. July 1999)

Department of the Treasury
Internal Revenue Service

Election by a Small Business Corporation
(Under section 1362 of the Internal Revenue Code)
▶ See Parts II and III on back and the separate instructions.
▶ **The corporation may either send or fax this form to the IRS. See page 1 of the instructions.**

OMB No. 1545-0146

Notes:
1. *This election to be an S corporation can be accepted only if all the tests are met under **Who may elect** on page 1 of the instructions; all signatures in Parts I and III are originals (no photocopies); and the exact name and address of the corporation and other required form information are provided.*
2. *Do not file **Form 1120S,** U.S. Income Tax Return for an S Corporation, for any tax year before the year the election takes effect.*
3. *If the corporation was in existence before the effective date of this election, see **Taxes an S corporation may owe** on page 1 of the instructions.*

Part I Election Information

Please Type or Print

Name of corporation (see instructions)	**A** Employer identification number
Number, street, and room or suite no. (If a P.O. box, see instructions.)	**B** Date incorporated
City or town, state, and ZIP code	**C** State of incorporation

D Election is to be effective for tax year beginning (month, day, year) . . . . ▶   /   /

E Name and title of officer or legal representative who the IRS may call for more information

F Telephone number of officer or legal representative
(   )

G If the corporation changed its name or address after applying for the EIN shown in **A** above, check this box . . . . ▶ ☐

H If this election takes effect for the first tax year the corporation exists, enter month, day, and year of the **earliest** of the following: (1) date the corporation first had shareholders, (2) date the corporation first had assets, or (3) date the corporation began doing business . . . . ▶   /   /

I Selected tax year: Annual return will be filed for tax year ending (month and day) ▶ -
If the tax year ends on any date other than December 31, except for an automatic 52-53-week tax year ending with reference to the month of December, you **must** complete Part II on the back. If the date you enter is the ending date of an automatic 52-53-week tax year, write "52-53-week year" to the right of the date. See Temporary Regulations section 1.441-2T(e)(3).

J Name and address of each shareholder; shareholder's spouse having a community property interest in the corporation's stock; and each tenant in common, joint tenant, and tenant by the entirety. (A husband and wife (and their estates) are counted as one shareholder in determining the number of shareholders without regard to the manner in which the stock is owned.)	**K** Shareholders' Consent Statement. Under penalties of perjury, we declare that we consent to the election of the above-named corporation to be an S corporation under section 1362(a) and that we have examined this consent statement, including accompanying schedules and statements, and to the best of our knowledge and belief, it is true, correct, and complete. We understand our consent is binding and may not be withdrawn after the corporation has made a valid election. (Shareholders sign and date below.)		**L** Stock owned		**M** Social security number or employer identification number (see instructions)	**N** Share-holder's tax year ends (month and day)
	Signature	Date	Number of shares	Dates acquired		

Under penalties of perjury, I declare that I have examined this election, including accompanying schedules and statements, and to the best of my knowledge and belief, it is true, correct, and complete.

Signature of officer ▶   Title ▶   Date ▶

For Paperwork Reduction Act Notice, see page 2 of the instructions.   Cat. No. 18629R   Form **2553** (Rev. 7-99)

Part II   **Selection of Fiscal Tax Year** (All corporations using this part must complete item O and item P, Q, or R.)

O   Check the applicable box to indicate whether the corporation is:

   1. ☐ A new corporation adopting the tax year entered in item I, Part I.

   2. ☐ An existing corporation retaining the tax year entered in item I, Part I.

   3. ☐ An existing corporation changing to the tax year entered in item I, Part I.

P   Complete item P if the corporation is using the expeditious approval provisions of Rev. Proc. 87-32, 1987-2 C.B. 396, to request **(1)** a natural business year (as defined in section 4.01(1) of Rev. Proc. 87-32) or **(2)** a year that satisfies the ownership tax year test in section 4.01(2) of Rev. Proc. 87-32. Check the applicable box below to indicate the representation statement the corporation is making as required under section 4 of Rev. Proc. 87-32.

   1. Natural Business Year ▶ ☐ I represent that the corporation is retaining or changing to a tax year that coincides with its natural business year as defined in section 4.01(1) of Rev. Proc. 87-32 and as verified by its satisfaction of the requirements of section 4.02(1) of Rev. Proc. 87-32. In addition, if the corporation is changing to a natural business year as defined in section 4.01(1), I further represent that such tax year results in less deferral of income to the owners than the corporation's present tax year. I also represent that the corporation is not described in section 3.01(2) of Rev. Proc. 87-32. (See instructions for additional information that must be attached.)

   2. Ownership Tax Year ▶ ☐ I represent that shareholders holding more than half of the shares of the stock (as of the first day of the tax year to which the request relates) of the corporation have the same tax year or are concurrently changing to the tax year that the corporation adopts, retains, or changes to per item I, Part I. I also represent that the corporation is not described in section 3.01(2) of Rev. Proc. 87-32.

Note: *If you do not use item P and the corporation wants a fiscal tax year, complete either item Q or R below. Item Q is used to request a fiscal tax year based on a business purpose and to make a back-up section 444 election. Item R is used to make a regular section 444 election.*

Q   Business Purpose—To request a fiscal tax year based on a business purpose, you must check box Q1 and pay a user fee. See instructions for details. You may also check box Q2 and/or box Q3.

   1. Check here ▶ ☐ if the fiscal year entered in item I, Part I, is requested under the provisions of section 6.03 of Rev. Proc. 87-32. Attach to Form 2553 a statement showing the business purpose for the requested fiscal year. See instructions for additional information that must be attached.

   2. Check here ▶ ☐ to show that the corporation intends to make a back-up section 444 election in the event the corporation's business purpose request is not approved by the IRS. (See instructions for more information.)

   3. Check here ▶ ☐ to show that the corporation agrees to adopt or change to a tax year ending December 31 if necessary for the IRS to accept this election for S corporation status in the event (1) the corporation's business purpose request is not approved and the corporation makes a back-up section 444 election, but is ultimately not qualified to make a section 444 election, or (2) the corporation's business purpose request is not approved and the corporation did not make a back-up section 444 election.

R   Section 444 Election—To make a section 444 election, you must check box R1 and you may also check box R2.

   1. Check here ▶ ☐ to show the corporation will make, if qualified, a section 444 election to have the fiscal tax year shown in item I, Part I. To make the election, you must complete **Form 8716,** Election To Have a Tax Year Other Than a Required Tax Year, and either attach it to Form 2553 or file it separately.

   2. Check here ▶ ☐ to show that the corporation agrees to adopt or change to a tax year ending December 31 if necessary for the IRS to accept this election for S corporation status in the event the corporation is ultimately not qualified to make a section 444 election.

Part III   **Qualified Subchapter S Trust (QSST) Election Under Section 1361(d)(2)***

Income beneficiary's name and address	Social security number
Trust's name and address	Employer identification number

Date on which stock of the corporation was transferred to the trust (month, day, year) . . . . ▶   /   /

In order for the trust named above to be a QSST and thus a qualifying shareholder of the S corporation for which this Form 2553 is filed, I hereby make the election under section 1361(d)(2). Under penalties of perjury, I certify that the trust meets the definitional requirements of section 1361(d)(3) and that all other information provided in Part III is true, correct, and complete.

_____   _____

Signature of income beneficiary or signature and title of legal representative or other qualified person making the election   Date

*Use Part III to make the QSST election only if stock of the corporation has been transferred to the trust on or before the date on which the corporation makes its election to be an S corporation. The QSST election must be made and filed separately if stock of the corporation is transferred to the trust after the date on which the corporation makes the S election.

Instructions for Form 2553
(Revised July 1999)

**Department of the Treasury
Internal Revenue Service**

Election by a Small Business Corporation

Section references are to the Internal Revenue Code unless otherwise noted.

General Instructions

Purpose. To elect to be an S corporation, a corporation must file Form 2553. The election permits the income of the S corporation to be taxed to the shareholders of the corporation rather than to the corporation itself, except as noted below under **Taxes an S corporation may owe.**

Who may elect. A corporation may elect to be an S corporation only if it meets all of the following tests:

1. It is a domestic corporation.

2. It has no more than 75 shareholders. A husband and wife (and their estates) are treated as one shareholder for this requirement. All other persons are treated as separate shareholders.

3. Its only shareholders are individuals, estates, exempt organizations described in section 401(a) or 501(c)(3), or certain trusts described in section 1361(c)(2)(A). See the instructions for Part III regarding qualified subchapter S trusts (QSSTs).

A trustee of a trust wanting to make an election under section 1361(e)(1) to be an electing small business trust (ESBT) should see Notice 97-12, 1997-1 C.B. 385. Also see Rev. Proc. 98-23, 1998-10 I.R.B. 30, for guidance on how to convert a QSST to an ESBT. If there was an inadvertent failure to timely file an ESBT election, see the relief provisions under Rev. Proc. 98-55, 1998-46 I.R.B. 27.

4. It has no nonresident alien shareholders.

5. It has only one class of stock (disregarding differences in voting rights). Generally, a corporation is treated as having only one class of stock if all outstanding shares of the corporation's stock confer identical rights to distribution and liquidation proceeds. See Regulations section 1.1361-1(l) for details.

6. It is not one of the following ineligible corporations:

a. A bank or thrift institution that uses the reserve method of accounting for bad debts under section 585;

b. An insurance company subject to tax under the rules of subchapter L of the Code;

c. A corporation that has elected to be treated as a possessions corporation under section 936; or

d. A domestic international sales corporation (DISC) or former DISC.

7. It has a permitted tax year as required by section 1378 or makes a section 444 election to have a tax year other than a permitted tax year. Section 1378 defines a permitted tax year as a tax year ending December 31, or any other tax year for which the corporation establishes a business purpose to the satisfaction of the IRS. See Part II for details on requesting a fiscal tax year based on a business purpose or on making a section 444 election.

8. Each shareholder consents as explained in the instructions for column K.

See sections 1361, 1362, and 1378 for additional information on the above tests.

A parent S corporation can elect to treat an eligible wholly-owned subsidiary as a qualified

subchapter S subsidiary (QSSS). If the election is made, the assets, liabilities, and items of income, deduction, and credit of the QSSS are treated as those of the parent. For details, see Notice 97-4, 1997-1 C.B. 351. If the QSSS election was not timely filed, the corporation may be entitled to relief under Rev. Proc. 98-55.

Taxes an S corporation may owe. An S corporation may owe income tax in the following instances:

1. If, at the end of any tax year, the corporation had accumulated earnings and profits, and its passive investment income under section 1362(d)(3) is more than 25% of its gross receipts, the corporation may owe tax on its excess net passive income.

2. A corporation with net recognized built-in gain (as defined in section 1374(d)(2)) may owe tax on its built-in gains.

3. A corporation that claimed investment credit before its first year as an S corporation will be liable for any investment credit recapture tax.

4. A corporation that used the LIFO inventory method for the year immediately preceding its first year as an S corporation may owe an additional tax due to LIFO recapture. The tax is paid in four equal installments, the first of which must be paid by the due date (not including extensions) of the corporation's income tax return for its last tax year as a C corporation.

For more details on these taxes, see the Instructions for Form 1120S.

Where to file. Send or fax this election to the Internal Revenue Service Center listed below. If the corporation files this election by fax, keep the original Form 2553 with the corporation's permanent records.

If the corporation's principal business, office, or agency is located in ▼	Use the following Internal Revenue Service Center address or fax number ▼
New Jersey, New York (New York City and counties of Nassau, Rockland, Suffolk, and Westchester)	Holtsville, NY 00501 (516) 654-6954
New York (all other counties), Connecticut, Maine, Massachusetts, New Hampshire, Rhode Island, Vermont	Andover, MA 05501 (978) 474-5633
Florida, Georgia, South Carolina	Atlanta, GA 39901 (770) 455-2169
Indiana, Kentucky, Michigan, Ohio, West Virginia	Cincinnati, OH 45999 (606) 292-5289
Kansas, New Mexico, Oklahoma, Texas	Austin, TX 73301 (512) 460-4046
Alaska, Arizona, California (counties of Alpine, Amador, Butte, Calaveras, Colusa, Contra Costa, Del Norte, El Dorado, Glenn, Humboldt, Lake, Lassen, Marin, Mendocino, Modoc, Napa, Nevada, Placer, Plumas, Sacramento, San Joaquin, Shasta, Sierra, Siskiyou, Solano, Sonoma, Sutter, Tehama, Trinity, Yolo, and Yuba), Colorado, Idaho, Montana, Nebraska, Nevada, North Dakota, Oregon, South Dakota, Utah, Washington, Wyoming	Ogden, UT 84201 (801) 620-7155
California (all other counties), Hawaii	Fresno, CA 93888 (559) 443-5030
Illinois, Iowa, Minnesota, Missouri, Wisconsin	Kansas City, MO 64999 (816) 823-1975

Alabama, Arkansas, Louisiana, Mississippi, North Carolina, Tennessee	Memphis, TN 37501 (901) 546-3900
Delaware, District of Columbia, Maryland, Pennsylvania, Virginia	Philadelphia, PA 19255 (215) 516-3414

When to make the election. Complete and file Form 2553 **(a)** at any time before the 16th day of the 3rd month of the tax year, if filed during the tax year the election is to take effect, or **(b)** at any time during the preceding tax year. An election made no later than 2 months and 15 days after the beginning of a tax year that is less than 2½ months long is treated as timely made for that tax year. An election made after the 15th day of the 3rd month but before the end of the tax year is effective for the next year. For example, if a calendar tax year corporation makes the election in April 2000, it is effective for the corporation's 2001 calendar tax year.

However, an election made after the due date will be accepted as timely filed if the corporation can show that the failure to file on time was due to reasonable cause. To request relief for a late election, the corporation generally must request a private letter ruling and pay a user fee in accordance with Rev. Proc. 99-1, 1999-1 I.R.B. 6 (or its successor). But if the election is filed within 12 months of its due date and the original due date for filing the corporation's initial Form 1120S has not passed, the ruling and user fee requirements do not apply. To request relief in this case, write "FILED PURSUANT TO REV. PROC. 98-55" at the top of page 1 of Form 2553, attach a statement explaining the reason for failing to file the election on time, and file Form 2553 as otherwise instructed. See Rev. Proc. 98-55 for more details.

See Regulations section 1.1362-6(b)(3)(iii) for how to obtain relief for an inadvertent invalid election if the corporation filed a timely election, but one or more shareholders did not file a timely consent.

Acceptance or nonacceptance of election. The service center will notify the corporation if its election is accepted and when it will take effect. The corporation will also be notified if its election is not accepted. The corporation should generally receive a determination on its election within 60 days after it has filed Form 2553. If box Q1 in Part II is checked on page 2, the corporation will receive a ruling letter from the IRS in Washington, DC, that either approves or denies the selected tax year. When box Q1 is checked, it will generally take an additional 90 days for the Form 2553 to be accepted.

Do not file Form 1120S for any tax year before the year the election takes effect. If the corporation is now required to file **Form 1120,** U.S. Corporation Income Tax Return, or any other applicable tax return, continue filing it until the election takes effect.

Care should be exercised to ensure that the IRS receives the election. If the corporation is not notified of acceptance or nonacceptance of its election within 3 months of date of filing (date mailed), or within 6 months if box Q1 is checked, take follow-up action by corresponding with the service center where the corporation filed the election. If the IRS questions whether Form 2553 was filed, an acceptable proof of filing is **(a)** certified or registered mail receipt (timely postmarked) from the U.S. Postal Service, or its equivalent from a designated private delivery service (see Notice 98-47, 1998-37 I.R.B. 8); **(b)** Form 2553 with accepted stamp; **(c)** Form 2553 with stamped IRS received date; or **(d)** IRS letter stating that Form 2553 has been accepted.

End of election. Once the election is made, it stays in effect until it is terminated. If the election is terminated in a tax year beginning after 1996, the corporation (or a successor corporation) can make another election on Form 2553 only with IRS consent for any tax year before the 5th tax year after the first tax year in which the termination took effect. See Regulations section 1.1362-5 for more details.

Specific Instructions

Part I

Note: *All corporations must complete Part I.*

Name and address of corporation. Enter the true corporate name as stated in the corporate charter or other legal document creating it. If the corporation's mailing address is the same as someone else's, such as a shareholder's, enter "c/o" and this person's name following the name of the corporation. Include the suite, room, or other unit number after the street address. If the Post Office does not deliver to the street address and the corporation has a P.O. box, show the box number instead of the street address. If the corporation changed its name or address after applying for its employer identification number, be sure to check the box in item G of Part I.

Item A. Employer identification number (EIN). If the corporation has applied for an EIN but has not received it, enter "applied for." If the corporation does not have an EIN, it should apply for one on **Form SS-4**, Application for Employer Identification Number. You can order Form SS-4 by calling 1-800-TAX-FORM (1-800-829-3676).

Item D. Effective date of election. Enter the beginning effective date (month, day, year) of the tax year requested for the S corporation. Generally, this will be the beginning date of the tax year for which the ending effective date is required to be shown in item I, Part I. For a new corporation (first year the corporation exists) it will generally be the date required to be shown in item H, Part I. The tax year of a new corporation starts on the date that it has shareholders, acquires assets, or begins doing business, whichever happens first. If the effective date for item D for a newly formed corporation is later than the date in item H, the corporation should file Form 1120 or Form 1120-A for the tax period between these dates.

Column K. Shareholders' Consent Statement. Each shareholder who owns (or is deemed to own) stock at the time the election is made must consent to the election. If the election is made during the corporation's tax year for which it first takes effect, any person who held stock at any time during the part of that year that occurs before the election is made, must consent to the election, even though the person may have sold or transferred his or her stock before the election is made.

An election made during the first 2½ months of the tax year is effective for the following tax year if any person who held stock in the corporation during the part of the tax year before the election was made, and who did not hold stock at the time the election was made, did not consent to the election.

Each shareholder consents by signing and dating in column K or signing and dating a separate consent statement described below.

The following special rules apply in determining who must sign the consent statement.

• If a husband and wife have a community interest in the stock or in the income from it, both must consent.

• Each tenant in common, joint tenant, and tenant by the entirety must consent.

• A minor's consent is made by the minor, legal representative of the minor, or a natural or adoptive parent of the minor if no legal representative has been appointed.

• The consent of an estate is made by the executor or administrator.

• The consent of an electing small business trust is made by the trustee.

• If the stock is owned by a trust (other than an electing small business trust), the deemed owner of the trust must consent. See section 1361(c)(2) for details regarding trusts that are permitted to be shareholders and rules for determining who is the deemed owner.

Continuation sheet or separate consent statement. If you need a continuation sheet or use a separate consent statement, attach it to Form 2553. The separate consent statement must contain the name, address, and EIN of the corporation and the shareholder information requested in columns J through N of Part I. If you want, you may combine all the shareholders' consents in one statement.

Column L. Enter the number of shares of stock each shareholder owns and the dates the stock was acquired. If the election is made during the corporation's tax year for which it first takes effect, do not list the shares of stock for those shareholders who sold or transferred all of their stock before the election was made. However, these shareholders must still consent to the election for it to be effective for the tax year.

Column M. Enter the social security number of each shareholder who is an individual. Enter the EIN of each shareholder that is an estate, a qualified trust, or an exempt organization.

Column N. Enter the month and day that each shareholder's tax year ends. If a shareholder is changing his or her tax year, enter the tax year the shareholder is changing to, and attach an explanation indicating the present tax year and the basis for the change (e.g., automatic revenue procedure or letter ruling request).

Signature. Form 2553 must be signed by the president, treasurer, assistant treasurer, chief accounting officer, or other corporate officer (such as tax officer) authorized to sign.

Part II

Complete Part II if you selected a tax year ending on any date other than December 31 (other than a 52-53-week tax year ending with reference to the month of December).

Box P1. Attach a statement showing separately for each month the amount of gross receipts for the most recent 47 months as required by section 4.03(3) of Rev. Proc. 87-32, 1987-2 C.B. 396. A corporation that does not have a 47-month period of gross receipts cannot establish a natural business year under section 4.01(1).

Box Q1. For examples of an acceptable business purpose for requesting a fiscal tax year, see Rev. Rul. 87-57, 1987-2 C.B. 117.

In addition to a statement showing the business purpose for the requested fiscal year, you must attach the other information necessary to meet the ruling request requirements of Rev. Proc. 99-1 (or its successor). Also attach a statement that shows separately the amount of gross receipts from sales or services (and inventory costs, if applicable) for each of the 36 months preceding the effective date of the election to be an S corporation. If the corporation has

been in existence for fewer than 36 months, submit figures for the period of existence.

If you check box Q1, you will be charged a user fee of up to $600 (subject to change—see Rev. Proc. 99-1 or its successor). Do not pay the fee when filing Form 2553. The service center will send Form 2553 to the IRS in Washington, DC, who, in turn, will notify the corporation that the fee is due.

Box Q2. If the corporation makes a back-up section 444 election for which it is qualified, then the election will take effect in the event the business purpose request is not approved. In some cases, the tax year requested under the back-up section 444 election may be different than the tax year requested under business purpose. See **Form 8716,** Election To Have a Tax Year Other Than a Required Tax Year, for details on making a back-up section 444 election.

Boxes Q2 and R2. If the corporation is not qualified to make the section 444 election after making the item Q2 back-up section 444 election or indicating its intention to make the election in item R1, and therefore it later files a calendar year return, it should write "Section 444 Election Not Made" in the top left corner of the first calendar year Form 1120S it files.

Part III

Certain qualified subchapter S trusts (QSSTs) may make the QSST election required by section 1361(d)(2) in Part III. Part III may be used to make the QSST election only if corporate stock has been transferred to the trust on or before the date on which the corporation makes its election to be an S corporation. However, a statement can be used instead of Part III to make the election. If there was an inadvertent failure to timely file a QSST election, see the relief provisions under Rev. Proc. 98-55.

Note: *Use Part III only if you make the election in Part I (i.e., Form 2553 cannot be filed with only Part III completed).*

The deemed owner of the QSST must also consent to the S corporation election in column K, page 1, of Form 2553. See section 1361 (c)(2).

Paperwork Reduction Act Notice. We ask for the information on this form to carry out the Internal Revenue laws of the United States. You are required to give us the information. We need it to ensure that you are complying with these laws and to allow us to figure and collect the right amount of tax.

You are not required to provide the information requested on a form that is subject to the Paperwork Reduction Act unless the form displays a valid OMB control number. Books or records relating to a form or its instructions must be retained as long as their contents may become material in the administration of any Internal Revenue law. Generally, tax returns and return information are confidential, as required by section 6103.

The time needed to complete and file this form will depend on individual circumstances. The estimated average time is: **Recordkeeping,** 8 hr., 37 min.; **Learning about the law or the form,** 3 hr., 11 min.; and **Preparing, copying, assembling, and sending the form to the IRS,** 3 hr., 28 min.

If you have comments concerning the accuracy of these time estimates or suggestions for making this form simpler, we would be happy to hear from you. You can write to the Tax Forms Committee, Western Area Distribution Center, Rancho Cordova, CA 95743-0001. **DO NOT** send the form to this address. Instead, see **Where to file** on page 1.

MINUTES OF DIRECTOR MEETING TO ELECT S CORPORATION STATUS

Pursuant to the laws of the state in which this corporation is organized, and its bylaws, a meeting of the Directors of the above named Corporation was held at the offices of the corporation. The meeting was held on the   day of   at   o'clock   M. Present at the meeting was a quorum of directors, and all have signed their names below. As evidenced by their signatures, the directors hereby waive any meeting notice that may be required. The meeting was duly called to order and the following items of business were resolved.

1. It is decided that in the best interest of the stockholders the Corporation should elect federal taxation treatment under Subchapter S of the Internal Revenue Code as provided by the Internal Revenue Service, which would allow the Corporation to be taxed as a partnership, with the income or loss of the Corporation "passing through" to the stockholders. Consent and agreement of the stockholders will be evidenced by their signatures on Federal Tax Form Number 2553, a copy of which shall be included in the records of the Corporation. By electing tax treatment under Subchapter S, the Corporation will be required to use a calendar year with the tax year ending December 31, of each year.

2. All directors hereby approve of the action.

Having concluded all current business, the meeting was duly concluded.

Date:

Signature of Corporate Secretary _____

Glossary

Articles of incorporation

The centerpiece of the incorporation process is the "Articles of Incorporation." Filing this document with your state brings a corporation to life and begins the process of organizing your business. The Articles of Incorporation is usually a basic form that contains information about your corporation, the stock it issues, its appointed representative, and its organizer. It is filed with a state agency responsible for corporations. The articles of incorporation go by different names in some states. It may be called a certificate of incorporation, charter, articles of organization, or similar title.

Assumed name

Sometimes a corporation may want to transact business under a different name than its corporate name. This is referred to as using an assumed name, or assumed corporate name. Some states refer to it as a fictitious name, or tradename (not trademark). Some simply call it a d.b.a., or "doing business as," as in ABC Corp., doing business as, "Dean's bookstore." Using an assumed name, allows you to present yourself to the public as different entities, while using only one corporation and keeping only one set of books.

Authorized shares

This is the total number of shares your corporation will ever have. This number is stated in the articles of incorporation. You can only change this number with the approval of a majority of shareholders and by amending the articles of incorporation. When authorized shares are "given out" to the shareholders, they become "issued" shares.

Board of Directors	The directors that oversee the affairs of the corporation are referred to collectively as the Board of Directors. The board may consist of one or more persons.
Bylaws	Bylaws are the internal rules by which the corporation operates.
C Corporation	The term C corporation is an IRS tax classification. It refers to a corporation that reports its income on IRS form 1120. The C corporation is responsible for and pays its own taxes. After your corporation is organized, the IRS recognizes it as a "regular" or C corporation.
Capitalization	Capitalization is the amount of money or property that a corporation has when operations are begun.
Certificate of incorporation	See articles of incorporation.
Charter	See articles of incorporation.
Controlling interest	See majority interest.
Common stock	There are two different types of stock (shares) your corporation can issue, common and preferred. Common stock is what corporations usually issue to shareholders. Common stockholders receive a pro-rata share of the corporation's assets upon its dissolution. Common stock can be voting, or nonvoting. Holders of voting common stock get to elect the directors of the corporation, and thereby exercise control of the corporation. Holders of nonvoting common stock do not get to elect the directors, but they still receive their pro-rata share of the corporation's assets upon its dissolution. Common stockholders are eligible to receive quarterly dividends if corporate profits allow.
Corporation	A corporation is a body of persons granted a charter legally recognizing them as a separate entity having its own rights, privileges, and liabilities separate from those of its members. It is a separate and distinct entity that acts for, or on behalf of a person or group of people. A corporation can consist of one person.
d.b.a.	See assumed name.
Delayed effective date	A delayed effective date is put in the articles of incorporation so that the filing won't be effective until that date. If you are incorporating toward the end of the year, you may want to include a delayed effective date of incorporation so that your corporation won't begin until the first of the upcoming year.
Department of state	See Secretary of State.
Directors	Directors are people who oversee the affairs of the corporation on behalf of the shareholders, to protect the shareholder's interests. They meet from time to time to review the actions of the corporate officers who run

the corporation on a day-to-day basis. Directors do not have to be shareholders, but in a small corporation, they are usually one in the same.

Dividends

Dividends are bonuses paid to shareholders based on the number of shares that person owns. They are usually paid on quarterly basis as corporate profits allow.

Duration

The duration of the corporation is simply how long it will exist. If you are using the corporation to pursue a single project, you may wish to limit its life span to the length of the project.

Employer ID number

See Federal tax ID number.

Federal tax ID number

This number is assigned by the IRS. It is an identifying number, essentially a social security number for your business. A Federal tax ID number is obtained by filing a form SS-4 with the IRS.

Fictitious name

See assumed name.

Form 2553

See S corporation.

Form SS-4

See Federal tax ID number

Incorporator

The incorporator is simply the person who files the articles of incorporation with the state. The incorporator really has no rights except appointing the initial corporate directors. After the directors are appointed, the incorporator resigns.

Issued shares

This is the number of authorized shares that are actually "issued" out to the shareholders.

Medical reimbursement plan

An employee benefit plan that allows the corporation to reimburse employees for medical and dental expenses. The reimbursement is non-taxable to the employee, and is a tax-deductible expense for the corporation.

Majority shareholder

A shareholder who owns 51 percent or more of the corporation stock. The majority shareholder controls the corporation. See majority interest.

Majority interest

An owner of more than 51 percent of the corporation stock is said to have a majority interest in the corporation. By having a majority interest, a shareholder controls who is elected as directors of a corporation, and thereby controls the actions of the corporation. A majority interest may be gained by combining the ownership of one or more shareholders.

Minutes

Whenever a meeting of directors or shareholders is held, a record of what was discussed is kept. This record is known as the minutes of the meeting.

No par value stock

See no par stock.

No par stock	No par stock is stock without par value, or a fixed price per share. No par stock can be issued at any price (what buyers will pay for it) since it does not have a fixed "face" value.
Nonvoting stock	See common stock.
Officers	Officers are responsible for running the corporation on a day-to-day basis. They answer to the directors of the corporation. Officers include president, secretary, treasurer, etc.
Organizational meeting	The organizational meeting is held after the articles of incorporation are filed with the state. At the organizational meeting the directors and officers of the corporation are appointed. Stock is also issued. Any other organizational matter is taking care of here.
Par value	Par value of stock is a bookkeeping term that basically equates to price. That is, the par value of a share of stock is usually the price per share that a shareholder must pay to the corporation when buying the stock. To buy 1,000 shares of stock with a $1 par value, will cost you $1,000.
Perpetual duration	A corporation with perpetual duration is one that exists forever, or until the shareholders terminate it.
Preemptive rights	Preemptive rights allow existing shareholders too purchase additional shares of stock before shares are issued to new shareholders. Having preemptive rights allows existing shareholders to maintain their current ownership percentage despite the issuance of additional shares.
Preferred stock	There are basically two different types of stock your corporation can issue, common and preferred. Common stock is what corporations usually issue to shareholders. Preferred stock, on the other hand is more like a bond or promissory note. It carries a fixed dividend percentage rate. Holders of preferred stock get paid dividends first. If there are profits left after paying the preferred dividends, then dividends are paid to the common shareholders. That's why it's called preferred stock, dividends on it are paid first. There is a drawback however. As a trade-off for getting dividends first, preferred shareholders don't get to vote on matters affecting the corporation. *Preferred stock is nonvoting*.
Purpose clause	A purpose clause is sometimes required in the articles of incorporation. This tells the state when your corporation will do for a living. Some states require this purpose clause to be specific. While others allow the use of a "general" purpose clause, which basically says the corporation will engage in any legal business activity.
Registered agent	A corporation's registered agent is the person appointed to accept legal documents on behalf of the corporation. If someone sues you, the papers will be served on the registered agent at the "registered office." Some states use the term "resident" agent.
Registered office	See registered agent.

Resident agent	See registered agent.
SEC	Securities and Exchange Commission, a federal agency that oversees the issuance of stock and other securities to protect investors.
S Corporation	S Corporation is an IRS tax classification. It refers to a corporation that reports its income and expenses on IRS form 1120S. Although the S corporation is a separate legal entity, its net profit or loss is shown on the shareholder's personal tax return. To become an S Corporation, file form 2553 with the IRS. You may also have to file a similar form with your State Department of Revenue.
Secretary of State	In most states, this is the state agency that is responsible for the formation and regulation of corporations. In some states, it is known as the department of state, or bureau of corporations.
Shares	See stock.
Shareholder	A shareholder is an owner of a corporation. Shareholder is used interchangeably with the term "stockholder." Since someone has to own the corporation, a corporation must have at least one shareholder.
Stock	Stock is issued to a corporation's shareholders (owners) to show that they own a part of the enterprise. The term stock is used interchangeably with the term "share."
Stock certificate	Used to evidence a person's ownership of stock in a corporation.
Stockholder	See shareholder.
Voting stock	See common stock.

Index

A

Accounting 55
Articles of Incorporation 24, 189
    completing 24
    duration 24
    incorporator 27
    name 24
    office 24
    purpose 27
    registered agent 27
Assumed name 22, 189
Authorized shares 25, 189

B

Benefits 11
Board of Directors 190
Bylaws 38, 190

C

C Corporation 14, 190
Capitalization 26, 190
Certificate of incorporation 190
Charter 190
Common stock 190
Company obligations 11
Consideration 33, 35
Controlling interest 190

Corporate kit 41
Corporate name 21
    availability 23
    state requirements 21
Corporate outfit 41
    making 41
Corporate records 41
Corporation 10, 190
    advantages 10
    background 19
    benefits 11
    disadvantages 13
    S Corp. vs. C Corp. 14
    tax benefits 12

D

d.b.a. 22, 190
Delaware corporation 20
Delayed effective date 27, 190
Department of state 190
Directors 190
    electing 28
Dividends 191
Double taxation 13
Duration 24, 191

E

Effective Date 27
Employees 55
Employer ID number 191
Existing business
      incorporating 45

F

Federal Employer ID Number 52, 191
Fictitious name 191
Fictitious names 22
Form 2553 . . . . .53, 191, appendix
Form SS-4 . . . . .191, appendix
Free help 55

I

Incorporating 21
    an existing business 45
Incorporating Process
      Step 1 21
      Step 2 23
      Step 3 24
      Step 4 28
      Step 5 41
Incorporator 191
Insurance 54
Internet address 2
IRS Form 2553 52
Issued shares 191

L

Limited liability 11
Limited Liability Companies 15

M

Majority interest 191
Medical reimbursement plan 191
Meetings 43
Minutes 191

N

Nevada corporation 20
No par stock 192
No par value stock 191
Nonvoting stock 192

O

Officers 192
      appointing 30
Organizational meeting 28, 192

P

Par value 192
Partnership 9
    advantages 9
    taxes 9
Permits 54
Perpetual duration 192
Preemptive rights 192
Preferred stock 192
Property transfers 36
Purpose clause 192

R

Real estate 16
Record Keeping 42
Registered agent 192
Registered office 192
Resident agent 193

S

S Corporation 14, 193
S Corporation Election 52
SEC 193
Secretary of State 193
Shareholder 193
Shareholder meetings 43
Shareholders 30
    equal ownership/equal consideration. . . 34
    equal ownership/unequal consideration. 34
    unequal ownership/unequal consid. . . . 34
Shares 193
Sole Proprietorship 8
    advantages 8
    taxes 9
State taxes 13
Stock 25, 193
    authorized vs. issued 33
    classes 26
    common vs. preferred 25
    consideration 35
    par value 26
    registration 37
Stock certificate 193
    issuing 37
Stockholder 193

V

Voting stock 193

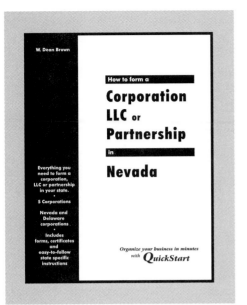

How to Form a Corporation, LLC, or Partnership Series

Forming a corporation, limited liability company (LLC) or partnership is easier than you think. If you can put your name and address on a form, you can do it.

Choosing the right type of business organization is important because it determines what your business can and cannot do, what happens if someone sues your business, and how your business is taxed. This book not only lists the advantages and disadvantages of the most popular types of business entities, but it will actually help you decide which is best for you.

While most books tell you basically how to organize a corporation, LLC or partnership. This book will show you exactly how to do it. Most importantly, it includes the full size 8½ x 11 inch forms required by state and Federal law, plus the stock or membership certificates that you'll need. (For Delaware, see *How to Form Your Own Corporation Without a Lawyer for Less Than $75* below.)

Available States:

Alabama	Arkansas	Arizona	California	Colorado
Florida	Georgia	Illinois	Indiana	Kansas
Kentucky	Maryland	Massachusetts	Michigan	Missouri
Nevada	New Jersey	New York	North Carolina	Ohio
Oklahoma	Oregon	Pennsylvania	Tennessee	Texas
Virginia	Washington	Wisconsin		

W. Dean Brown - 142 pages - (disk is available) $24.⁹⁵

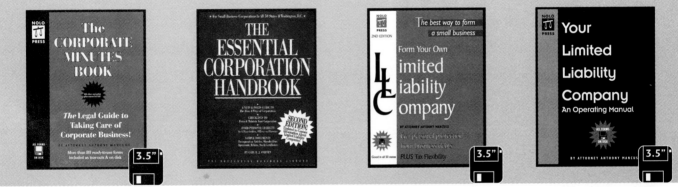

The Corporate Minutes Book
Shows you how to take care of day-to-day corporate business and comply with state law requirements for keeping corporate records. It explains how to hold corporate meetings, keep and prepare corporate minutes, pass board and shareholder resolutions, legally document corporate transactions, amend articles and bylaws, prepare buy/sell provisions to control the sale of corporate stock and more.

608 pages., disk $69.⁹⁵

The Essential Corporation Handbook
An "owner's manual" for your corporation, this book explains all the hows and whys of corporations. It covers everything from incorporating to dissolution. Subjects include—piercing of the corporate veil, shareholder buy/sell agreements, securities law, the roles of officers and directors, mergers, bylaws, proxies and more. It also includes checklists to properly form and maintain your corp.

Atty. Carl Sniffen - 262 pages $19.⁹⁵

How to Form Your Own LLC
This best-seller covers how to set up a limited liability company in any state. Subjects include choosing a name, preparing articles of organization and filing them with your state, setting up a member or manager managed LLC, and taking care of ongoing legal and tax paperwork. All forms are included on 3.5" disk.

Atty. Anthony Mancuso - 336 pages, disk . $34.⁹⁵

Your Limited Liability Company
This indispensable manual gives business owners all they need to maintain the legal validity of their LLC. It also helps them document important legal, tax and business decisions, prepare minutes of manager and member meetings. It includes more than 80 ready to use forms in the book and on a 3.5" disk.

Atty. Anthony Mancuso - 400 pages, disk . $49.⁹⁵

The Corporate Forms Kit
Here's a condensed and affordable answer to the challenge of keeping corporate records. This book includes the most popular corporate minute forms that you'll need, such as minutes of shareholder meetings, changes in governance, declaring dividends, fringe benefits, employee benefit plans and more.

149 pages, disk $24.⁹⁵

How to Create a Buy-Sell Agreement
Control the destiny of your business if a partner in your corporation, LLC or partnership dies, retires, or sells his/her share of the business. This book carefully explains each step of the process, providing all the tax and legal information needed to draft a buy-sell agreement to insure the smooth transition of ownership.

Mancuso/Laurence - 250 pages, disk $49.⁹⁵

How to Form your Own Corporation w/o a Lawyer for Less Than $75
In its 26th edition, this book has incorporated more businesses than any other. If you want to incorporate in **Delaware**, this is the book for you. It has everything you need including the certificate of incorporation, minutes, bylaws, and step-by-step instructions.

Nicholas / Melvin - 160 pages $19.⁹⁵

How to Form a Nonprofit Corporation
Explains everything you need to know to start and operate a nonprofit corporation. A special appendix includes the specific requirements for incorporating your organization in your state. It also includes complete instructions for obtaining tax–exempt and public charity status with the IRS.

Anthony Mancuso - 368 pages, disk $39.⁹⁵

The Partnership Book
This book is considered *the* authority on the subject of partnerships. It covers forming, running and selling your partnership in any state. It also covers important partnership issues like cash and property contributions, tax liability and buy-outs. Draw up your own partnership agreement using standard clauses, or use the ready-to-use forms provided on paper or disk.

Atty. Fred Steingold - 304 pages - disk $34.95

The Legal Guide for Starting & Running a Small Business
This book is a must-have comprehensive legal handbook for entrepreneurs. It covers all areas of operating a business including corporations, partnerships, business purchases, contracts, licenses, permits, leases, contractors, hiring & firing, customers, ind. contractors, insurance, taxes and more.

Atty. Fred Steingold - 432 pages $24.95

Consultant & Independent Contractors Agreements
Here's the perfect guide for today's consultant filled workplace. Comprehensive and up-to-date, this book helps both contractors and business consultants learn how to put everything in writing, avoid disputes, get paid on time, and avoid costly lawsuits.

16 forms, tear-out and disk $24.95

Smart Start Series
This is the best one-stop resource to *current* state and Federal regulations that affect your business. It'll help you cut through the red tape in your state and get you started off on the right foot. It includes extensive checklists and information on permits, licenses, business taxes, insurance, employees, payroll & unemployment taxes, workers comp., and more.

PSI Staff - 350 pages $19.95

Trademark—Legal Care for Your Business & Product Name
By far the most comprehensive do-it-yourself trademark book available—a user friendly guide to the laws that govern commercial names. This book will show you how to choose a name competitors can't copy, conduct a trademark search, register your trademark with the U.S. Patent and Trademark office, protect your trademark from infringement and more.

Attys. Elias / McGrath - 352 pages $34.95

Patent it Yourself
This book contains all the forms and specific step-by-step instructions that you'll need to patent your invention in the United States - including provisional applications. It explains the entire process from the patent search to the actual application. It also covers licensing to others, marketing of your invention and how to deal with infringement.

Atty. David Pressman - 512 pages $46.95

The Employer's Legal Handbook
This is the most comprehensive resource available that covers your questions about hiring, firing, and everything in between. Its 456 pages include topics like—discrimination, privacy rights, employee rights, workplace health and safety, employee benefits, wages, hours, tips and commissions, sexual harassment, termination, taxes, liability insurance, and safe hiring practices.

Atty. Fred Steingold - 456 pages $31.95

How to Write a Business Plan
Your banker, investors, and the Small Business Administration need your business plan, but where do you start? Used by SBA offices around the country, this 272 page best-seller comes complete with examples, forms, and work sheets that show you how to write a winning business plan in only *one* day. It will help you present your business opportunity to bankers and investors in a format they'll understand.

Mike McKeever - 272 pages $24.95

Tax Savvy for Small Business
Fully revised and updated, this book will show you how to make the most of your small or home-based business tax deductions. It will also show you how to maximize your fringe benefits, what records to keep, how to document expenses, and how to survive an audit. A must for every small business.

Atty. Frederick Daily - 352 pages $29.95

Business Owners Guide to Accounting & Bookkeeping
This is a nontechnical, easy to understand book that will teach you the basics of accounting and how to keep your own books. Not only will it teach you how to prepare your own financial statements, but it'll also show you how to make them look their best for creditors.

Placencia, Welge, Oliver - 184 pages $19.95

Plan Your Estate
The most comprehensive guide to estate planning & trusts available. It covers topics from basic planning to sophisticated tax saving strategies. It's the only book that shows you how to create an estate plan tailored to your needs. Good in all states except Louisiana. Includes durable powers of attorney, and living wills too!

Attys. Clifford / Jordan - 480 pages $24.95

Stand Up To The IRS
A hands on guide to battling the IRS and coaxing favorable decisions from agency personnel. It shows you how to defend yourself in an audit, challenge an incorrect tax bill, negotiate an installment plan, appeal an audit decision, file delinquent tax returns, support your deductions, and represent yourself in tax court.

Atty. Frederick Daily - 400 pages $24.95

Order Form

Ship To:

name

address

suite or unit number

city   state   zip

area code & telephone number — in case we have a question

Credit Card Orders:

name on card

card number   exp. (month/year)

signature

Books & Software

Quant.	Description		Price Ea.	Total
	Business Owners Guide to Accounting and Bookkeeping		19.95	
	Consultant & Independent Contractor Agreements		24.95	
	Form Your Own Limited Liability Company		34.95	
	How to Create a Buy-Sell Agreement		49.95	
	How to Form a Corporation, LLC or Partnership in…	*Specify state:*	24.95	
	How to Form a Corporation, LLC or Partnership forms on disk	*Choose one:* ☐ MAC ☐ IBM-Windows	10.00	
	How to Form a Nonprofit Corporation		39.95	
	How to Form Your Own Corporation w/o a Lawyer for Less than $75—Delaware		19.95	
	How to Write a Business Plan		24.95	
	Legal Guide for Starting and Running a Small Business		24.95	
	Patent it Yourself		46.95	
	Plan Your Estate		24.95	
	Smart Start Your *(state name)* Business	*Specify state:*	19.95	
	Stand Up to the IRS		24.95	
	Tax Savvy for Your Small Business		29.95	
	The Corporate MINUTES Book		69.95	
	The Corporate FORMS Book		24.95	
	The Employer's Legal Handbook		31.95	
	The Essential Corporation Handbook		19.95	
	The Partnership Book		34.95	
	Trademark, Legal Care for Your Business & Product Name		34.95	
	Your Limited Liability Company		49.95	

Record Keeping Supplies

Quant.	Description			Price Ea.	Total
	Basic Outfit	*(seal, certificates, binder, etc.)*	black	58.00	
	Deluxe Outfit	*(seal, certificates, binder, etc.)*	*Choose color:* ☐ black with burgundy trim ☐ green	95.00	
	Heavy Duty Outfit	*(seal, certificates, binder, etc.)*	*Choose color:* ☐ black ☐ green ☐ brown	85.00	
	Leather Outfit	*(seal, certificates, binder, etc.)*	*Choose color:* ☐ black ☐ burgundy	199.00	
	Standard Outfit	*(seal, certificates, binder, etc.)*	*Choose color:* ☐ black ☐ green ☐ tan	64.00	
	Standard Outfit	*(seal, certificates, binder, etc.)*	black with burgundy trim	73.00	
	Blank Stock Certificates - package of 10 *(without company name)*			8.00	
	Customized Stock Certificates *(certificates only)*		*($36 for the first 20 certificates, each additional 20 is $10)*		
	Seal Only		*Please specify:* ☐ Desk black/chrome $39 ☐ Desk brass $54 ☐ Pocket $30		

Information For Company Outfits and Seals

company name as it will appear on the outfit — either ALL CAPS – Initial Caps – or any combination of caps and lower case letters.

date of organization	state of organization	number of AUTHORIZED shares (corp. only)	par value (corp. only)	is it common stock ? (corp. only)

Since the time of printing, some of the information in this catalog may have been updated. Printed 1/1/00.

Subtotal _____
** Tenn. sales tax _____
Shipping _____
Total _____

**Tennessee only. Multiply subtotal by .0825.

Record Keeping Supplies

Well kept records are the sign of a properly organized company and can serve as evidence to protect its legal status. To store your company records, we offer the finest outfits available. They are custom made for any type of corporation or LLC with their corresponding forms.

Personalized especially for you, all of our outfits feature:

- A sturdy, handsomely designed turned-edge **binder** made with leather grained vinyl – includes a matching slipcase.*

- A heavy duty, chrome-plated **embossing seal** engraved with your company name, state and year of organization.

- 20 custom printed and numbered stock or member **certificates** imprinted with the company name and share or ownership information, with certificate transfer ledger.

- Your company name embossed in **gold lettering** on the spine of the binder.*

- **Preprinted minutes and bylaws.**

The Standard
Our most popular outfit features an attractive turned-edge binder made from a rich leather grained vinyl.
Black, Tan, or Green $64
Black with burgundy trim $73

Outfits ship within 24 hours, including the seal.

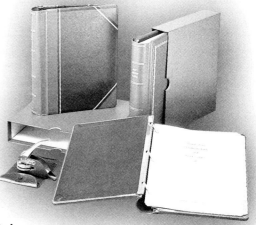

The Deluxe
This outfit features a heavy, substantial binder that looks and feels like real leather. It has a rounded library spine and a three post binding.
Black with burgundy trim, or Green $95

The Basic
This outfit includes a heat-seamed vinyl binder. The company name is typeset and viewed through a window on the spine. *Black* $58

Next day delivery is also available.

Company Seal
All our outfits include a company seal. Seals are also available alone. Engraved with your company name, year and state of organization.
Pocket Seal (hand-held with pouch) $30
Desk Seal - Black & Chrome $39
Desk Seal - Brass $54

The Heavy Duty
This outfit has an impressive binder with a metal hinge for added durability. It also features a rounded spine.
Black, Green, or Brown $85

*See the description for the Basic outfit.